The Dream Society

The Dream Society

How the Coming Shift from Information to Imagination Will Transform Your Business

ROLF JENSEN

McGraw-Hill

New York   Chicago   San Francisco   Lisbon   London   Madrid
Mexico City   Milan   New Delhi   San Juan   Seoul
Singapore   Sydney   Toronto

Library of Congress Cataloging-in-Publication Data

Jensen, Rolf.

    The dream society : how the coming shift from information to
imagination will transform your business / Rolf Jensen.

       p.   cm.

    Includes bibliographical references and index.

    ISBN 0-07-137968-1

    1. Business forecasting.   2. Twenty-first century—Forecasts.
3. Competition, International. I. Title.

HD30.27.J47   1999

658.4'0355—dc21   99-10353

                                                               CIP

McGraw-Hill

A Division of The **McGraw·Hill** Companies

1 2 3 4 5 6 7 8 9 0 DOC/DOC 0 4 3 2 1

ISBN 0-07-137968-1

This is the paperback version of ISBN 0-07-032967-2.

Printed and bound by R. R. Donnelley & Sons Company.

McGraw-Hill books are available at special quantity discounts to use as premiums and
sales promotions, or for use in corporate training programs. For more information, please
write to the Director of Special Sales, McGraw-Hill Professional, Two Penn Plaza, New
York, NY 10121-2298. Or contact your local bookstore.

Contents

Introduction

The sun is setting on the Information Society—even before we have fully adjusted to its demands as individuals and as companies. We have lived as hunters and as farmers, we have worked in factories, and now we live in an information-based society whose icon is the computer. We stand facing the fifth type of society: the Dream Society!

This book is a blueprint for the successor to the Information Society—the Dream Society—pinpointing consequences for the workplace, the marketplace, and leisure. The book is addressed to everybody interested in business—everybody wanting to understand market developments, everybody who does not want to become stuck in the Information Society while markets, consumers, and employees are all charging into the Dream Society. It is a book for everybody interested in the future, in life in the twenty-first century.

There is, in fact, an answer to how long the harsh logic of the Information Society will last, how long company management will still have to focus on purely technical and rational thinking.

The answer is that the Dream Society is emerging this very instant—the shape of the future is visible today. Right now is the time for decisions—before the major portion of consumer purchases are made for emotional, nonmaterialistic reasons. Future products will have to appeal to our hearts, not to our heads. When this has happened, the prevailing societal model in the affluent countries will no longer be the Information Society, but the Dream Society. Now is the time to add emotional value to products and services. This book should prove an indispensable guide to understanding the marketplace and the company of the future.

Chapter 1 is an introduction to the logic of the Dream Society. Companies will miss out on the major part of coming market growth if they do not adjust to this new logic. The Dream Society will arrive like a glacier—slowly, but surely. If you choose not to budge, you will be flattened. Chapter 2 is about the marketplace, about storytelling, and about the six emerging, emotionally defined markets. A new logic serving as inspiration for strategic deliberations, generously peppered with detailed examples, makes its bid for early recognition. Chapter 3 deals with the company and its employees—the company of the future, its mission, its vision, and its strategy. The company is viewed as a tribe, complete with rituals, myths, and stories all its own. Chapter 4 meets with the consumer and the employee at home and at leisure. Here we envision how people will spend their spare time in the future, and look at the relationship between work and free time. Chapter 5 deals with the global picture, with relationships between the affluent countries, the emerging global middle classes, and the developing countries. Also described are the wealthy consumers, comprising slightly over one billion, and the four billion who, for a while, will still remain poor.

My native land is Denmark, also the birthplace of Karen Blixen and Hans Christian Andersen. This book is about how storytelling is reaching out from the books and into the product markets.

Rolf Jensen
www.cifs.dk

Acknowledgments

The thoughts contained in this book are the result of a decade and a half's work at the Copenhagen Institute for Futures Studies. The manuscript was drafted in my busy Copenhagen office, not at a retreat in an isolated mountain cottage. For this reason, the book as it stands is—to an even greater extent than usual—the result of ideas and inspiration received from many colleagues. Among the many who have contributed are Carsten Beck, Anders Bjerre, Niels Bottger-Rasmussen, Marie-Therese Hoppe, Jesper Bo Jensen, Soren Jensen, Tine Jensen, Liselotte Lyngso, Niels Birkemose Moller, Axel Olesen, Soren Steen Olsen, Johan Peter Paludan, Uffe Paludan, Finn Ole Ramstad, Erica Skafdrup, and Steen Svendsen.

The student interns at CIFS have been helpful in editing and finding figures and examples. Thanks are due to the following for helping me meet my deadlines: Signe Aggerbeck, Lene G. Andersen, Troels Theill Eriksen, Jan Jensen, Anders Norgaard, Lotte Aa. Ostergaard, Mette Peetz-Schou, and Elise Seck Porning.

The CIFS secretariat has been of assistance by correcting proofs and by keeping my spirits up in intermittent moments of disquiet: Peter Andersen, Elna Hansen, Jette Lauritsen, Hanne Lindahl, and Ellen Mauri.

Martha Jewett, Literary Services and Representation (www.martha-jewett.com), wrote me with the suggestion that I expand an article in *The Futurist* into a book. A fine suggestion, and one that was followed up with indispensable support and loving critique along the way. Thank you.

Member corporations of CIFS have had the opportunity to follow this project as it developed, and many executives and employees from these companies have contributed valuable ideas and constructive criticism. Furthermore, along with Martha Jewett, they have seen to it that the book did not end up as scholarly treatise.

Mark Hebsgaard has translated the book into English; ours has been a valuable and congenial collaboration. Writing page upon page over a six-month period while still holding on to your first *apercu* as well as your sense of proportion is not always an easy task. Editor Mary Glenn made this possible, offering numerous suggestions, all phrased so I felt they were my own ideas.

Chapter 1

A Few Words About Futurism and How We Will Get to the Dream Society

The ideas for the Dream Society began one chilly autumn morning during a meeting with two of our major clients, a telecommunications firm and a leading bank. The clients listened to our presentation describing market changes and the business environment 5 to 10 years into the future. What were they to prepare for and how would their markets develop? After the presentation one client asked: "What comes after the Information Society?"

Our answers betrayed our sense of confusion and uncertainty. Don't worry about that, we told them. The Information Society will be around for a long time, and meanwhile the main concern is to apply new technology—the way we had just outlined. We did, however, promise to call our clients if we found an answer. We called them. We came up with the answer. That is what this book is about.

What's coming next is the Dream Society. It's a new society in which businesses, communities, and people as individuals will thrive on the basis of their stories, not just on data and information. The Dream Society is not so far off; its signs have begun to

1

appear in many of the world's businesses. This book will show you what the Dream Society is, why it is coming, what it will mean, and how to thrive in it.

Being asked "What comes after the Information Society?" was the best thing that could ever have happened to us. Good ideas are born under pressure and through challenge. We felt pressured by the question and it offered a challenge. It was logical; it demanded an answer. It was the best question we have ever been asked.

Here are a few basic assumptions we as futurists have made that will help you begin to apply Dream Society logic to your business today.

1. *The future pays you a daily visit!* The past is receding from us at a dizzying speed. The future is heading toward us with increasing velocity. You might say that the future is drawing closer—it is almost becoming part of the present. You need to think a few steps ahead of the competition.

2. *The days of the Information Society are numbered.* We then looked at the different types of societies and found that the pace of development from one societal type to another is accelerating. The agricultural society originated 10,000 years ago, the industrial society between 200 and 100 years ago, the information-based society 20 years ago. Who knows how many more years the logic and economics of the Information Society will last? Something new will replace it. Nowadays, a major part of the workforce is engaged in knowledge processing; we are in the midst of an information economy. How long will this last? The answer is that soon we will probably see the birth of a new type of society, a new economic foundation for businesses.

3. *Whatever can be automated, will be automated.* The Information Society will render itself obsolete through automation, abolishing the very same jobs it created. The inherent logic of the Information Society remains unchanged: replacing humans with machines, letting the machines do the work. This is reflected in the three waves of the electronics

2

industry. The first wave was hardware. The second wave was software (where we are now). The third wave will be content; that is, profit will be generated by the product itself, not by the instrument conveying it to the consumer.

What follows is an example of how Dream Society logic is being used today.

In Denmark, eggs from free-range hens have conquered over 50 percent of the market. Consumers do not want hens to live their lives in small, confining cages; they want hens to have access to earth and sky. Consumers want what could be called "retroproducts"; they desire eggs to be produced under the technology and methods of our grandparents—the old-fashioned way. This means that the eggs become more expensive—more labor-intensive—but consumers are happy to pay an additional 15 to 20 percent for—for the story behind the egg. They are willing to pay more for the story about animal ethics, about rustic romanticism, about the good old days. This is what we call classic Dream Society logic. Both kinds of eggs are similar in quality, but consumers prefer the eggs with the better story.

What has happened? The egg is a fine, traditional product that has been part of our diet for centuries. Now, however, a story has been attached to the egg. That's an irrational element insofar as it does not reflect any difference in quality. But it's a profitable element too, since it turns out that the consumer is prepared to pay 15 to 20 percent more for the added story. We concurred that here was a new and important trend. In 5 to 10 years this could be the way eggs will be produced everywhere. Eggs from hens stuffed into tiny cages will be a rare occurrence; such cages will probably be outlawed. The new story about animal welfare and rustic romanticism will be victorious. The egg market has acquired a new dimension; it no longer consists of a standardized commodity, mass-produced at the lowest possible cost.

With the egg, we had spotted a track leading to the future. Could this hold the key to the future of business and selling consumers products and services? After we debated the issue and stockpiled 50 other examples, the conclusion became evident: Stories and

3

tales speak directly to the heart rather than the brain—so went the overall theory. In a century where society is marked by science and rationalism, by analysis and pragmatism, where symbol analysts hold the highest positions of society—this is precisely where the emotions, the stories and narratives, the values all return to the scene. The term Dream Society suggested itself. The market for dreams would gradually exceed the market for information-based reality. The market for feelings would eclipse the market for tangible products.

Initially we figured that the Dream Society would be a challenge facing the coming generation, dawning in the year 2025, and thus well beyond the event horizon of most businesses. But we soon changed our minds. When we made presentations to clients about the Dream Society, we realized that the Dream Society is happening now. Our clients reacted in the same way: "You have provided us with a structure and a description about what we are already doing in our company. Now we know *why* we're doing it and that we're doing the right thing."

However, many organizations are still immersed in the reality of the Information Society, focusing on electronics, automation, and the processing of knowledge. So in many ways modern companies operate in two simultaneous societies.

> *The Information Society.* Its sun has reached its zenith in the 1990s, but it will be afternoon and evening at the beginning of the twenty-first century. Until then, it remains a central part of the business environment.
>
> *The Dream Society.* Its sun has already risen, but it is still morning. This sun will shine on the marketplace with an ever-increasing strength. It will permeate strategies and visions with a growing force until it finally prevails, and the term for the society in which we live will be the Dream Society.

Therefore, modern companies face a twofold challenge: two coinciding revolutions in the same marketplace. One diminishes in significance while the other increases. This is also how the industrialized society morphed into the Information Society. Hardly noticeable, gradually, it came in with the pace—and strength—of a glacial movement. Momentous societal changes do not transpire over a weekend, neither technologically nor, in particular, mentally. For a period, they exist simultaneously.

We started reflecting on our own daily lives. During a heated argument we might accuse one another of using emotional lines of reasoning. It usually works. However, considering the significance of opinions and values, we decided it was not always reasonable to limit ourselves to the objective, easy-to-measure corporeality. Instead, we tried: "Your line of reasoning is entirely overshadowed by facts." The dialogue changed character; opinions and values were now permitted. Another question arose: Do we do our shopping using our hearts or our brains? This question has in fact been posed to consumers. The answer when only the decision makers—the heroes of the Information Society—were asked was that ordinary consumers do their shopping with their brains. When the same ordinary consumers were themselves asked, however, the answer was the opposite: We buy groceries with our hearts.

The marketing expert will usually tell you that we consumers buy with our hearts and rationalize with our heads afterward. We purchase the expensive brand-name product and then reflect: "This can be washed again and again." We insert a false rationality into our purchasing behavior. Words like *rational, reasonable,* and *objective* are cornerstones in our behavioral model. Let us partition people as follows: Person 1 is the rational, planning being, and Person 2 is the emotional and story-buying entity. The present century has disowned and repressed Person 2—a rejection that is not strange in a technological era boasting scientific advances, enormous strides in health science, growth in prosperity, cars, planes, radios, televisions, computers, space travel, and microwave ovens. Now, as the century of materialism is waning, Person 2 is once again back in town: in the shops, on the Internet, in the companies, in politics, in economics, and even in science.

This book provides examples—taken from modern-day companies—revealing lessons learned and decisions made concerning new businesses and new markets in which stories and products are integrated. But this is a book about the future. The future cannot be verified. Besides, if we were certain about the future, running a business would not be exciting. So we will try to make our case and to convince the reader through examples, theory, and circumstantial evidence. If we are right, the Dream Society will be the successor to the Information Society; and the future has begun.We as futurists have discussed the Dream Society with numerous business executives. They have all contributed to the theory—and they have also confirmed our belief that the story of the egg reveals the beginning of the future. The confirmation is not without reservations, however; a theory has been proposed and is now open to discussion. Until the future becomes the present, we will have to make do with opinions. The future is the ultimate judge. Facing the future, we can only present our case and join in the journey to the Dream Society. We can visit a future more exciting than most geographical destinations. The prerequisite for any plane getting off the ground is the bolt down the runway. Likewise, we need to do a full-throttle before we can break through to the future. Our preliminary run covers no less than the spectrum of human history, yet it is surprisingly short. Let's go for it.

A Sprint Through the History of Humanity

Let the machines do the work for us! It all began the first time we used a stone to crush the nut we had decided to eat. It continued when we let horses and oxen do our ploughing for us or hoist our water from the well. Later, we proceeded to let the might of the rivers and the winds alleviate the hard toil of grinding down our corn to flour and irrigating our fields. By the time we reached the eighteenth century, our knowledge of the laws of physics had reached a level enabling us to construct steam engines that were able to transport people and products over great distances. In the present century, oil has been the most important source of energy. Today, only a small part of our energy needs rely on muscle power.

Muscle power has, by and large, been supplanted by machines. In affluent countries, muscle work is more likely to be done for fun

6

than out of need. Most of us are more likely to experience physical exhaustion at play than at work. Our brow becomes more sweaty outside the workplace than inside.

In the second half of the present century, our brains and our senses become next in line to have their tasks automated. Computers and intelligent machines no longer simply perform routine chores; they get a crack at even the most advanced assignments. Computers have freed the weather watchers from the tedious parts of forecasting; scanners have taken over an ever-increasing number of doctors' tasks, and our highways are lined with automatic patrols, videocameras that observe, record, and keep track of the speed demons—even issuing them tickets. The automation of brains and senses will have more in store for us that is yet to be seen, but we can begin to imagine the shape of things to come.

When summarized in this manner, 100,000 years of history will bring us to the conclusion that for much of the world, the focus on acquiring more and more of the material aspects of life is drawing to an end. Instead, we have a growing interest in humankind's emotional side. There are, however, three provisos to be mentioned. First, the past societal types did not cherish the material aspects of life as we do in the present, so we cannot assume we are merely returning to values we once honored. The average American is at least 40 times more wealthy than individuals from the ancient societies of hunter-gatherers—and that wealth makes all the difference.

Furthermore, the agrarian society, as well as the industrial society, may have all but automated its way out of existence, and the same is beginning to happen with the Information Society; yet our material needs remain considerable and are not likely to be reduced. The point, then, is simply that the material aspect of living will receive less attention—we will cease to define ourselves through physical products, relying instead on stories and feelings. Here lies the historic watershed.

We stand on the shoulders of our forebears; each generation has learned from the previous one—though not always. There have been constructive as well as destructive ages; happily, the constructive ones also proved to be the most enduring—history has been one long learning process. Only modernists would think of calling the master builders of the Pyramids "ancient" Egyptians; they, of course, viewed their own culture as the pinnacle of a long evolution, beginning with the beginning. Similarly, we must view the Dream Society as a result of the entire history of humankind and not merely as the fruit of the last few generations' efforts.

So we must ask what contributions our immediate ancestors have made to our future, to the Dream Society. We can understand the Dream Society only when we realize that it is rooted in the past as well as in the present. History may be viewed as an elongated carpet to which a yard is added every year. So today we already stand with a 100,000-yard carpet, but in order to weave the next great expanse we will have to investigate the threads and patterns already woven. The pattern we will elaborate upon already exists—we cannot start an entirely new one. We began this carpet as hunters and gatherers; as such, we laid down the fundamental patterns and if we estimate human history to be 100,000 years old, then 90 percent of this carpet was woven by hunters and gatherers.

In the following section, we shall see exactly how the values characterizing the hunter-gatherer society will become significant for people in the future. We will have a lot in common—a good deal more than was the case in the twentieth century.

The Hunter-Gatherer Is a Good Storyteller

We lived from day to day as nomads with a time horizon of one or two days. All senses were needed for survival. This is a way of life that still exists, in isolated parts of the world: a few thousand individuals preserving a past way of life. They constitute a valuable social time capsule. Anthropologists study this mode of living because it shows us our roots. Experience was important, therefore the oldest member of the tribe, the one who had experienced the most springs and seen the most rainy seasons, was usually chosen as the leader. Or it might have been the member who was most familiar with tribal myths and rituals. The spiritual element, the stories were important in these societies.

The hunter-gatherers may teach modern-day companies a lesson: respect for myth and stories. Modern organizations are beginning to rediscover their past. The History Factory, a company in Virginia, offers consultations on how to utilize a firm's history—stories of victories, of initiatives that accomplished success—as a means to create the culture that builds corporate winners.[1] "Unlock the Power of the Past," it says in the company presentation. "We help corporations use their past to cultivate their present and create their future." Contemporary business enterprises are insufficiently aware of the strength that lies in myths, the value of the "old storytellers" who use tales to communicate what behavior is appreciated by the corporation. We ourselves have had discussions with organizations whose executives were more or less custodians of a vision formulated many years ago. We drew their attention to the fact that their business originally grew big because of an idea of how to do things innovatively, not how to do the same things better. In an attempt to conserve fundamental values, these values had, in fact, been betrayed.

The Disney Corporation is built on innovation. The company sticks to this tradition. "It is about creating change before it creates you," says CEO Michael Eisner in the 1996 Disney annual report, adding that nearly half of Disney's growth during the past 10 years has been generated by business that did not exist in 1985.[2] Tradition is renewal.

The notion of team building, with employees getting to know one another as human beings—not merely as colleagues—has grown popular in recent years, complete with courses in which departments build kites, construct bridges over streams, and race one another over rough terrain. The notion of a "casual Friday" is similar in spirit. The tribal community sense is strengthened. A seasoned hunter from southern Africa or a Punan hunter from the rain forests of Borneo would give an approving nod to "tribe building" of this sort. He would understand it, saying "That's the way we do it."

Fifty years ago, hunter-gatherers were considered "primitive." Today we possess a better understanding of their values. Why? Maybe because we are heading toward the Dream Society where myths, rituals, and stories are once again fully appreciated; where material prosperity is no longer the be-all and end-all of our lives. In the twenty-first century, the human race will probably feel a closer degree of kinship with the hunter-gatherer, closer than is felt today and entirely different from how things were around the year 1900. In those days, hunter-gatherers were considered "backward" because we viewed them in relationship to their technology and their comparatively low level of material wealth. They were considered to be in need of the "civilizing influence" of affluent countries. According to this line of reasoning, colonizing such tribes was in their own best interest. Attitudes like this, which may seem obvious in a materially focused society, are now being consigned to history books.

In 1992, the Australian high court acknowledged for the first time that common law recognizes native title where indigenous people have maintained their connection to the land. More than any previous society, the Dream Society will empathize with the hunter-gatherer society. This trend has already begun in the USA, Canada, and Australia.

The contribution made by the hunter-gatherer to the future now facing us may be summed up as follows: Humankind really is a part of nature. Thus we should, in our own interest, respect the laws of nature; we should be living in compliance with nature rather than dominating it. Native Americans of the northwestern seaboard saw "killer whales" as sacred animals to be treated with awe and respect. We are beginning to adopt similar views. In the Dream Society, such an outlook will once again be considered innate to all of us.

The tribal myths and stories served as guidelines for the social community. There were no organizational diagrams, but certainly a set of fixed core values. Modern corporations are gravitating toward a similar line of thinking; namely, that core values are more important than "core business." You may diversify into other lines of business or domains, but the company's fundamental values need to be secured.

10

The hunter-gatherer societies were not materialistic societies. Sure, fundamental needs had to be met, but from then on, values were of a spiritual and nonmaterialistic nature. A lot of time was spent on storytelling—time that could have been spent on garnering greater stockpiles of supplies or building better dwellings. Life had a different set of priorities. We will experience this same set of priorities in the Dream Society, because the material needs have been met for an ever-increasing part of the population. The price of a wristwatch reflects its functional value (a precise indication of time) plus an added story about who the owner is. That last, added value—the story value—normally accounts for about half the price of the watch. The hunter would understand this way of prioritizing, whereas the rational ways of modeling our needs typical of the Information Society are somewhat flummoxed by nonmaterial requirements.

The organization of society will gravitate toward value communities of limited size—in principle, no greater than so as to permit personal contacts. These kinds of communities will become more widespread in the Dream Society. This is equally true of corporations—to an increasing extent, they will be comparable to tribes (see Chapter 3); and it also applies to the many communities of interest flocking to share their passion, be it sports, the great outdoors, or entertainment. They will meet at big shindigs, but they may also stay in touch via the Internet. These are the so-called *cybernations*.

When Experience Doesn't Change: The Farmer's Era

About 10,000 years ago agriculture emerged, and with it came the unremitting effort to subjugate nature and achieve mastery over it. The farm now comprised the production unit. Family life and production took place under the same roof. The predominant part of the global population still perpetuates this way of life. Lived in its traditional way, this kind of life possesses no concept of future—time simply means the changing of the seasons. Therefore, experience is still an important leadership quality.

Progress was made in the methods of cultivation, but new tools and improvement of livestock by breeding arrived only slowly over the centuries. The individual human being—with an average life expectancy of less than 50 years—did not register these changes. Only at the end of the nineteenth century did agricultural development really begin to accelerate, through large-scale farming and, above all, through mechanization. The next agrarian revolution occurred in the 1990s and it is called gene technology, also leading to improvement of livestock and crops—only not through generations of breeding, but in a matter of a few years, by splicing genes.

The victory over nature and its whims has gradually become complete. Until about 15 years ago it was considered one of humankind's great victories; all nature's resources were now at agriculture's disposal, and in huge areas of the globe the battle against hunger had been won. All was well until the advent of this story, old and new at the same time: humankind is not master, but an integral part of nature. Now we have gone one step further. We should not rule and dominate nature, but respect it. Ancient hunters and the contemporary green movements have in common the entire understanding of humanity's relationship to nature.

Though the contribution made by the agrarian society to our future may not be as conspicuous as that of the hunter-gatherer society, it is still part of our patrimony, part of the future's foundations. Today we may thank the agricultural society for providing the idea of multiple tools, for the additional energy-alleviating manual labor improvements in the fields, for workhorses, mills, and the plough. If, at some point in the future, working at home should once again become widespread, then the separation of home and workplace will have been only an insignificant, brief interlude in world history, lasting a mere 100 to 200 years.

Some 10,000 years ago, when the idea arose to grow crops and keep livestock, this meant that humans were placing an investment in the future—realizing that today's endeavors would not yield results until a certain number of months had passed. The concept of production had been born. Production requires patience—an ability to postpone the gratification of needs, as well as an ability to think beyond a basic hand-to-mouth time frame. Along with the concept of investment came the notion of interest, which, strictly speaking, really amounts to the price of impatience.

With the advent of animal husbandry in production (and the dog for guard duty) the amount of energy available in the quest to satisfy human needs was significantly increased. Later, the water mill arrived, again leading to a considerable increase in available energy. The idea of letting the energy of animals and nature replace muscle power was born.

The Beginning of Wealth: The Age of the Industrial Worker

We can thank the industrial revolution—which gave birth to the third type of society, emerging around 1750 in Great Britain—for our cities, infrastructure, and wealth. More than anything else, the industrial revolution established Europe's position of material predominance in the world. The unequal distribution of global wealth in the modern age is due to the fact that the Atlantic societies were the first to establish industry-based economies.

Here the idea of future and progress was truly founded; it would be different from the present, and better. Time now was no longer cyclical but linear—and it pointed toward a golden future brimming with products that would make life easier and packed with prosperity and technological advances. The notion "men of a new era" goes back to the end of the nineteenth century. They were inventors, scientists, capitalists—all the individuals who forged a new epoch through their visions, an epoch without poverty and dirt, illnesses and crime.

As a purely commercial enterprise, the incorporated company has a long history, dating back to the fifteenth century. But the truly modern company came into being with the industrial revolution; the shareholder-owned company with many employees, rationally planned production, and plenty of machines. The machine enabled a worker to bend steel. The modern company is a relatively new construct from a social and economic point of view. In a 1997 *Harvard Business Review* article, Arie de Geus, former group planning director of Royal Dutch/Shell Group, compares the average life span of human beings and corporations. Western corporations have an average life span of approximately 20 to 30 years, which is roughly equivalent to that of the hunter-gatherer. Companies have as yet to acquire the ability to ensure themselves a really long and healthy life. "The corporation is still in the Neanderthal age. It has not yet realized its potential," de Geus argues.[3]

The large industrial corporations also invented the organizational chart—the detailed description of who reports to whom, the minutely detailed assignment of tasks and responsibilities. The French painter Magritte—almost as a comment on the organizational chart—once painted a pipe. A beautiful pipe it is. Below the picture of the pipe, the text reads: "This is not a pipe." Magritte, of course, is right: it is not a pipe. And the organizational chart is not an organization.

Management was conducted from the top down; the top was where decisions were made. Management constituted the eyes, ears, and brain; the workers were the body, the muscle. The Western world is consigning this type of organization to the museum. An industrial romanticism is dawning in the great cities of Europe. One of the first examples of this is the Pompidou Center in Paris.

Western countries are nearing the end of their period of industrialization; a number of developing countries are standing at the threshold of theirs. This is true of these major countries: China, India, Indonesia, and Nigeria. They will not have reached the stage of true information economies until 50 years from now. Their period of industrialization will be briefer than was the case for the countries that started it all, but they must pass through it; there are no shortcuts.

We have put the agricultural and industrial economies behind us, thanks to automation. They have automated themselves into the history books. There aren't any people left on the shop floors in modern companies. Just a few people running a large number of machines are capable of making the products that are in demand. Never before has there been such a proliferation of agricultural and industrial products. But these economies are about to be relegated to the past, because jobs have become scarce and have moved to the Information Society.

With the industrial society—the era of the worker—a comprehensive, global perspective was, for the first time, brought to bear on history. It created the prevailing gap of inequality between the affluent countries and the poor; the poor being those countries that did not undergo an industrial revolution. The fact that China's per capita level of prosperity equals only 10 percent of the USA's is, obviously, attributable to many factors, but the primary reason is that China's industrialization came very late and has been interrupted by strife. The twenty-first century and the Dream Society of the affluent countries will choose to focus more on the relationship between rich and poor countries in the world.

The industrial society gave birth to the idea of progress—the notion that things were bound to develop along an even path leading ever onward and upward, with the future inevitably outshining the present. It also engendered the inbred faith that humankind was capable of creating its own future. Time was no longer cyclical, influenced by ups and downs, composed of different periods with no prevalent trends. Planning further ahead than just one year became possible; the time horizon for any given investment was increased.

The truly global markets started to evolve during the nineteenth century and at the beginning of the present century; the prerequisites were widespread use of mass production and a highly specialized division of labor within a hierarchical management structure. An added factor was the most outstanding achievements of the industrial society: its sophisticated means of transportation (trains, steamships, automobiles, and airplanes). Only globalization and these advanced means of transportation seem to form part of the inheritance we will have use for in the future.

The industrial society gave rise to the large concentrations of city dwellers. This urban boom in turn facilitated the personal exchange of ideas between many individuals—a precondition for a dynamic society where the idea of constant change comes naturally. With the urban areas representing more static and traditional elements, the cities remain more dynamic and geared to change (see Chapter 5).

The big political ideologies—socialism, liberalism, and nationalism—grew out of the industrial societies. They have exerted great influence upon the world our children will one day inherit; yet it is unlikely that these ideologies will be an inheritance that many will find useful. The future and the Dream Society will prefer the abundance of different stories on offer, while fewer people will share in any given set of values (see Chapter 2).

The Information Society

Most people will say that the fourth type of society—the Information Society—began in the 1960s. Around that time, desk jobs started to outnumber production jobs. As with previous periods of transition, new victorious companies were created. IBM, Hewlett-Packard, and Motorola are all among the 25 largest U.S. companies, measured in gross sales. Knowledge becomes more important than capital, and as the British scholar Charles Handy has pointed out, Marx and communism were proved right at last—by the Information Society. The workers have taken over capital because it is intellectual, not physical. It resides in our heads, not in bank accounts or in machines. The worker can bring it with her when she switches jobs.

Regardless of the Information Society, accountants today calculate only a company's physical assets. The accountant is measuring the company's capital at night—that is, when all employees have gone home. Nonetheless, many annual reports describe employees as the company's greatest asset. Yet when you turn to the balance sheets, this asset goes unmentioned. The industrial society's way of reasoning still remains, long after it has become irrelevant and even downright erroneous. The Swedish insurance giant Skandia has devised a way of summing up intellectual capital and in-house training, entering these into the books as investments. Skandia, by the way, is a highly successful company.

The Information Society assigns great value to academic learning. Never before has so high a premium been put on the ability to sit still for long hours, the ability to plan and control emotions. Spontaneity, the joy of the moment, is not permitted. You are supposed to focus on problems that may arise later on. You are wiser to think of them now. Numbers are better than words because they are concrete; they reflect measurable, physical realities. Pictures—possibly our most efficient means of communications—are not allowed in books of learning. Pictures are not considered appropriate. If you win a lottery prize, you should deposit it in the bank and use it for a new roof. Ethics committees are comprised of people who have completed long educations—as if the length of education and the ability to decide on ethical questions have anything to do with each other. The logic of the knowledge society permeates our set of values.

The rational Western world has won the global materialistic contest thanks to a Zeitgeist that valued change, and thanks to the ability to suppress emotions. The struggle against poverty and disease seems closer to being won than ever before. On top of this, rich countries are the absolute leaders in military might. After all, mastery of information technology today means military supremacy as well.

This will not last; a new era is coming. A new battle for the market has begun, with a new logic. The reason is that the Information Society, by definition, is abolishing itself. Its purpose is automation, letting the machines—computers and scanners— take over cerebral and sensory work. Exactly the way the purpose of the industrial society was to abolish our manual labor.

Information technology is advancing by leaps and bounds; companies in this sector will gradually come to dominate the Fortune 500 list. Current Fortune 500 companies have held on to their position on the list, and will be able to do so in the future, only to the extent that they make efficient use of information technology, for automation and for freeing the workforce to do more relevant work.

The modern-day Information Society, with its prevailing logic, still dominates the affluent societies and will continue to do so for some time to come. Gradually, it will be superseded by a new logic—that of the Dream Society. How far into the future can we extrapolate from the Information Society? First and foremost, we may base our assumptions on the material prosperity created during the present and the previous centuries. This state of plenty constitutes the basis of the Dream Society. Apart from this, however, our children and grandchildren will be assimilating only a few values from the Information Society. As already mentioned, they will, in many ways, be learning more from the hunter-gatherer society.

The Information Society, with its multiple TV channels, computers, and omnipresent telecommunications, has created a near-global market not only for the exchange of knowledge and data but for ideas as well. Chapter 5 deals with the new, global media and the adherent, open market for ideas and values. Seen as a whole, these developments probably constitute the greatest contribution that the Information Society will make toward shaping the future.

The many knowledge workers in charge of consummating the incipient automation of tasks previously handled by the brain and the senses will still have to evaluate and execute systems development—the great majority of jobs will not become emotional in substance before, say, the middle of the twenty-first century. Until then, the rigid logic of the Information Society will continue to be important. In the coming decade, this will be evident in the digitizing, communication, and mapping of the human genome.

When all is said and done, the brief reign of the Information Society still falls within the overall domain of the obsolescent materialistic societal type. Thus it is very conceivable that within 20 years, this type of society will be rejected as being anachronistic and cheerless—precisely the way many people today view the industrial society with its smoking chimneys and relentless, monotonous drudgery as negative. Years later, we may come to see the

Information Society in a romantic light—exactly the way some people today feel a sense of nostalgia for the agrarian society.

Someone once philosophized that time is what keeps everything from happening all at once. So it is; and as mentioned previously, our conception of time has changed through history, as it will continue to do in the future. This is why, before turning to the company in the Dream Society, we will look at the way time is perceived in the future. It is unlikely to be the same as today.

What Is Time?

The future arrives at the speed of 60 minutes an hour, and as this book enters the market there are fewer than 365 days remaining before New Year's Eve 1999. We also know that the future—happily—arrives only one day at a time. This is the mechanical time measured by our watches and calendars. We can also measure time celestially and through the changing of the seasons—cosmic time.

Time—As We Choose to Measure It

But time is also subjective. The year 2000—the great sea change ushering in a new millennium—is a human construct, as is the fiscal year or, for that matter, the Gregorian calendar. Will January 1, 2000, be a day like any other? No, it certainly will not. That day has a dream built into it. The dream is about taking stock. What have we achieved? What results do we have to show for it—we as humanity, as nations, as companies, as individuals? Have we yielded a profit? Of happiness? Of prosperity? But the dream is also about the future: a new millennium, replete with new possibilities, new goals. We will both settle old accounts and open new ones.

The countdown to 2000 has commenced on a digital clock outside the Pompidou Center in Paris. In Hanover, Germany, 40 million people are expected to visit the millennial world fair, Expo 2000. Events will be arranged at all of humanity's great monuments—

19

to wit, at the Great Pyramid of Khufu, at the Acropolis in Athens, at the Eiffel Tower in Paris, at St. Peter's Square in Rome, at Times Square in New York. Airlines will offer as many as three New Year's celebrations: first in New York, then at the international dateline, and finally in London. You had better stock up on champagne well ahead of time. Producers of the genuine article cannot adapt their vineyards to the exigencies of new millennia; they are too rare an occurrence. This will be expensive bubbly.

Older readers will recognize the familiar feeling that New Year's Eve seems to be happening every two weeks. A day offering many novel experiences—such as the first day of a vacation trip—is longer than "another day at the office." The fact that time appears to pass slowly when you are young (to a six-year-old, next year seems to be on the other side of the time barrier) and quickly as you grow older may be because there are fewer novel experiences and more repetition as you mature. Mechanical time and subjective time are two different things.

The future has always been around—as subjective time. During the Middle Ages, the peasants of Europe had a cyclical perception of time, governed by the changing of the seasons. Time repeated itself; it moved in circles rather than along a straight line. No wonder, there was no such thing as development. Not until around 1300 did people begin to think in terms of a future, a possible change ahead, in terms of the future as being potentially different from the present.

As we will discuss later in this chapter, in the present century, the ideology of progress has held sway over the Western world. The prevailing philosophy has been that the future will inevitably be better, that our children will be more prosperous than ourselves, and that our parents had a poorer and less attractive lifestyle than we do.

Let's consider time as a car driving us into the future. Until about 20 years ago, everyone in the car wanted it to go faster. The more changes, the better it was, because changes meant progress: progress in health care, machines that made work easier, bigger and better cars. Then, a visionary book about the future, Alvin

Toffler's *Future Shock* was published in 1970.[4] The book centered on the idea that people in the West were exposed to too many changes. The book argued that, unless we quickly learned to control the rate of change in our personal affairs as well as in society at large, we were "doomed to a massive adaptational breakdown." The book described an ominous paucity of under-pinnings in modern life. The relationship between the familiar and the unknown had gone haywire, putting the mental balance at risk. The car heading toward the future was speeding a bit out of control. Many were still complacent about the high speed of change, but an increasing number of people felt that the car speeding into the future was going at least a little too fast.

Is the need to slow down the reason for the ecological wave? Is this the reason so many products today are marketed using nostalgia, visions of the past, and rustic romanticism? Products from before the world went awry, from when life still had its permanent bearings. Back when you understood the surrounding world. The answer does not come easy, but let's venture a cautious "Yes, Toffler was right." His vision turned out not to be a flash in the pan; it offered a glimpse of the future seen from a distant perspective.

Three Reactions to Change

We react to the steady increase in the speed of change by "turning retro." Also, today we hold different views of time: How do we react to new products and how do we react to change in general?

> *Neo-Luddites.* One group reacts negatively to anything new. They are against it, they point to risks, they see "frightening perspectives." Modern-day Luddites may be more numerous than their predecessors in the English factories. This group shows a marked skepticism about biotechnology, the Internet, escalating consumption, and new technology in general. Things were better before.
>
> *Deniers.* A large group, comprised of those oriented toward the present, declines to contemplate the future. The

present is what counts, and the future will probably turn out to be more or less like the present anyway. When asked about the future, a member of the denying group might reply: "Well, this fall we have our silver wedding anniversary."

Early adapters. The last group, those oriented toward the future, can't get enough change; they are the early adapters who welcome all things new as an opportunity rather than as a risk. They are the first to buy new products, the first to use new technology. For their vacations they always seek out new destinations.

Some studies as well as personal observations would suggest that there are comparatively more people oriented toward the future in the USA than in Europe. The reason may be found in the annals of U.S. history, which hinges on values that welcome the future. Most of you will belong to the last group—those oriented toward the future. Otherwise you wouldn't have bought this book.

All three perceptions of time are fine, but in a period with a rapid speed of change, it is unwise to be oriented toward the past or the present. That brings too many disappointments.

The theory regarding the increased speed of change cannot be proved through objective methods. Yet few people can be in doubt that the car speeding toward the future is, in fact, rapidly increasing its velocity and that this will also hold true in the future. "The good old days" will be last year. One measure of the speed with which things are developing might be the waves of "revival" within music and fashion. In the 1970s revival meant the twenties or thirties (a 40-year time span), in the 1990s it is the seventies and eighties (a 20-year time span). The days of yore are yesterday.

The propensity for looking back in time instead of ahead is dealt with in Chapter 2, in the section The Market for Peace of Mind. Let us conclude by trying to imagine the subjective perception of time in the year 2020—as it may emerge if the present trends continue to prevail. If they do, our faith in progress will have disappeared. The vast majority of people living in the affluent countries will turn their gaze back in time, longing for the past. More to the point, they will pine for their fantasy of how the past was. At best, the future of the future will be a continuation of our present future; at worst, it will seem menacing. This means that most products will have to refer back to the past and that the word *modern* can no longer be used as a marketing slogan. A further consequence is that a new option for market segmentation will suggest itself according to demarcations following historical epochs. Some consumers, say, will be Victorian-age buffs, others will be Wild West enthusiasts, and some will swear by the dark period in the 1930s that gave rise to the heavy industries. The market will no longer be constrained to the present and the future; it will cover the entire spectrum of time. Time will truly have become a relative concept; "2020" will merely be the designation of a year happening to be on the calendar, while values and products often belong to an entirely different era.

Can a given civilization develop without belief in a better future? Probably not; we will perhaps witness a more radical separation between mechanical time (clock time) and subjective time.

We will be less apt to see time as a front advancing like a tank, conquering the future one day at a time and leaving it behind as dead past. We will no longer be living only in the present moment, and the notion of our society as steadily improving thanks to progress in technology and ingenuity will vanish. We will once again think of time the way the hunter-gatherer did: There are changes, but they do not progress in any single direction. The difference in relation to the world of the hunter-gatherer lies in the sheer multitude of changes as well as the liberty to choose our own sets of values. By contrast, the twenty-first century citizen's idea of time will have very little in common with that of, say, the European immigrants coming to the USA a century ago. They carried with them the notion of a dark past in the old country, of a present rife with opportunity, and of a golden future awaiting when the farm had been built and would yield prosperity to the whole family.

We have not yet reached 2020, but we are clearly beginning to use the concept of time as a means of creating fixtures for our lives—we merely change the year on the calendar.

If You See the Future as an Obstacle, You Are Walking in the Wrong Direction

If we limit ourselves to thinking in terms of realities, facts, and knowledge, we have got the future all wrong, because it is made, not of certainties, but of dreams. The future does not exist in the physical world but is present in our thoughts and in our dreams only. That is why futurology is not solely an exact science. Far too many companies search for the future in the rear-view mirror, because that is where certainties are found. There we find the part of reality that can be verified. The strict scientific model of logic is a trap that prevents us from looking ahead.

The idea of producing a Walkman was not the result of exhaustive market research by Sony. It was an idea, a dream, and is now a reality, shared today by millions of people all over the world. The airplane was a dream—the dream of moving in the world of birds. Without that dream, no one would have sacrificed life and limb in order to make the dream come true. The dream of landing a man on the moon motivated tens of thousands of collaborators back in the 1960s to push themselves to the limit, mentally as well as physically. The lunar landing served as an inspiration to billions of people all over the world.

Behind every technological breakthrough there lies a dream. Behind every new product there lies a dream. Dreams create realities—through hard work.

Think of the future as a realm of possibilities, as a realm of dreams—a large, three-dimensional space within which the future will take place. A company's products must be placed somewhere inside this vast realm. The danger lies in underestimating this space. Far too often, the range of possibilities is assessed to be the size of the present, with a few extras added.

The future's realm of possibilities is always bigger than you imagine.

What is the realm of possibilities for ice cubes? Not overwhelming, you might say. Ice is a commodity. Ice cubes are used to cool our drinks, and this modest role is reflected in their modest price. It is a standard product for which price is the determining factor. Wrong! In 1996, Copenhagen Airport imported pieces of the Greenland ice cap. The ice cube was transformed into a story about millennia and millennia of ageing. The bubbles in the ice cubes contain air from the time before the Pyramids were built. Pure air in new drinks. The realm of possibilities for a trivial product, the ice cube, has been expanded. You order an ice age ice cube, and it even comes with a drink included! The story was the product.

Dreams are the stuff the future is made of. The future is uncertain. Yet companies seek certainty in their investments; shareholders must be convinced of solid dividends on their shares. Still we have to acknowledge that dealing with the future is dealing with uncertainty. For this reason, organizational deliberations concerning the future should consist of structured dialogues, often with an alternate voice, which could typically be a futurist acting as participant or moderator. A structured dialogue is chosen because there are no exact answers, because decisions have to be made before developments can be ascertained. This book will help you structure such a dialogue.

A structured dialogue about the future grows from pertinent questions. *Newsweek* posed one such question in January 1997. It began like this: President Lincoln was a great orator. He was a great communicator; people listened, and they understood what he was saying. President Roosevelt came across as an imposing speaker on radio; his "Fireside Chats" in the 1930s—the golden age of radio—were outstanding. The consummate TV presidents were, above all, John F. Kennedy and Ronald Reagan. The pertinent question asked, then, was this: Who will be the Internet president? Who will understand how to utilize this, our newest means of communication, to its utmost capabilities?

Needless to say, because you must get rid of as many uncertainties as possible through research, that is also part of the structured dialogue about the future. Population development is one such area where research is feasible. In five years, how many consumers will be 40 to 50 years old? This question can be answered pretty decisively. All countries can offer excellent statistical forecasts. You can also project the future—extrapolate, assuming that the present rate of development will continue unaltered for the next 10 years. If this is applied to Internet users, the answer will be that nearly everybody in affluent countries will be online in 10 years.

You may also ask when the people of China will reach the same standard of living as that of the United States if the current growth rate in China of 10 percent per annum proves enduring. The answer is around 2030. The growth will occur mainly toward the end of this time span—since we are dealing in percentages—which is why consumer growth in the coming 10 years, measured in absolute numbers, will not be all that impressive. This calculation can be used to conclude that a veritable mass market for cars in China lies 15 to 20 years ahead.

Forget About Your "Strategy"

In a stable world, a company's strategy (strategy in the sense of a consciously chosen path of development) can be permanent. In a slightly less stable world that involves some changes in the company's market, periodic strategy revisions will be needed—perhaps every five years or so. The point is that along with an increased speed of change the need for strategy revisions also increases.

Many companies have experienced how a detailed strategy originally conceived as a *plan* becomes obsolete in no time. Market developments raced ahead of it long before the planning horizon was reached. The three-year plan became a one-year plan instead. So numerous companies have already felt it imperative to concentrate on more basic objectives.

The Mission: "Why are we in business? What would be missing from the market if we weren't around?"

The Vision: "Where will our company be in 10 years? What products will it be offering?"

Strategies that define a very specific path of development often get in the way of initiatives and block possibilities of acting swiftly as openings in the market appear. No strategy is stronger than the market. Strategy is supposed to be a beacon, and the idea behind it is to let employees know what actions and decisions management supports. The problem arises because the market is mercurial. Even the most alert executives cannot adapt strategies at a pace that keeps up with the market; they will always lag slightly behind, unless they forget about their determined strategy and adapt to the wider and more commodious concept of *vision* as the company beacon.

Strategy meetings should be downplayed; the company's future is at stake if market opportunities are stalled and strangled by the iron grip of strategy. The market is in a continual state of movement, you need to flow with it, to keep ahead of the market. Trends can no longer be handled by market research; it covers a past that is increasingly different from the future. Regulated planning for the future virtually guarantees losing out to companies better poised for change.

The road to the future leads away from strategy, toward emphasis on the market and its possibilities, from strategy-guided control toward inspiration from the vision, from management control to guidance by the many eyes of employees and staff all focused on the market and its possibilities.

Planning on the Future: Fiction with No Plot

Businesses need to imagine their futures, the way good novelists imagine their stories. Georges Simenon, the renowned Belgian writer of detective stories, is a fine storyteller capable of evoking images of Paris through his descriptions of sounds, music, dance halls, and bistros. When you read his books it's like being there yourself. He is master of the *mise en scène* with all its props and backdrops. He also makes his characters exude mystery right to the very last page. Similarly, business scenarios are a stage and the market is the play with its actors. The futurist sets the stage for the play that will unfold in the market of the future. That the word *scenario* is etymologically related to *scene* is no wonder. The scenario is the background for the drama of the market. Operating with scenarios makes it easier to answer companies' questions about the future: What stage are we to act on, what does the scenery look like, what color is the backdrop? In science fiction, the scenery is often the most important ingredient; describing the distant future is more important than the plot—except of course in good science fiction. The *Star Wars* saga is both a depiction of an alien galaxy whose civilizations are battling—a brilliant scenario—and also a heart-rending myth about the victory of good over evil.

The comparison of scenario planning to the world of theater and fiction is no accident. Building scenarios is not merely an analytic exercise, a stringent and technical process. It is also part drama and part dream. The future demands that you manage uncertainty, and scenarios are the proper tools—alternative visualizations of the market in 3 to 5 years, in 5 to 10 years. For many years, Shell of London has paved the way in using scenarios for planning company development. Nowadays, most large firms use scenarios in some form or another, because the future is uncertain, because the realm of possibilities is vast, because only a structured dialogue can lead to a conclusion solid enough to form the basis for investment.

The Can of the Future

One example. One of our large clients asked us: "What is the future of canned foods? Will the can be made obsolete by a desire for fresh foods and frozen products? Should we invest in new machinery for manufacturing tin cans? The time horizon is 5 to 10 years."

We were unable to produce a forecast, predicting what consumers would choose, so we decided to work out four scenarios capable of filling out the realm of possibilities.

1. *The green scenario.* The green, ecologically aware consumer is the future. In 5 to 10 years nearly every consumer will be thinking in terms of environmental soundness. All products will have to be nature-friendly. The green wave is hitting Europe and the United States with great force. We have only just seen the beginning. In 10 years, additives will be illegal, recycling a matter of course, and products required to emanate nature-friendliness and rustic romanticism.

    The packaging challenge: The green, environmentally sound can—what does it look like?

2. *The busy, "intelligent" consumer scenario.* The busy, technologically aware consumer is the future. In 5 to 10 years, nearly all products will come with built-in chips. The products will be "intelligent." The consumer will be connected to the Net, live in a high-tech house, buy prefabricated food—and will often eat meals alone. Eating in groups will be a rarity, because of the fast pace of life.

    The packaging challenge: The high-tech can—what does it look like?

3. *The story scenario.* The consumer buys feelings, experiences, and stories. This is the postmaterialistic consumer demanding a story to go with the product. Food that is of good quality, tasty, and nutritious will no longer be sufficient. It must appeal to the emotions with a built-in story of status, belonging, adventure, and lifestyle.

    The packaging challenge: The can with a story to tell—what does it look like?

4. *The stable, business-as-usual scenario.* Consumer preferences will remain unchanged for the next 5 to 10 years. The can will enjoy a stable and traditional place within the consumption pattern. The consumer buying canned foods may have grown a little older but we should not expect dramatic

upheavals. There will always be a demand roughly equivalent to the present.

The packaging challenge: Avoid product development.

The scenarios above are extreme because they have to cover the
entire realm of possibilities and have to include all consumers,
who will have a somewhat higher standard of living than today.
In addition, they envision new technology that might threaten
the can itself.

The initial result was that we rejected the fourth scenario on the
ground that no one believed in business as usual; there would certainly be a change. Next, the green, environmentally sound can
was put out to pasture. It didn't cover the essentials. Recyclability
and eco-friendliness were important, but too feeble as guiding
principles. Greenness was a side issue. After a couple of further
meetings the conclusion was clear. We had developed a forward-
looking scenario in which everybody believed—a shared vision of
the future market. Product development could commence,
investments could be made. The final conclusion remains the
property of our client, but readers may feel free to draw their
own. What do you think?

The Bank of the Future

A question was posed to us by a large European company: "What
do you think? What will the bank of the future look like in 5 to 10
years? Which expectations will we face from business clients and
from private customers? We need you for inspiration; of course,
we have our own ideas, but we want you to be our alternate voice.
Maybe you can point out possibilities we have overlooked." We
agreed to use a scenario process.

1. *The systematic bank scenario.* The bank customer is price-
   conscious. The future lies in automation of all data processing, and employees will become increasingly fewer and
   farther between. The systematic bank is one comprehensive
   system where the customer rarely, if ever, will encounter an

employee. This may seem impersonal, but costs are lower than in less automated banks. Systematic banks will be the most competitive, and given the economy of scale involved, we must expect larger banks to be victorious—in 10 years there will be very few banks in Europe. The systematic bank will win in the future.

2. *The segmented bank scenario.*   Bank customers aren't all the same. The successful bank will be the one best able to tailor its services to fit customer segments; perhaps by dividing customers into 8 to 10 groups according to age, income, and family status. The bank most skillful at segmentation will be the winner, just as product variation has replaced mass production and standard merchandise on the market for tangible products. The segmented bank will win in the future.

3. *The customer's bank scenario.*   Bank customers demand attention, advice, and personal service. Money is an important part of life, and people are willing to pay for advice. Customers should be treated as individuals; service at the counter must be replaced by more personal relations, including counseling. We should strive toward banking as it was conducted a century ago, when there was time to have a chat with the customer. The customer's bank will win in the future.

The stage was set. All agreed that most banks in Europe were pursuing a strategy equivalent to scenario 1 and moving away from scenario 3. Scenario 2—the segmented bank—was something many banks were working on. We tried to argue in favor of scenario 3. Particularly if you happen to be a smaller bank, following a strategy that is based almost solely on economies of scale would be disastrous. The problem, of course, lay in getting the customers to part with their money willingly for financial advice. We felt this was a challenge that needed to be met. The conclusion we reached is that very few banks are moving against the tide. Doing things in a different way from everyone else is risky—after all, others have also done some thinking on the matter. Adhering to conventional wisdom is the safest thing to do. Risking the entire company on the basis of a controversial strategy might be called courageous by some, but seen as sheer foolhardiness by others, especially if things go wrong. Again, uncertainty is what makes business exciting.

The Product Becomes Secondary

All the above scenarios are designed for specific companies and their markets, and bear the distinguishing marks of the Dream Society.

We've Become Rich but Dissatisfied

There has been a sixfold increase in affluence in the twentieth century, a momentous revolution that will never be repeated and has never previously been seen in world history. We in the so-called rich countries have gone from rags to riches within the span of a century—despite two world wars. The result has been an immense focus on the material things in life. GNP growth and individual happiness do not go hand in hand, yet in the twentieth century we have assumed that this is so. We are now discarding our material fascination. Measurable quantities, logic, and academic learning have held sway in the evaluation of human qualities, especially within the world of science and education. Companies are aware that skills come in a variety of shades and nuances. One book has given this Zeitgeist a little nudge.

In *Emotional Intelligence: Why It Matters More Than IQ*,[5] which rose to the top of best-seller lists in the United States and Great Britain, Daniel Goleman quotes Aristotle by way of introduction: "Anyone can become angry—that is easy. But to be angry with the right person, to the right degree, at the right time, for the right purpose, and in the right way—that is not easy." The message, of course, is that IQ comprises only a small part of human potential and that this is particularly pertinent to modern business, where efficiency means the ability to convey a message from A to B quickly and succinctly. The key word is *communication*.

In Henry Ford's factories at the start of this century, the name of the game was the amount of tangible products manufactured, measured in time and quality, because the company's manufacturing plant and its manufactured goods were its assets. The modern-day, knowledge-intensive company is far more of a social construct, because its corporate culture—its people and their know-how—are its assets.

The employee with the highest IQ is often not the manager. Many other factors are valued highly, factors like emotional intelligence, including self-control and the ability to get along with people. Aristotle was right. As Goleman writes in his book: "The market forces that are reshaping our work life are putting an unprecedented premium on emotional intelligence for on-the-job success; and toxic emotions put our physical health as much at risk as does chain-smoking, even as emotional balance can help protect our health and well-being." We all know this, but it needed to be expressed in words.

People Who Tell Stories

The one-sided deification of the IQ is truly a thing of the past. The valuable employee of the future will possess the ability to create, cooperate, motivate, incite, and catapult initiatives. The successful employee of the future is a virtuoso at acquiring and conveying knowledge, at coalescing and improving the work environment. The employee who, through telling stories about the organization's results, manages to strengthen corporate culture will be considered a valuable asset. Nothing so inspires an organization as an enlivening story relating how the whopping contract was finally won, despite adversity and horrendous odds. The storyteller creates corporate culture. Social skills create cooperation. None of these skills relate solely to IQ. Today, even research is carried out by teams—in research environments— the results of which depend on participants' collaborative skills. The need still exists for the isolated genius—the individualist relentlessly opposed to living in close social quarters—but you want only one or two of them around.

Who Makes the Money?

Another objective indication that we are heading toward the Dream Society can be seen in the executive remuneration. Which employees receive the highest salaries? A survey of the highest-salaried individuals of 1997 suggests that these people are not exclusively high priests of the Information Society or executives from Fortune 500 companies. Among the Top 10, we also find people from the Dream Society. Figures from *Business Week* (surveys of executive pay) and from *Forbes* magazine (highest-paid athletes) demonstrate this fact. Four athletes have made it into the *Business Week* Top 10 league. Their high-salaried tenure may be shorter than that of the top executives, but they make their killing earlier in life. Their wealth can accumulate interest for many years. And this is without taking into consideration candidates from the world of film and music. Madonna, for example, is essentially a storyteller advancing on the global market.

What we are witnessing is a beginning. Storytellers from the world of sports and entertainment are becoming the top wage earners—a clear and objective indication of the shift from the Information Society to the Dream Society. In just a few years, athletes and artists will head the Top 10 list of earnings. The era of storytellers has begun: athletes who can tell a story of success, of the will to achieve results regardless of the costs. We need this story in our everyday lives, and we are willing to pay for it. Companies buy a story for their products and pay top dollar to have this story attached to their products.

Products That Tell a Story

Wristwatches today are very accurate and reliable. They are long-lasting and are of good quality. If you want a watch that will keep the exact time, the price is $10. Unless you are after a story. If the watch is to appeal to the heart, to bespeak a certain lifestyle, status, or adventure, the price can go up as far as $15,000.

In the *Rolex Awards for Enterprise Journal*, the Rolex people explain how they have endowed their watches with a story: "The spirit of enterprise, our raison d'être, is sometimes a difficult thing to explain. It defies strict definitions, and words don't ever seem to do it justice. For clarification, we often turn to the individuals who embody it—that gives the best idea of what is meant by the spirit of enterprise." The Rolex award is presented to individuals who tell the Rolex story through their spectacular achievements. The story has many buyers—and you get a watch along with it.

Machines Will Move Us— Emotionally, Not Physically

For centuries, we've used machines to help us survive physically. Ever since the first water mills were constructed in the Nile delta to facilitate irrigation of the fields along the river, we have concentrated our efforts on inventing machines capable of supplanting our muscles. Up until modern times, 99 percent of the energy at our disposal was derived from human toil. Mills supplied us with energy but we still had to work them. Then the steam engine and later the internal combustion engine arrived, suddenly providing undreamed-of amounts of energy. The industrial revolution was more important than the French revolution. It changed the material conditions of life fundamentally. Today we must face the fact that machines have taken over 99 percent of muscle-powered labor.

Thus, most of us use our muscles only for amusement. The market for sports equipment, fitness paraphernalia, and athletic footwear is booming as a result of automation. Our urge to sprint along streets and roads in order to achieve physical fatigue would be incomprehensible to inhabitants of the nineteenth century. They would ask: "How come you are running when you've got cars and you aren't going anywhere, anyway?"

When the Information Society set in, we began to automate our communication and our senses. Communication no longer needs to be transmitted in person or in writing: we have phones and TV. Calculators and computers have supplanted a major part of the brain's work. We have now come one step further. We are automating not only muscle labor but brain power as well. We have robots that paint, cut, and feel; sensors that keep cars on the road and at a proper distance from other cars. Again we let machines do the work for us.

What's next is cerebral and sensory work for amusement purposes in the beginning of the twenty-first century. Just as we saw a market appear, based on muscle work for fun, we will have a market for cerebral and sensory work for fun. When driving a car has been rendered clear of all danger—and thus boring—by microchips, those 80 percent of adult males who claim they are better than average drivers will be willing to pay in order to prove their abilities, on large ranges with curves and hills—even at realistic race tracks. Younger people have already adopted sensory work for entertainment—witness the computer games, laser games, and virtual reality. Soon adults will be permitting themselves the same indulgence on a large scale. Were we to single out a growth industry for the twenty-first century, it would have to be cerebral and sensory work for fun.

People living in a society of hunter-gatherers had to use every human skill at their disposal just to survive. Intelligence, experience, eyes, ears, nose, muscles—all senses had to join forces. The prerequisite for survival was that all senses were intact. Modern people are not that different from the hunters. We also want to use all our senses. When machines take over our work and make some of these senses superfluous we will use them anyway—for fun.

The Victorious Companies of the Twenty-First Century

How to build a story into your business? Let us try to furnish an outline describing some victorious companies of the twenty-first century, the ones that will go to the top of the global company list.

36

The market for athletic footwear is worth $7 to $8 billion in the United States alone. Nike, the current market leader, paid $400 million for the right to sponsor the Brazilian national soccer team. Nike is a global company able to tell its story across linguistic and cultural borders. It is skillful at attaching a story to a pair of sneakers. It is a Dream Society company. Nike works from the basic tenet that the issue is not athletic footwear, but a story of youth, success, fame, and triumph. Wear Nike and you, too, will be a "rebel with a cause."

In the years lying ahead, the market for fairy tales will see a booming expansion. A large number of companies will gradually be entering the market. We will have to abandon our way of categorizing products according to their immediate function. The tobacco giants have understood this. Marlboro and Camel come not only as cigarettes, but also as watches, shoes, and apparel. Their story can be sold with a whole range of products, the products themselves being secondary. The tobacco companies were compelled to take on the role of Dream Society advocates, presumably because of the risk that cigarettes would eventually be spurned by consumers—or outlawed. They had to ask themselves: "How do we avoid losing our considerable investment in the story?" The answer suggested itself quickly: by relocating it to other products. Cigarettes and watches thus share the same slot in the market.

The traditional English motorcycle makers—Norton, Triumph, Royal Enfield, and BSA—although illustrious and venerable, all lost out to the Japanese competition in the 1970s. The Japanese products offered better means of transportation—cheaper, faster, and demanding of less maintenance. They were technologically superior. So the English motorcycle is a thing of the past. Wrong! Even in Europe, motorcycles are ceasing to be a means of transportation carrying you from point A to point B. They are embodiments of a lifestyle, of adventure and speed. To put it a bit schematically, at the threshold of the Dream Society, lifestyle value outranks transportation value. Technology becomes secondary compared with the story.

This is why the industry is now experiencing a rebirth—the story of these proud motorcycles is being picked up again, dusted off, and relaunched as a lifestyle. The same is true of the glorious American motorbikes, Harley-Davidson and Indian. The market for stories resembles other markets in that the demand for certain types of stories may change. Sales figures for Rolls-Royce and Bentley, those two distinguished English luxury automobiles, have been cut in half since 1990. It would appear that the market for a story about status, luxury, and prestige has seen a decline in demand. Wealth, and the need to flaunt it, has decreased. Perhaps the story about extreme affluence and abundance is not part of the future. The reason may well be that we are entering the Dream Society, where life's material aspects are of less significance.

In the twenty-first century, the transportation market will see the same development in cars and trains. The first Dream Society train is already in operation—between Vienna and Istanbul—it is called the Orient Express. These aren't trains you take because you are going from one place to another. They are a fairy tale being offered, a fairy tale about old-world charm, about champagne and caviar, about romance. The tickets are not cheap—romance and charm cost more than transportation.

One story in particular from this century, that of the *Titanic*, is told over and over again in books, in musicals, and in movies. It is not unthinkable that the *Titanic* could be rebuilt and possibly relaunched in 2012, the centennial of the dramatic shipwreck. An ocean liner with a story, nostalgia, drama, and status. Of course it would come with the stipulation that now its safety must be impeccable. That would also provide the perfect setting for a future film about the loss of the *Titanic* on that freezing April night when 1600 people perished.

Five miles south of the Magic Kingdom at Disney World lies Celebration, a complete city with room for 20,000 residents.[6] The first dwellings were offered for sale on Mickey Mouse's birthday, November 18. A city with a theme, a philosophy, a story. This is not a theme park, but a themed town. Disney is very adept at appealing to our hearts. Every old city of Europe—big and small—also has a story just waiting to be told. In Ireland, inhabitants of some of the smaller villages have congregated to build a home page on the Web. They tell the stories behind their villages, through pictures, through the elderly citizens' memories of a town's myths and legends. Does a market exist for this? Yes, apart from the millions of Irish residents now living in the USA, Canada, and Australia who are yearning to know more about their roots, there are millions more who would like to know the story behind the tune "It's a Long Way to Tipperary."

Among the most dynamic Dream Society companies will be sports teams, Grand Prix racing teams, the Olympic Games, and sports stars. The German Grand Prix racing star Michael Schumacher makes approximately $25 million a year. This income is global because the story is global. Even European sports celebrities make astonishing amounts by displaying their stories of audacity, courage, speed, and technology.

Anyone seeking success in the market of the future will have to be a storyteller. The story is the heart of the matter. The story content might be, say, how you avoid product development. The company should decree a ban on any product improvement. Otherwise, the story is ruined.

The English AGA stove has had no product development since 1922.[7] The price is in the $10,000 to $15,000 range, installation not included. Yearly sales are at 7000 units, but the stove has a clear future because of nonexistent product development. *Time* magazine quotes marketing manager Ian Heath as saying, "What other kitchen appliance can promise family together-ness? They (the customers) want family life and AGA is at the center of that wish. They see the AGA in a very emotional sense." This is not a status appliance, although the price tag would seem to indicate otherwise. It is a lifestyle appliance with a story of family togetherness, something that abounded in the old days, back when family values and gender roles were not up for discussion and before mass production robbed products of their spirit.

The Most Important Raw Material of the Twenty-First Century

In the age of the industrial worker, the raw materials were coal, oil, and steel. In the era of the farmer they were soil, fields, and livestock. In the epoch of the information experts and symbol analysts, the raw materials consist of data, information, and knowledge. Production of knowledge increases daily; any attempt at a comprehensive overview will inevitably prove futile. The number of objective facts has expanded toward infinity.

Data are figures and letters in various combinations. Today, knowledge is stored as letters; we learn through the alphabet—this is the medium of the Information Society. Most likely, the medium of the Dream Society will be the picture. The paleolithic cave paintings in northern Spain and the southwest of France show beautiful, colored figures of horses, bulls, and other animals. They were created by some of the first Europeans 20,000 to 30,000 years ago. They constitute the Homo sapiens' first successful attempt to store information outside of memory; these messages depicting the coveted prey could be "read" from generation to generation independently of oral tradition. Even after the written languages came into being in the Middle East more than 30,000 years ago, images remained an important means of communication. The written word and the image were rivals in communication until Gutenberg. When along came the ability to mass-produce the written word in books, images started to lose ground. In medieval Europe, literacy was the exception to the rule. Most people received the Christian gospel through oral transmission—as well as images. Only during the nineteenth century did the majority of Europeans learn to read and write. In our age, the written word has taken over completely as the medium for information storage. The written word has won over the image.

The advent of television in the 1950s challenged the dominance of the written word for the first time since the age of Gutenberg. Television is the first truly global medium; it is available to the great majority of the population even in less developed countries (see Chapter 5). In the affluent countries, we spend a daily average of 3 to 4 hours watching images on TV. The relationship between receiving information through the written word as opposed to images has shifted; we view relatively more images than we did 50 years ago. The revolutionary theory is that we are approaching a situation where images will once again become the most important medium for information storage, where the written word will lose ground. The primary rationale behind this theory is that images transcend linguistic barriers. This proliferation of different languages is one of the barriers blocking globalization and may partially be overcome through images; not just through TV, but through computers and advertising as well. A smile, anger, sorrow—all are illustrated more easily through images. This is a development that will require many years, but it is quite possible that a century from now, our "Gutenberg period" will be over and that the Dream Society's primary means of communications will be images.

Through his highly ambitious project Corbis, Bill Gates, Microsoft founder and CEO, is establishing a vast, global library of stored images. Freed from the constraints of the book and accessible through the Internet, Corbis is a digitized world of pictures aimed at serving the needs of the twenty-first century.

Another type of raw material is stories, myths, and legends. Where may they be found in large concentrations? The answer is obvious: among the populations least affected by modern society's rational world view, the inhabitants of less developed countries. They live in Africa, in India, along the Polar Circle, in South American rain forests, and on the Pacific isles. It is high time they claim copyright ownership of their own myths, the ones told around the campfire and passed down from generation to generation. All indigenous peoples who have held on to their traditions have access to the raw material of the future.

Currently, Western scientists are searching the Amazon region for plants that could be of use in the pharmaceuticals industry. In the twenty-first century, experts from major companies will be traveling to the same areas. Their objective will be to buy myths

41

from the natives. Affluent countries are rich in a material sense, yet they are poor in myths and legends. Let us entertain the thought that in 2025, Greenland's main export will be legends and fairy tales; that Australia's primary product industry will have been surpassed by aborigines selling their legends. The notion is not farfetched. Though Hollywood is today's undisputed world leader in story merchandising, it still needs more and better raw materials for its movies. The Western world's own artists are, of course, also a source of wealth. Just as the European soccer players who were appallingly underpaid in the 1950s are envious of current megastar, high-salaried soccer players, contemporary writers will have reason to envy the storytellers of the future. Had the two great Danish storytellers, Karen Blixen and Hans Christian Andersen, written their books today, their financial situations would have been very different.

The World as a Theme Park

The large companies of the twenty-first century will launch themes. Jurassic Park is a good example. A universe has been created, narrated through a film and a theme park. The theater for which Shakespeare penned his plays, The Globe, has been rebuilt in England; the palaces of the Indian maharajas have been partially transformed into hotels. Our demand for stories is greater than can be met at the present. The drama is beginning to evaporate from even the most imposing of nature's huge monuments. Mount Everest in the Himalayas is climbed by 80 people a year, some tagging along as paying tourists. The story created by the locals, the Sherpas, insisting that the summit is a holy place possessing powers that transform men, has been drowned by empty cans and plastic wrappers littering the eternal snow. We are running out of real fairy tales so we have to dream up new ones.

In some areas of the great national parks of Africa, animals have grown entirely accustomed to the daily caravans of ogling tourists passing by. Substantial amounts of money are spent on saving the endangered species. But if they do become extinct we will have to stage some new fantastic stories, like the dinosaurs of Jurassic Park.

The last remaining natural habitats of the orangutan (which means "forest-human" in Indonesian) on Borneo and at the northern tip of Sumatra are at risk. In 50 years, these areas will be a global tourist attraction, drawing many visitors from all over the world. The rain forest will no longer be a virgin natural haven where myths flourish unfettered; T-shirts will be sold along with the experience of seeing a "forest-human" clinging to the highest branches in the treetops.

The great sights to see in the theme world of the twenty-first century will be attractions that are genuine, and recognized as such. The Great Pyramid of Khufu in Egypt has experienced the longest payback horizon in world history. It was built nearly 3000 years ago, as a religious monument in a spiritual world where such a prodigious effort to construct something with no (material) purpose came naturally. Only now, in the twentieth century, is the investment yielding a return through mass tourism. In the twenty-first century, it will probably be considered unusual if you haven't visited the Pyramids at least once and learned about their history.

Doing Well by Doing Good

In the Dream Society, companies will do well by doing good, but in a different way than today. Already today, many big companies adhere to declared goals that do not directly contribute to profits. Money is given to charities. The idea is to build up "political capital"—tantamount to investing in confidence and reputation. This effort is directed at employees, customers, and regulating authorities alike. The traditional, for-profit-only company is on its way to becoming a thing of the past. In 10 years, a company whose only objectives are reflected on the bottom line may well become a not very attractive business associate. The same is true of the market for daily groceries. Consumers will be politically aware, choosing products from companies that exhibit attitudes similar to their own. The political consumer will play a major part 5 to 10 years from now.

At the same time, the big Dream Society companies will encompass those that specialize in selling sympathy, compassion and aid, or assistance, like the Red Cross and other organizations, large and small, currently collecting donations for charitable purposes. They should be considered to be companies precisely because all companies of the future will be selling emotions. Thus they are not fundamentally different from the other market players. What is the size of the market for compassion? We will be facing a market with considerable growth in the twenty-first century: support in favor of the poor, the environment, human rights, democracy, freedom of the press, and animal welfare. Of course, we shouldn't anticipate all these companies going public, trading shares, and so on. The majority of these companies will steer clear of the stock exchange, which will be reserved for the old production firms and companies with profit as their sole objective. Greenpeace might well become one of the twenty-first century's important Dream Society companies, selling firmly held convictions about environmental issues. The company will open an office in China before 2000, and it is getting ready to customize its sale of convictions to Chinese tradition. Greenpeace wishes to avoid open confrontation. A large global market for convictions is on the horizon.

Many visions of the future involve outer space and its conquest, including the possibility of visiting or even colonizing Mars. The purveyors to this market are science fiction writers and the entertainment industry at large. However, NASA also contributes. The American space administration's official vision is as follows: "NASA is an investment in America's future. As explorers, and pioneers, and innovators, we boldly expand frontiers in air and space to inspire and serve America and to benefit the quality of life on earth."[8] This is remarkably reminiscent of the famous vision that is introduced at the beginning of every episode of *Star Trek*. It demonstrates NASA's real product: adventure.

Bloodless Wars

In an often quoted 1996 article from *Foreign Affairs,* professor Samuel Huntington advanced the theory that wars of the future will be wars of culture, wars of values within a world subdivided into six to eight great areas of culture—rather than nation states.[9] These cultural areas will have competing values. It has also been suggested that whereas World War II was an industrial war where the nation with the highest industrial capacity won, the Gulf War was predominantly an information war, a war of hardware and software. The war of the future could be a content war—of ideas and values. The information monopolies have been broken; the Internet recognizes no boundaries. Victory will be won by the culture that can sell its values, its ideological foundations, to the adversary. The war of the future can be perceived as a battle of mentalities and will involve no deaths or casualties. The combatant with the best stories rules the world—and the world market.

The war of cultures, of stories, and not of bodies is a Dream Society war of the future. Like the laws of physics, the Dream Society theory is all-encompassing, and in order to be validated must prove itself applicable to all cases covered by the theory. If it does not apply to all social aspects, then it is flawed. Wide-ranging transformations do not happen from one year to the next, not even from decade to decade. Transformations take place all the time, however. We might draw a comparison to the USA in the 1880s. True, the farming economy was predominant, but there could be no doubt that within the span of 10 to 20 years, industry would account for the greater part of the economy and industrial work would become the most common type of employment. The transformation leading to the Dream Society will proceed more swiftly, since the velocity of change has accelerated dramatically during the twentieth century.

But this applies only to affluent countries and to the rapidly growing affluent middle class in the urban areas of developing countries. These countries are generally still in the age of the farmer or on their way toward a period of industrialization. Therefore, they are not the focus of this book. They face other problems; their future is different. The reason the Dream Society still has relevance for developing countries is that it describes the nature of their relationships with affluent countries. We have to envision these developing countries as the industrial areas of the world—the producers behind the products onto which companies in affluent countries attach their stories. Of course, no one can rule out that the less developed countries will also acquire the ability to tell stories through their products. Their challenge, however, will lie in getting these stories to cross over the cultural boundary into affluent countries that possess the purchasing power.

The Alternatives

The Dream Society is a theory about the future; therefore it cannot be verified. Let us discuss other theories it is competing with. What are the alternatives?

The Green Society

In an ecological future that emphasizes taking care of nature, sustainability and recyclability will be unequivocal political guidelines. We will live happy lives in harmony with nature. We need to learn from nature's laws and must understand that we have only borrowed this planet from our children. It is our duty to return it in good condition and to safeguard its many treasures. Ruthless exploitation of fossil fuels and forests is out of the question. New technology may be used only for further protection of the environment. When we are faced with a choice between jobs and environmental priorities, the environment wins.

This scenario for the future is preferred at the moment by many citizens and by some futurists. Some go as far as to say that unless our future is green, we don't have any at all.

The green approach is part of the Dream Society—one story among many that will determine the future—but it is not an overall theory. When whales are no longer food, but beautiful animals that people sail to sea in order to photograph, then a new story is unfolding. A green story to be sure, but still a story. The green movement will be able to explain only part of the changes taking place in the market of the future—but it is part of the big picture.

A World of Conflict

Two major world wars and a history proving that wars have always been a part of human societies—sometimes, the destructive forces are the strongest—make a conflict scenario a very distinct possibility. In the long run, however, wars are only exceptions from the main path of development. Thomas Edison and the Wright brothers did more to change the world than did Napoleon and Hitler. They merit longer chapters in the annals of history than the great warmongers. Thus the conflict scenario is not a scenario proper, but an occurrence—one that unfortunately cannot be excluded.

No Changes

The Information Society with its emphasis on knowledge and technology will continue for the next 50 years. This is the scenario adopted by the great majority of futurologists, the great majority of people interested in the future. Most futurists are busy analyzing the consequences of the Information Society to prepare companies for the future. This book argues that the sun is setting on the Information Society and that the key to looking forward is to look for the dream. This approach puts it at odds with the majority view, with conventional wisdom as it were.

After the Dream Society

Will the Dream Society turn out to be the last societal type? Powered by an accelerating development, the future might create a new era—based on the automation of emotions. If the grandchild of chess computer Deep Blue were a music computer, if it were fed with the score for every musical ever written, if this computer were self-tutoring and advanced—might such a sophisticated, electronic entity defeat Andrew Lloyd Webber in a musical-writing contest? We cannot rule out that a computer might write music more popular than that of Lloyd Webber. But we can be certain that a human will receive the accolades usually given to the songsmith—regardless of the fact that the computer did most of the work. We will not relinquish our creative ability.

Equally unthinkable is Grand Prix racing with computer-driven race cars. The drama would be sorely lacking—spectators and TV viewers would stay away in droves. Automation stops at logic, at cerebral work.

However, if feelings can be automated—indeed, *if*—then the Information Society is also an important part of the twenty-first century. It will be more important than it is today, because digital technology will be able to satisfy more of our needs. There will be many new tasks for the advanced computers of the future to solve—writing novels, composing music, directing movies, and maybe even laying strategies and crystalizing visions for companies. This outcome cannot be entirely excluded. Many can envision how increasing computer efficiency will continue to startle most people, and how computers will in fact be able to do things that today are thought to be within reach of only the human brain. After all, we have been continually astonished until now. Ten years ago, who would have expected that the world's greatest chess player would turn out to be a computer? One may raise the objection that chess is a closed system with a vast, but not infinite number of possible combinations. A novel, on the other hand, is an open system—the number of possible combinations of words and descriptions is infinite. In any case, the challenge will be many times greater and, as is the case with the chess computer, there has to be a group of humans behind it. The program code behind the novel must adhere to a number of rules that can be laid down only by real, nonvirtual people.

In 20 years, we may conceivably see novels with introductory acknowledgments in which the grateful author thanks her agent, her spouse—and the computer program Bookmaker. A similar situation may arise within other fields of artistic endeavor, but the author, director or composer will still get the credit for the work in question. The problem with this conjecture is precisely that it is nothing *but* conjecture as to where developments will lead us. We cannot be sure that things will not develop much further—into a world where the computer gradually takes over areas previously handled by the human brain. The present author, however, believes that we will prefer to keep certain functions to ourselves—more precisely, our emotions. But the jury is admittedly still out on this question, and will remain so for the next 20 years.

The only caveat to keep in mind regarding the Dream Society is that the Information Society may continue insofar as it not only solves logical tasks but enters into emotional, and thus unrestricted, areas. And this is a rather important caveat, since it means fewer jobs in storytelling; on the other hand, it does not preclude that consumers will increasingly demand stories to go along with their products. The theory still has validity because of the increase in prosperity and the automation of production.

Thus the Dream Society is the ultimate societal type. All previous societal types were materially defined—based on the way products were made. There is no turning back to the industrial or the agrarian society; we would have to reduce our level of prosperity by half and "forget" scores of technological advances. No such thing has ever happened in Western Europe or North America, despite many wars; it borders on the unthinkable. As long as we cling to a division of societal types based on modes of production and products, the Dream Society presents itself as the fifth and final type, and there will be no successors. A material definition is natural when we are dealing with history. Hitherto, humankind's lot has been dominated by the struggle for food, clothing, and shelter. This struggle has not ceased for the multitudes living in the developing countries—the majority of the world population. Nor has it ended for poorer citizens in the affluent countries, but the struggle is changing from basic survival toward welfare and nonmaterial consumption.

However, this material way of defining society becomes less relevant when the large majority of consumers in affluent countries are spending increasing amounts of their income on stories. When the Dream Society has come to dominate markets in affluent countries, such material definitions will have outlived their usefulness. In this—and only in this—regard, the Dream Society is the final societal type.

Let us try to imagine the shape of things to come, beyond! A fairly educated guess is that the twenty-first and twenty-second centuries will subdivide the phases of society's evolution according to the emotions dominating the marketplace. One epoch may be characterized by a yearning for adventure, while another may reflect the longing for peace of mind. A third possibility is that people will go retro, emulating the lifestyles of yesteryear. Living the life of a farmer could become popular, a throwback to the beginning of the present century. If so, it will be a game involving the deliberate abstention from technological advances—provided you can afford such abstemiousness. People will have the wherewithal to produce foodstuffs using non-state-of-the-art technology.

In other words, you may say the Dream Society marks the end of humankind's multimillennial epoch of material domination; at the same time, it is the first postmaterialistic era—the beginning of something new.

The aim of this book is to describe the transition from Information Society to Dream Society—to point out just how our daily lives will be confronted with a new logic and how this new logic is not a gleam in the distant future, but developing right here and now. The question of what lies beyond the Dream Society has been touched upon above; it is indeed an interesting question, but one whose answer is best left to a writer of H. G. Wells' stature: someone who, using knowledge and especially intuition, is able to discern the distant future and win accolades for it 50 years after his death. At the very best!

Chapter 2

The Market for Stories and Storytellers

Chapter 1 examined how we are entering the Dream Society, underscoring the importance of futurism to long-range planning for business. Since every picture paints a story, this chapter will take a look at the story behind the Dream Society: the emotional market. The chapter will provide you with a fuller understanding of the trends that are currently shaping the future of your business. This is uncharted territory for many businesspeople, and this market is evolving as we speak.

Chapter 2 presents six market profiles:

1. Adventures for Sale
2. The Market for Togetherness, Friendship, and Love
3. The Market for Care
4. The Who-Am-I Market
5. The Market for Peace of Mind
6. The Market for Convictions

Taken together, these profiles comprise the most important aspects of the Dream Society. In the Information Society, our work has been driven by information technology; in the Dream Society, our work will be driven by stories and emotions, not just by data. Research at the Copenhagen Institute for Future Studies shows that the major growth in consumption in the future will be of a nonmaterial nature, making it even more crucial that every company gear itself to corralling the growth of these emotional markets right now. Obviously, there will always be a certain demand for the practical value of products. We will still need toasters and refrigerators to toast and refrigerate, but the *story* side of the product will become an ever-important part of the decision to buy.

Although the market itself is still amorphous and ever changing, this chapter does offer real-time advice in terms of individual products—ideas you can use right here and now so that your business will be poised to take advantage of the megatrend.

Let's start with a working definition of a *story*. In the present context, stories are defined as *value statements*—in other words, they are not subject to the same standards of scientific truth. They may be stories about the universe and humankind's place in it, or they may be little everyday stories about who we are and who the others are. These stories may be transmitted orally, in written form, through images, in plays or movies, or through the very products we choose to be surrounded by.

The next question is: Why do we crave stories? From time immemorial, human beings have lived for and with myths, fairy tales, and legends—communicated at first through an oral tradition as well as through images and, subsequently, through the written word. All people throughout the ages—from the nomads and the ancient Greeks up to and including our own era—have had their stories and legends, just as people have always used tools and sought food and shelter. In other words, the craving for stories is part of what it means to be human—integral to any definition of the Homo sapiens. We have always lived in a spiritual as well as a physical world.

Until the beginning of the twentieth century, the stories we told through our material surroundings—through our clothing, our belongings, our homes—usually drew their defining power from the interrelationship between different layers of society: peasants, artisans, merchants, nobility, and royalty. The clothing you wore revealed the social standing into which you were born; the story about who you were was written in stone from the day you were conceived. These stories were determined by tradition and there was no freedom to choose others. In most societies there were fixed rules about attire: Peasants could not dress up as artisans or as nobility—regardless of whether they could afford to. Materially as well as spiritually, these were static societies—social classes. But today, stories are no longer bound to any one tradition. Regardless of age, profession, and nationality we are free to tell any story through the products we buy: clothes, transportation, leisure products, vacations, homes. So we do just that—according to financial status and needs. We will not be ridiculed for choosing stories other than the ones we were born into.

This is why the market will gradually be emotionally defined. Pushing it a bit to extremes, we could say that the product itself (its content or utility value) will become secondary—the product will be an appendix, the main purpose of which is to embody whatever story is being sold.

1. Adventures for Sale: Small–Medium–Large–Extra Large

How little we actually know about emotional requirements may be illustrated by the current state of affairs in advertising. Anyone with knowledge of the business knows that the name of the game remains "hit or miss," and this will not change. The explanation is that advertising appeals to our emotions and is not susceptible to analysis. Many companies express the adventure in the following way: "Only half of all advertising is effective, only we don't know which half." This is a pity, considering that global expenditure on advertising is estimated at $291 billion—according to Zenith Media, a London-based consulting firm.[10] Needless to say, this figure is growing rapidly. If we could, in fact, determine which advertisements were effective, all would be well and companies could slash their advertising budgets in half.

Humans have always craved adventures. The difference now is that stories and adventures are demanded and supplied like products themselves—in various sizes too. The market for stories in the twenty-first century will be vast, and many companies will grow big and become global by entering this market—just as Microsoft grew big in the short time that the Information Society prevailed.

So far, all this is in the beginning phase. Hot-air balloons as a means of transportation date back 200 years, but hot-air ballooning is a novel entry in the story market. The market, so far, is still modest. The English newspaper *The Economist*[11] estimates that 1000 balloons are produced annually (most of them, incidentally, made in Great Britain). This market will grow as it becomes clear that ballooning is in itself a story, an adventure. Attempts to circumnavigate the globe by balloon are ongoing; until that goal is achieved, efforts will be made to beat the distance record, and the record for staying aloft for the longest time. At the close of 1998, this record stood at 6 days, 2 hours, and 54 minutes. The contestants have corporate backing, as the names of their airships clearly suggest: *Virgin Challenger* (with the English airline's CEO, Mr. Richard Branson, aboard) and the *Breitling Orbiter.*[12] Breitling is a watch manufacturer.

Flying a balloon is indeed a story in itself, and as demand steadily grows and affluence increases, the market will grow as well. The pioneers show us how the stories are properly staged; feeding fantasy with examples, they become market trailblazers. It has all only just begun. When the earth has been circumnavigated by balloon, there await new goals: over the South Pole, over the North Pole, over the Himalayas, over the rain forests and deserts of Africa.

Mountaineering did not become commercialized until the 1950s. The world's barren and forbidding peaks will, in the Dream Society, become a gold mine for the countries that have them within their borders, and for the companies providing services for the mountain climbers. Mountains will surpass farmland in value. The biggest adventure story is, of course, Mount Everest— because at 29,000 feet it stands as the highest peak in the world, and because fewer than 1000 men and women have made it to the top. But it also constitutes a story, because (so far) 156 mountaineers have perished attempting to reach this pinnacle. The Mount Everest Story is available only in Extra Large. Happily, the mountaineering story can be procured in other sizes too— in the Alps, in the Andes, and elsewhere. The point is that the market for stories is played by rules other than those of the Information Society. The source is irrational. According to cerebral logic, climbing mountains is crazy, and submitting yourself to pain, freezing cold, and mortal danger is decidedly nonlogical. Thus we have the classical reason given for climbing the mountain at all: "Because it's there." That is to say, "I wanted to put myself and fate to the challenge—I wanted to tell myself, and others, a story—an adventure story."

Mountaineering is in itself an adventurous story market. But the climbers may also sell their stories to companies that offer products within that market—products that seek association with a thirst for adventure. The Rolex "Spirit of Enterprise" watch and the Breitling example mentioned above illustrate tailoring a product (and company) to the market for adventure stories. When any watch will give you the time of day with total accuracy, timepieces must be sold through an appeal to the emotions; adventure stories are one possibility. Phil Knight, the Nike executive, explains to *Fortune* magazine that his firm allows sponsored athletes to make statements on what they actually feel committed to. "From there, we don't think it's a big leap to connect the athlete with the product."[13]

Stories can also be sold as therapy and educational material. Increasingly, mountain climbing is utilized in halfway-house efforts aimed at helping young criminal offenders adjust. Stories as alternative treatment—here, the market abounds with opportunities. Let's forget about the old business sector divisions that separate mountaineering, ballooning, watches, movies, and books into completely different product categories; they all belong in the market for adventures. They are not so different. Stories are what is in demand; stories are what suppliers supply. More important, these suppliers are engaged in an ever more fierce competition, vying for the consumer's attention. If you are operating in the market for stories, well, then you are joining a throng of other offers to pick and choose from. A few years hence, market analysts will have classified the story offerings into the subcategories Small, Medium, Large, and Extra Large. Within each subheading will be found a whole array of wares. It is not hard to imagine that in the year 2005 you will be choosing among these offerings on the Internet under STORIES, ordering and paying for your selection online.

Today most of the story market lies within the sports industry. *Fortune*[14] has estimated total costs in connection with the 1996 Olympic Games in Atlanta at $1.7 billion. More than 10,000 athletes participated in the event, covered by 15,000 journalists and photographers. About 25 percent of revenues came from ticket sales, while 64 percent were generated by sponsorship deals, marketing sales, and TV rights. A plethora of unfolding events, happening right this instant, gave us the euphoria of victory and the agony of defeat. It was human theater capable of competing in intensity with that offered by the greatest dramatists throughout the ages: an Olympic drama, surpassing even great writers in terms of attention paid and financial prowess. NBC bought the rights for broadcasting the Olympic Games until the year 2008, for the sum of $3.6 billion. We may assume that the 2000 Olympics in Sydney will be seen on TV by far more viewers than the 3.5 billion people who watched all or part of the 1996 games. Approximately two-thirds of the total world population will take part in this drama. Sports has come a long way from being the meeting place of amateurs, to becoming the great, commercial market for adventures—and the future is looking good. We will demand an increasing number of stories, particularly those with high intensity, unfolding instantaneously as we watch. We do not know how it ends until it ends.

The Olympic Games are universal in appeal. Many products are impeded by cultural boundaries; this is not true of stories. They are in demand in all cultures. In a world where globalization is the buzzword it is important to note that we are dealing here with a global product. People's need for stories recognizes no cultural or national boundaries.

In Europe, the German conglomerate Kirch has forked out $2.6 billion to obtain the TV rights, outside the United States, to the World Cup soccer finals in the year 2002, as well as in 2006.[15] Unlike Hollywood—where each picture has to compete with every other, and where all expenditures are payable in advance— the soccer clubs and the national leagues have an effective monopoly; there is only one Premier League, only one World Cup. We must therefore conclude that shares in the European football clubs will remain strictly blue chip for the next decade. Clubs will become wealthy, through sales of T-shirts, but especially through sales of TV rights and sponsorship deals. The same is true in the USA, where even more sports are competing for the highest viewership. Sports clubs and teams will be among the truly major players in the story market.

The players will become wealthy—the stars—by telling their stories about success, about competing, about surmounting difficulties. In the twenty-first century, many multimillionaires 25 years old or even younger will have earned their fortunes selling stories in the Dream Society. Many of these nouveaux riches would not have made it far in the Information Society. Their muscles, their agility, their ability to make drama happen, all these things will make them rich. They will become superbrands in their own right. Some of them will go public; others will take out patents on themselves as individuals (Eric Cantona, an eminent, if controversial, European footballer has already applied to the U.K. patents office for a patent on himself as a person). We are talking about a market that has already grown too large to ignore, and that, at the same time, works according to an emotional logic.

The big film stars also belong to the adventure market. In 1997, two books on Humphrey Bogart were published. Today, 40 years after his death, at least 10 books have been written about this hero, "the silent winner." A myth rather than a myth maker, he is still a storyteller. In a review dealing with the latest two volumes, *The Economist*[16] attempts to provide one explanation for the

Bogart mystique. In the end, the conclusion reached is that no such explanation exists, but "perhaps, after all, it was that unforgettable corncrake voice." Could be, but the main point remains that the story, the magic, is emotionally rooted and that all the knowledge mavens of the Information Society are at a loss—so long as they seek to explain such phenomena using scientific methods. Unfortunately, these methods do not apply to the story market. Here we are tackling myths and the telling of tales.

The Bogart market encompasses more than just films and books. This particular story is sold to companies and associated with products. According to *The Economist,* the story has been bought by Four Roses Bourbon, Lufthansa, Hyundai, Pan American Airways, and a number of hotels and restaurants for use in connection with their products and services. What, then, are they buying? Nostalgia, adventure, peace of mind, and ethics. A many-chaptered story.

The James Bond market is not limited to Jamaica's "James Bond Jamaica Festival"—it comprises the clothing and auto markets as well.[17] We need "007" on numerous occasions where an adventure story is required to sell a product, be it an Aston Martin or a BMW. These cars are not simply means of transportation, but stories. You may write the actual story yourself, or—maybe better still—buy one already on the market.

"We race on Sunday and sell on Monday," said Henry Ford. That worked in the early twentieth century and helped make his cars popular. Today, Grand Prix race car driving is in itself a story industry in the multimillion-dollar league. Professional Grand Prix racing with millions of TV viewers in nearly all the world's countries is a story that began in 1950, and we can expect it to become one of the biggest-selling adventure stories of the coming century. It has already gone public, and with the bright prospects of both pay-per-view sales and digital television making it possible to order images from the actual camera following a favored vehicle, there is great adventure in the air.

Grand Prix racing offers stories in the Extra Large category, by allowing participation in the event, as well as in size Small, by watching it on TV. The story even comes in Medium: You purchase a PC-based racing simulator and, thanks to ever-increasing computing power, according to the publication *Wired*,[18] you feel almost as if you are colliding head on with reality.

The technology, the excitement, the risks, the speed, the people behind the wheel—all are elements suited to a drama writ Extra Large. Sponsors are eager to buy this story for association with their products, whether they be car manufacturers, tobacco companies, or financial institutions. Ferrari and other auto makers have already built up a story halo around their products using Grand Prix racing. And the story is the product—the rest is just production.

Of course, not all cars are part of the adventurous story market. Most are part of the market for security, identity, and togetherness. Some even remain, in part or in whole, within the transportation market—that is, the old, industrial market. The latter group of auto makers should expect a decline in sales in the future. Today 50 million cars are produced yearly for the global market. As this market expands, and a transition is made from selling means of transportation to selling stories, a large, emerging part of the Dream Society becomes evident. A portion of this huge market will be a story market.

Nature is part of the adventure market. Nature has moved from being merely a source of food and raw materials in the late twentieth century, toward becoming—in the affluent countries— a source of stories. The big whales—which up until a few decades ago were content to supply us with a raw material, animal oil— have become purveyors of stories. Taking pictures of these big mammals as they move about on the high seas is an expanding market. We study their communication, seeking to understand their form of life—we need the story of Great Mother Nature with all its attendant mysteries and forces. The same is true of those other great mammals and fish of the sea, the dolphins and the sharks.

If we cannot get enough stories from animals that actually exist, then we merely imagine some and tell stories about them. The

Loch Ness Monster and the Abominable Snowman are but two examples. Do they actually exist? Proving that they do not exist is impossible; therefore the mere chance cannot be ruled out. Just as we need the mysteries of outer space, we also need the mysteries of the sea and of faraway places. Great potential in the future market can be foreseen for the travel agency specializing in voyages into the Great Nature Adventure. Swimming with dolphins, understanding their language, and being healed by them is already a growing market, although small.

The unspoiled nature and the forests of Africa—these possess the stuff that stories are made of, just like the great mountains. The fight between the story market and the market for agricultural produce has already begun in Africa. Should villages expand their arable land at the expense of the wildlife refuges where elephants and lions live, roam, and hunt? India and China are faced with the question of whether fields and cities are to be allowed to confine the living spaces allocated to the tiger and the panda. In the long run there is no doubt as to the answer—the story market wins out because that is where the money lies. The value of one wild tiger still alive will exceed that of an entire village's annual production. Adventure-story seekers, particularly from the affluent countries, will gladly pay for catching a glimpse of one of nature's wonders. The problem, however, lies here: Who has the right to the income generated by the tiger? The local villagers living next door to the wildlife, or others living far away from them?

Nature's stories also come in different sizes. Size Large is a safari through the African savanna. Size Medium is a visit to a wildlife refuge or the zoo. Size Small is reading about it or buying a nature film. The story will be sold in all sizes, and the smaller sizes will also serve as commercials urging you to up the ante—to go for size Extra Large: buying camels and starting up an expedition, following the tracks of Tuareg salt caravans, all across the Saharan desert from Egypt to western Africa.

We seek our stories from other people, especially from people whose culture, lifestyle, and geography differ from our own. The people differing most markedly from inhabitants of today's affluent countries are found among the few remaining cultures of

60

hunter-gatherers. Interest in their cultures, their stories, and their values is already growing. It is growing in Greenland, as evidenced by the story market built around the ice cap. Here you may buy access to larger as well as more modest expeditions crossing the Greenland ice cap from east to west. Interest is also mounting in the indigenous sealers—their values, myths, sagas, and stories. We imagine that this market, around the year 2020, will exceed that of the fishing industry (including processing), currently crucial to Greenland's economy. We also imagine that in 20 years the inhabitants of the minute island of Siberut, off the coast of Sumatra, will be able to make a living just from telling their myths and stories. The trend in tourism is obvious: this is a growth industry. The interesting part, in this context, is that a rising portion of the growth is happening precisely in the story market. Tourism to the underpinning of the world, the South Pole, began as late as 1958, and today—according to *Royal Geographical Magazine*—between 7000 and 9000 visitors come yearly to the vast land of the penguins, of Scott and Amundsen. When adventure stories are traded, voyages tend to be long. Welcome to adventure tourism, size Extra Large. In size Small, we now have all the theme parks sprouting up across North America and Europe. At any given point in time, approximately 200,000 people will be passengers on board an airplane. Many of these passengers will be en route to a live story they have bought. Experts estimate that the annual number of plane trips, which stood at 1.8 billion in 1997, will treble to 4.5 billion over the next 20 years.[19] Many of these trips will also be made to encounter stories purchased.

By degrees, cruise vessels will cease to be merely floating hotels offering peace, relaxation, and spectacular sights. "Vacationers want to see themselves as actors. They take on roles during vacation and want to play a happier part. Vacation becomes comparable to a staged play," writes Horst Opaschowski in a trade journal.

The stories that we create a demand for as we sit in front of the TV are typically about good being victorious over evil. It's a story we never grow tired of, since we come upon it too seldom in real life. In the decades to come, world literature will be searched inside out for stories, for fairy tales. Most recently, we have seen renewed interest in ancient Greek literature,[20] with *The Odyssey* as a prime example. This story shows that the ancient Greeks were not always as rational and democratic as they have sometimes been portrayed. They wrote good "sword operas."

In the eyes of some analysts, the market for CD-ROM games and for "edutainment" has disappointed expectations. One of the explanations is that although the Information Society does provide us with new media, the result is not necessarily an increasing number of good storytellers. Wanted: stories.

A similar state of affairs may be prevalent in large corporations. It has become "open door" to create positions such as "chief knowledge officer," or to launch "knowledge initiatives," or to calculate the organization's "intellectual capital."[21] If we follow the theory of the Dream Society and the emotionally driven market, executives operating in the story market should boast a job title like "chief adventure officer." This is the person chiefly responsible for the story marketed by the organization. The company has a story to maintain, develop, and promote. The job demands a person with a feel for this particular story—someone who actually lives it, someone who has a true sense of what it contains, how it came to be, and where it is headed in the future. The chief adventure officer will necessarily rank among the highest in corporate management. She or he will be like the resident high priestess, the medicine man, the one in charge of explaining and explicating the story. When will this field be taught at Harvard Business School? The exact date is impossible to predict, but it will happen.

How to Infuse Stories Into Your Products and Services

Clearly, the simplest approach is to buy stories ready-made, to take your pick from what the market has to offer by sponsoring athletes, mountaineers, and racers—in short, people with a story to tell.

Another method involves arranging an adventurous story yourself—say, a sports event. That is what Camel has done with its

Camel Trophy Cup. The adventure part of the story lies in the grueling route—jeeps must traverse streams, deserts, and rain forests. Thus the Camel name is associated with the adventure story. Camel moves products like watches, shoes, bags, and cigarettes as a result.

A third possibility lies in the realization that you are really selling the story together with your customer, who becomes co-storyteller. In 1989, when Richard Teerling became head of Harley-Davidson, he inherited a story with a means of transportation attached to it. Since then, Harley Owners Groups have been established and now include 360,000 members among the rank and file. They tell the story to each other, they tell it to new owners—and they tell Teerling and his employees how they want the story to unfold.

A fourth prospect lies in letting the customer invent the story altogether. In a world filled with political correctness, the cigar has become a symbol of independence, freedom, and personality. This story was not originally told by the cigar producers; it was created by the customers themselves. The demand for the little story embedded in the cigar preceded the supply thereof. Only afterward did manufacturers go along with—the story.

If sales figures were aggregated in a way that enabled us to gauge developments within the story market, we would plainly see that this is a growth market meriting close attention. The absence of any such statistics is due to the fact that our mind frames are still lodged in the Information Society. We think rationally while the irrational market is blooming at our very feet. We are facing a radical transition in our Weltanschauung regarding markets and demand, a transition toward the Dream Society.

2. The Market for Togetherness, Friendship, and Love

As previously discussed, emotional fulfillment is a key aspect in the Dream Society. Companies in the Dream Society will become even more concerned with interpersonal relationships—

romance, family, friendship, neighbors—as they explore ways of tapping into the market for togetherness, friendship, and love. In this section we will look exclusively at the *symbols* attached to love and togetherness. Companies will be pleased to find that there is a market for these symbols. In the Dream Society these symbols will be in demand, they will have a price, and the smart companies will be the ones to supply them.

For companies looking at this market, a key question becomes: How can we create new symbols and new rituals to represent the ties that bind people together? Keep that question in mind as we take a look at current trends that point to the new logic of the Dream Society.

The Market for Togetherness and Friendship

Already the large telecommunications firms are promoting themselves as something more than providers of phone connections—any player in this field can do that. They might offer added service, but others can do that too. This is a market where me-too products can very swiftly be introduced. When making an operator-assisted, long-distance phone call in Texas, you will be asked which long-distance company you wish to use. Some 97 percent respond by naming a company, but 3 percent are indifferent—saying "just pick one" or "whoever." Ultimately the long-distance providers could compete on pricing—and end up in a situation where nobody makes any money. The way that the companies have gotten out of this predicament is by avoiding the Information Society's focus on technology, and instead defining their product according to the logic of the Dream Society.

Phone calls, especially private ones, constitute a form of togetherness. A phone call links two people together, overcoming geography and establishing or strengthening the bonds between them. Rarely is a phone call a mere technicality. "Building brand identity" is the key to a successful strategy for major companies. For instance, the "Dial 10-10-321" long-distance phone service campaign in the United States primarily focuses on the ease this service offers customers in staying close to their friends and relatives. It is only at the end that the low price is mentioned.

In the Dream Society, brand identity is about togetherness—the emotional market, which is about solidarity and interpersonal feelings. Phone companies need to build a profile in the togetherness market. Those companies choosing to remain mere providers of the specific service called phone calls will lose out to the competition. Feelings—not technology—are in the air. Phone companies don't just provide the hardware and software; they actually do *bring people closer together, symbolically.* More and more companies will need to think about how their own brand identity can be focused on the idea of drawing people together.

The bar and club market in the United States has a gross profit of about $15 billion, which amounts to $129 spent by every American between the ages of 25 and 59. Why do people go to bars and clubs? The answer, again, is togetherness; they do so in order to strengthen social contacts and to feel a sense of belonging. The Irish brewery giant Guinness sells beer all over the world. But, increasingly, this brewery has realized that the product it is selling is not beer but togetherness, conviviality. The key word is *craic,* Gaelic for congenial chatting and just generally being in good company. That is why Guinness, in collaboration with the Irish Pub Company and others, is selling "Irishness" all over the world. Pubs sporting names like James Joyce, The Dubliner, and O'Reilly's are marketed as a turnkey product, replete with Irish bartenders, Irish musicians, and, needless to say, a decor that is Irish to the core. According to *The Wall Street Journal,* this franchise is currently opening one Irish pub every day somewhere in the world, be it in the Ukraine, in Bangkok, or in Brussels.

Togetherness is a product quite different from beer, but then again, a lot of beer does go along with togetherness sales. The beer is the ritual; the pub is the stage upon which it unfolds. The pub guests are the participants, playing out the ritual. It would seem that we now face a quiet revolution in the market for bars and pubs; companies that have fully grasped the togetherness concept will gradually become global market leaders. Given the rise in worldwide travel and globalized TV, the best togetherness stories will carry the day. Guinness has managed to gain an invaluable head start. *Craic* is worth billions of dollars in the togetherness market. Happily, there is room enough for other togetherness stories; they just have to be very easy on the ear, they must appeal to the heart, and they must not water down as time goes by. The challenge will be for all kinds of companies— whether they produce consumables, necessities, luxuries, or services—to create the story behind their products. All stories need to be nurtured and taken care of, because they amount to a company's greatest and foremost asset. Make your togetherness story a strong one and convey your message to the entire world.

In France, there currently exist about 50 *cafés-philos*—places where a philosopher will raise a question for debate and preside over the ensuing discussion about, say, the relationship between good and evil, eternity as a concept, or people's relationship to nature. The rapport group will initiate a dialogue in which all are free to join. Naturally, this idea started in France, given the proud French philosophical tradition: a venerable form of togetherness clearly rooted in national identity. All it needs is to be picked up, brushed off, and marketed. In the old days of the industrial society, the French dug up coal as a great source of prosperity and wealth; in the Dream Society, the equivalent source of prosperity is stories. Our guess is that before the year 2000 more than 1000 *cafés-philos* will be found in big cities all over the world. Along with the ongoing dialogue on why we have been put on earth and what will happen after it's all over, food and beverages will be sold.

This attempt to describe the markets of the Dream Society is not new in the sense that people have always sought these kinds of stories. What is new is that our natural craving for stories will move away from the realm of books, movies, and entertainment and toward actual consumer retail products. This new logic of the Dream Society—and our growing freedom to choose different products depending on their emotional appeal—will dominate the marketplace.

Fortune[22] has noted the considerable success enjoyed by theme parks and malls. In the United States, Dave & Buster's has opened eight huge malls, 4500 square yards each, where you will find it all: restaurants, bars, golf simulators, pool tables, moneyless blackjack (with dummy $10,000 chips), and video games. The average turnover for these supermarkets of togetherness is in excess of $10 million. Just pick your favorite theme: What do you wish to socialize around, how will your bonds best be strengthened? Here lie many possibilities.

Restaurants and cafés—grossing more than $300 billion in the United States alone—also belong in the togetherness market. This is another, and far bigger market where we can anticipate a revolution. Once you acknowledge that restaurants are not merely places to eat you can proceed to create your own togetherness story. Make your togetherness pitch a strong one and convey your message to the entire world.

In the United States, the coffee market is worth about $6 billion (approximately $50 for every adult), or about half the size of the market for theme parks. If coffee is to secure its hold as a market leader, its purveyors need to realize that they operate not only in the coffee market but (and primarily) in the togetherness market as well. At least in Europe, any business meeting where no coffee appears is doomed to failure. Coffee is part of the ritual—the ritual meant to make us connect, the ritual meant to instill trust— an atmosphere of togetherness. If, as a participant, you choose not to take part in the coffee ritual you will be wise to have a good explanation handy. On the private front, coffee plays the same role; it brings people closer together. Tea, or water, may of course enter into the togetherness ritual, but so far coffee holds sway in the USA and in most of Europe. At CIFS in Denmark we serve coffee at all client meetings. Clients who request tea seem only half committed to the ritual.

Videoconferencing and e-mail will allow us to reduce the number of business meetings we attend—instead, we will meet electronically, saving time and money. This is what many people still believe the future will be like. But it will not come to pass—

because of our need for togetherness; because we learn more, communicate more, when we are together nonvirtually. The phone or the computer cannot render our body language. Some scientists claim that 80 percent of the brain's capacity is used to process visual impressions and that this is why—other things being equal—we prefer to be face-to-face with the person we are talking to, so we don't miss the body language. In any case, the volume of business-related travel has not declined, despite the many new electronic communications options. Videoconferencing has been on the market for 15 years and is still used only to a limited extent.

Togetherness explains why the event industry is growing. In May of 1997, the National Restaurant Association met at McCormack Place in Chicago. According to *The Economist*,[23] 102,000 people participated, and before leaving they spent $160 million. Each year, Chicago draws close to 3 million visitors to conferences and exhibitions. Only Las Vegas can boast a larger event industry. Obviously, all these restaurateurs cannot communicate with body language (which is said to make up 80 percent of human-to-human communication) or create physical contacts electronically. People have to meet in person.

In surveys of the togetherness market—as in the case of the story market—it is difficult to assess the exact numbers involved; the available statistics are still compiled using the principles of logic, and the business-sector divisions are applicable to the Information Society and to the industrial society, the latter in particular. So our purpose here is to provide, through examples, the market description that will be unique to the Dream Society. The purpose is also to show how, even today, this description may be more accurate than the traditional ones, more useful for understanding the market, and thus more valuable for creating growth and generating earnings.

We do not take pictures of each other incessantly. Actually, we prefer to do so on special occasions: Christmas and other red-letter days, birthdays, anniversaries, weddings, vacations. The key word underlying all these events is *togetherness*. Special days give us something around which to celebrate a feeling of togetherness;

68

Christmas, to name one, is a time for the family to affirm its mutual love and solidarity. This event is commemorated by taking pictures. The same is true of our vacations, where we spend entire days sharing experiences together. The average American consumer bought 3.6 rolls of film in 1996; industry analyst Euromonitor estimates that Eastman Kodak has a share of about 80 percent of this market. This surprisingly large share may be attributable to Kodak's clear understanding that the market for film is about togetherness—not about introducing newfangled, hi-tech solutions. Despite many efforts at technological innovations, the 35 mm print still reigns supreme, and, incidentally, has enjoyed its greatest growth rate in the 1990s. Taking snapshots—like making phone calls—is an emotional gesture and therefore belongs to the emotional, not the technological market.

The theme park is one of the growth industries of the twenty-first century. The theme parks provide a safe, well-defined experience. Some theme parks belong to the story market, but most of them, including the market leader, the Disney theme parks, belong to the togetherness market. They are for families, children, grandparents, and close friends. These are the people who, through visiting, strengthen their bonds by spending time together. Many theme parks have a global appeal. In 1996, Disneyland Paris had close to 12 million guests, twice as many as the Eiffel Tower. Tokyo Disneyland had 17 million guests; here, an adjacent theme park is being planned (Tokyo DisneySea). With shopping arcades, home videos, interactive computer games, and movies we can see the shape of tomorrow's giants in the togetherness market. Disney knows very well that togetherness transcends all traditional market boundaries.

Like the story market, the togetherness market seems to possess a truly global appeal. Of course the Disney theme park is not perceived in the same way by the Japanese as it is by the French, but the basic service rendered—the feeling of togetherness, the strengthening of the ties that bind—is universal. The emotional products of the Dream Society may well cut across cultural borders much more easily than did the products of the Information Society or the industrial era. A possible explanation is that the customer contributes his or her own content to the story of togetherness told by the company. The customer coproduces the story.

The Market for Love

Love, of course, does not constitute a market. It is about strong feelings occurring between human beings, and it is one of the feelings that science cannot define and should hold no monopoly in defining. Love is enchantment, fascination, and abandon, a subject that only the most skillful poets and writers can describe, making us exclaim, "Yes, that's how it is." Eternal stories about the one big love, from *Romeo and Juliet* to *Gone with the Wind*, are indispensable to our understanding of ourselves as human beings.

However, love is accompanied by a series of symbols and rituals, and in this regard it does provide a market—or, more precisely, it has become one in the twentieth century. As mentioned previously, the Disney Corporation operates in the togetherness market, but it is also active in the love market. According to *USA Today*, Disney World receives 18,000 requests for wedding reservations every year. However, capacity is limited to 2200 (amounting to six a day, all year round). Half of the couples come from the United States; the rest are predominantly Japanese. For $2000 you can even take a trip in a large Cinderella carriage (although it will not turn into a pumpkin). A wedding is a big and significant ritual; it needs the proper setting, and people do not mind paying a substantial amount of money for it. The symbols of love should correspond to the strong emotions giving rise to this occasion.

Substantial growth is characteristic of the market offering symbols of love, but the question every company should ask itself is this: How can we stage the ritual so that it best symbolizes love? The short answer is that the company should think of itself as purveyor of a romantic drama, a theatrical show. There are several scripts to choose from, and customers may select whichever suits them best. The company acts as director and provides all props for the drama. Every phase of the wedding ritual should

70

symbolize love—from the ceremony to the banquet, the limo, and the honeymoon. The wedding is transformed from an event made up of uncoordinated elements, with some socializing thrown in, to a package deal, focusing on what the customer is really after: symbols of love.

As mortal humans, we have one other major and symbol-laden ritual: the funeral. It is a necessary ritual allowing us to honor the memory of the deceased, giving us comfort and a chance to come to terms with our continued lives despite the loss. The symbols surrounding the funereal rites are a market. *The Economist*[24] estimates that the funeral industry in the affluent world grosses $20 billion annually. As is the case with weddings, funerals operate in the love market. They call up some of the strongest of human emotions—in this case, bereavement. How can these symbols be placed in the proper setting so they best reflect the sentiments of the grieving loved ones? An American company is offering—for a $1000 fee—to set up a memorial Web site on the home page of the bereaved, seeing the opportunity for an electronic shrine in lieu of a cemetery plot. The electronic tombstone.

The world's largest funeral company, the U.S.-based Service Corporation International, has gained a foothold in the U.K. market, and may be expected to set up shop in the rest of Europe as markets are continuously liberalized and privatized. In all probability, the coming century will see global business concepts vying for their share of the love market—as was the case with the togetherness market. These will be business concepts reflecting a careful enacting of the ritual and a deep understanding of its unique character and underlying emotional needs. Business concepts thought out along the lines of Information Society logic will lose out in the competition.

Gifts, as symbols of love, will often take the form of jewelry. Euromonitor estimates that the U.S. jewelry market grosses nearly $16 billion annually, or about $60 per capita. The figure reflects how much we need our expressions of love. Jewelry has traditionally been viewed as symbolic of wealth or prosperity, but today it is primarily symbolic of love; it belongs in the love market. How, exactly, does a piece of jewelry symbolize love? One way, of course, is that it is expensive, thus reflecting the intensity of love as measured in dollars. Another way is that the jewelry itself conveys the love message—say, a necklace with a heart—and can do so without a prohibitively expensive price tag that makes the expression of love possible only for the rich. In this respect, there is some doubt as to whether the small jewelry manufacturers (and this industry has many small manufacturers) have fully comprehended the nature of the market they are in. Many still adhere to the notion that jewelry can possess symbolic value only through its price. In any case, here too we can look for a market revolution when some company thoroughly analyzes the symbolic value of jewelry and the feelings with which it is bought and given.

Jewelry may also be seen as part of the Who-Am-I market (see below), and for the individual manufacturer it is, of course, vitally important to determine which market a product belongs to. We are dealing with completely different sets of emotions, with different needs. The jewelry found on the love market is sold by jewelers like Tiffany's. Who-Am-I jewelry is sold through chains and department stores.

Likewise, the market for cosmetics and perfume is part of both the love market and the Who-Am-I market. The gift market typically forms part of the love market. The fine French perfumes with their sophisticated scents revolve around love, around seduction. Just a short list of names on the labels will demonstrate that the makers have understood their market: True Love, Poison, Dolce Vita, Original Women, Eternity, Narcisse, Eden. These are symbols of strong emotions—so strong, in fact, that discount sales are out of the question. There can be no discounts on love and sensuality.

The U.S. perfume market is valued in the $3 billion range, and it is growing at a stable rate. Love is one of the most potent forces in our lives and its symbols have a firm hold on the market, provided that manufacturers understand that market and the feelings for which they are challenged to find the proper symbols and the visible expressions.

A significant segment of the film market involves stories about love, both blissful and star-crossed. These are stories in which we can see our own emotions reflected, stories we can identify with. A movie is an abstraction. We know that the actors in a movie are only acting; we know that the plot is unfolding in chiaroscuro on a two-dimensional screen—yet we let ourselves be carried off. With *Romeo and Juliet* we may cry—the story is many times stronger than our rational knowledge about the abstraction. The split between rational human being and emotional human being may sometimes be a complete one. A cautious guess—just surveying the movies offered—is that a little less than half of them tell stories about love; thus filmmakers are in the love market. The other half is predominantly in the story market and the market for seeing good win over evil. The latter story, apparently, is one that we rarely come across in real life, so we need to supplement reality with fiction. One explanation may be that we are only too accustomed to seeing evil emerge victorious; another may be the fact that, in our very complex society, we no longer see a clear opposition between good and evil, but shades of gray instead, making it difficult to single out heroes and villains. This is true of politics, of the judicial system, and of the struggles between interest groups.

The music market, on the other hand, seems to be overwhelmingly about love. All successful songwriters write about flirting and falling in love, about the one great love, about unhappy love, about missing, longing, and reuniting. The theme must have played in a million variations—in all the world's languages—but since this is the story we need to hear, there is no escaping it for those who want to stay in the market. Live music as well as recorded music has undergone a technological revolution during the last decade. The score can be controlled by computers, and software may help the composer—the longer-term perspective is electronic music composed and distributed without being touched by artistic hands. It is an option already offered by technology, but we might just possibly reject it. The market is already experiencing a reaction, a countercurrent. There is a demand for unplugged concerts, for music produced without technological assistance, and this is because we are looking not for music, but for emotions, for love.

Finally, we turn to the home. As prosperity grows, and as most of us find that we can afford the basic conveniences, our interior design urges have become more a question of how we set the stage for our emotions. The family feeling of love and solidarity requires symbols showing that we belong together. The bedroom's symmetrical furnishings (down to the twin reading lamps), the communal living room with a marked absence of things that belong only to one person (kids' toys, laptop computers)—all these are symbols showing us to be a real family.

The home is for showing off to ourselves and showing off to friends and acquaintances. Interior decorating will gradually cease to be a question of status symbols, of luxury; instead, it will be about feelings. This vast market, too, will need redefining. The market for home furniture alone is valued at more than $40 billion.

Love and togetherness—these are two pivotal marketing definitions in the Dream Society. Gary Hamel, management expert and professor at the London Business School, wrote an award-winning article on strategy for the *Harvard Business Review*.[25] Briefly put, the idea was that successful strategy consists of imagining what the market will look like in the future—and then adjusting the company's capabilities to suit this market. Or, as CEO Michael Eisner phrased it in Disney's 1996 annual report: "It is about creating change before it creates you." This section seeks to provide inspiration for creating change.

Creating change? Given the ongoing globalization and the trends presented in this chapter, we are looking at a scenario for the coming decade in which more and more large companies specialize in providing symbols for the love market. They will peddle weddings, jewelry, and funerals, and they will produce movies and computer programs. Synergy will be deployed in product development, and the potential for growth will be practically infinite. Let us, for the sake of experiment, create a mission, a vision, and a strategy for one such company. Let us call it Caring for Love.

Mission: "To provide the symbols that best strengthen and attest to the strongest bonds that exist between people."

Vision: "To develop capacity and do business in the world's major spheres of culture, and to be a market leader in three of these." Further: "To offer at least four new services each year."

Strategy: "To gain a deeper understanding of the strong emotions for which we are providing the symbols, and thereby make our services ever more competitive. This understanding is the company's capital. The company does not wish to own real estate, means of production, or any other kind of physical capital. Intellectual capital is the only capital at Caring for Love."

Remember, the Dream Society is a future scenario. We do not know the future; reputable futurists are not in the business of predicting. Rather, they provide sketches outlining scopes of possibilities, pictures of the future. The picture of the love and togetherness markets is, therefore, only a picture. But it is a sketch that is becoming clearer. At present, we can provide a preliminary drawing. The purpose of this chapter is to clarify these initial lines so that the drawing may become more well defined.

3. The Market for Care

This section is about the market for care; however, for an historical background on why emotional rather than materialistic concepts can be used to describe markets in the first place, we call upon one of the most eminent economists of this century, J. M. Keynes. In his now-famous essay from 1930,[26] "The Economic Prospects of Our Grandchildren," Keynes wrote: "In the not so distant future, I envision the greatest upheaval that has hitherto occurred in human history. Of course, it will happen gradually, not as a catastrophe. Actually, this development has already begun. What will happen is, quite simply, that the problems of economic necessity will be relieved for an increasing number of classes and groups of individuals." According to Keynes' estimate, this upheaval will take place within 100 years—in other words, by the year 2030.

When the upheaval has occurred, Keynes concludes that we will be "free to return to some of the most secure and durable principles of religion and traditional values—we must honor those who can teach us how best to benefit from the hour and the day, these admirable people who know how to enjoy things. Like the lilies of the field."

Keynes foresaw the Dream Society in 1930. He predicted it even though he was immersed in an English class society in the midst of the Great Depression, with mass unemployment and widespread poverty. However, human beings are not content with merely admiring the lilies in the field. Their emotional needs extend further than that. Another such need is to give, to show compassion, to comfort, to bestow healing, help, and happiness. People have a need to provide care. Some scholars explain this seemingly unselfish urge by taking into consideration the species, the survival of humankind—a collective instinct of self-preservation. In the present context, suffice it to say that we harbor a need to provide care—not all the time, not toward everybody, but often and in a great variety of situations.

Corresponding to our need to provide care is the reciprocal need to receive care, help, and comfort. This urge may be based on a material or an emotional need. We may be sick, helpless, hungry, or in distress—whatever the reason, we create a demand for help from our fellow human beings. What is intriguing about providing care, of course, is that the greater the joy is on the receiving end, the greater the joy of giving becomes. A need is met in both giver and recipient. A positive correlation exists.

The need to provide care and the need to receive care are both important factors in describing the Dream Society market.

Care—From One to Four Hearts

One of the recent, humongous hits in the toy market is the Tamagotchi; a little electronic "egg" demanding to be treated with care and attention. When thus treated, it becomes "a cute, happy little cyberchicken. However, should you neglect to lavish your

Tamagotchi with tender loving care it will grow into a horrid, ill-behaved monster," admonishes the manufacturer's instructions. The Tamagotchi comes from another planet, whither it will always return. Yet it knows human feelings: "in order for it to display four hearts on the screen, you must play with it and nurture it, keeping it happy and properly fed." This neat piece of technology the size of a key ring offers kids and adults an opportunity to provide care. We may call it an electronic pet, but the main point is that the Tamagotchi essentially has but one purpose: giving its owner a chance to provide care. Viewed within the framework of traditional, materialistic logic this product makes no sense. It has no function; it doesn't "do" anything. Viewed from the logic of the Dream Society, however, the product makes perfect sense. It fulfills an existing demand for providing care. Sales figures, empty shelves, and long lines of eager buyers all attest to the existence of a considerable demand, a need. A Dream Society product has been discovered. An answer to the question: How can we meet the demand for providing care?

Maybe care-centered products of the future should carry truth-in-labeling information, dealing not only with the environmental friendliness of the product but with information regarding its emotional dimension—ranking it from one to four hearts. The hearts would designate the intensity of the feeling of care that particular product—after being tested by a consumer agency—can be expected to inspire. Or you may return the product for a full refund.

Sales volume in the U.S. pet market lies close to $12 billion, most of it within the care market. People have had pets—or "companion animals"—for many thousands of years, as demonstrated by the inscriptions of ancient Egypt. Pets give us an opportunity to provide them with care. It is a beautiful relationship in which, if we give a lot, we get a lot. Pets are about feelings, but they are also about a market. Once again, the rational Information Society does not possess any theory capable of explaining the growing demand for pets. With the exception of hunting dogs and watchdogs, they are devoid of utility value. This market can be understood only from an emotional perspective.

The green movement also reflects our concern with animal rights. To an increasing degree we stress that the animals providing our foodstuffs must have lived their life according to nature. Hens should not be encaged while laying their eggs, pigs should be free to wallow in the fields; animals have a right to see the sky, to feel the sun and the breeze. The use of animals for scientific purposes—or for testing new cosmetic products—should be banned or at least restricted so no unnecessary harm is done to them. The notion of care has been extended from our pets to our livestock. That is not all. We must also protect wildlife. Whales are not to be caught using harpoons (with only a few exceptions, they are in fact safeguarded by global preservation rules), foxes may not be caught in traps, dolphins may not be drowned in fish nets. The modern-day urbanite living in the affluent part of the world is continuously extending her or his care needs to new areas.

The long-legged, fair-haired Barbie has acquired a dollhouse of friends. Her newest friend, called Becky, differs from Barbie in one respect—she sits in a wheelchair. The most successful doll of the century—Barbie—has expanded her emotional bandwith to encompass a possibility for children to provide special care.

A hotelkeeper in Stratford-upon-Avon, England, has added two dogs, both homeless Labradors, to his payroll.[27] Each dog has a leash hanging in the lobby so hotel guests may take "Digby" and "Snoopy" for a walk. It's what you might call a win-win-win situation (for the dogs, the hotel, and the patrons), with the need for providing care at its core.

On June 24, 1859, the Austrian and French armies fought a blood-drenched battle at Solferino in northern Italy. After the battle, which lasted a full 16 hours, 40,000 dead and wounded littered the battlefield. That same evening a Swiss traveler named Henry Dunant arrived at this scene. So deeply moved was he by the terrible display of death and carnage that he sought to organize help for the thousands of sufferers. In 1862 he published a book, *A Memory of Solferino,* which stirred the conscience of Europe. This, in turn, supplied the initial spark for setting up the International Committee of the Red Cross (ICRC). Today, some 170 national Red Cross committees exist, with a total of 10 million members. The mission is impressively described with force and grace in the seven cornerstones: "Humanity, Impartiality, Neutrality, Independence, Voluntary Service, Unity, and Universality." Many business organizations might rightly envy the ICRC for having encapsulated a vision as well as a strategy in such a poignant way.

A successful, humanitarian organization, the Red Cross is built around a simple principle: the firm belief that human beings are willing to provide care for those in distress, and that such care will be provided on a volunteer basis, without expectation of anything material in return. The Red Cross is not a for-profit organization, but along with the gradual blurring of the demarcation lines between profit-seeking companies and other organizations, the Red Cross will come to be seen as a prominent factor within the care market. It will have to compete with many other organizations for a share of the market for care. "Customers" will have to be convinced that the Red Cross product gives "buyers" (those giving a donation to the aid work) good value for their money—to wit, the satisfactory certainty of actually having helped. The Red Cross is not competing with Becky, or with the Tamagotchi— there's room enough for both types of products, but they are in the same market.

The International Red Cross may serve as a bellwether for the marketplace of the twenty-first century in other ways. The organization is global; like the purveyors of stories (the Olympic Games, Grand Prix racing, the international soccer organization FIFA), it works unfettered by national boundaries. All are global organizations with rules of their own that will not give in to demands or special considerations at the national level.

McDonald's, on the other hand, is not an organization in the care business. All the same, the company's home page tells us that "Ronald McDonald House Charities has awarded over $150 million in grants to thousands of organizations serving children." The explanation lies in "doing well, by doing good." The company wants to be thought of as an organization that not only makes money, but also has a heart, also wants to be caring. The message is aimed not only at customers, but at employees as well. As a McDonald's employee, you can take pride in knowing that your work goes beyond making money for the shareholders. The demarcation lines separating organizations that exclusively sell the opportunity for providing care and organizations that rely on care as a facilitating part of their strategy are still present; but the sharp, dividing line between for-profit companies and charitable organizations is headed toward obsolescence.

We must anticipate that all companies, in principle, could market their products as an opportunity for providing care. As an example, an ad for Seagate[28] proclaims that since the company is a "leader in data storage technology, much of the data on the Internet is stored on our disk drives." The ad shows a picture of a boy cradling his baby brother. The boy says: "This is my baby brother. I'm writing a book about him. It's not very long. Yet. I've only got 3 weeks of stuff. When he gets older, he can read it. On his home page. I'm saving everything." The ad has got it right. The touching story about the elder brother caring for his newborn sibling can be stored on disks. Disks are thus part of the care market, right! Because we are on our way to the Dream Society, where all products—even computer disks—have to have an emotional appeal. Seagate has claimed its stake in the care market.

The Salvation Army is one of the major companies in the care market and is also seeped in tradition, like the Red Cross. Founded in London in 1865, it established its purposes as "the advancement of the Christian religion...of education, the relief of poverty, and other charitable objects beneficial to society or the community of mankind as a whole."[29]

The Salvation Army operates in over 100 countries and in more than 140 languages. With 352 hospitals and clinics, 780 homes for the elderly, and more than 2000 food distribution centers, as well as many other types of care activities, this is a truly global company within the care market. Care is provided by volunteers to the sick, the poor, the homeless, and those whose lives have lost their meaning. Members of the Salvation Army, known as Salvationists, wear a uniform that forges a bond among them. Together they constitute "an international fellowship knowing no barriers of age, sex, or race." This clear and unmistakable spirit of community is precisely what so many large companies with worldwide activities aspire to. The crucial esprit de corps is already in place within the Salvation Army. The comparison seems farfetched only if you are using the artificial market partitioning of the Information Society, placing for-profit companies and charitable organizations in totally separate categories. The Salvation Army should be used as a case study in business education for the twenty-first century.

The San Francisco Bay Area Volunteer Information Center has a "hot list" of 139 different organizations where you may sign up as a voluntary, nonsalaried provider of care. Likewise, volunteer organizations in Europe are experiencing an upswing. The state is no longer presumed to be the sole provider of care for its citizens. Private organizations built on volunteer work succeed in establishing a more direct and straightforward rapport—care with an emotional meaning for the provider. This trend is particularly noticeable in northern Europe, where the state has traditionally been allocated the role as sole provider of care for society's poor and infirm members, on behalf of the community at large. There is still a need for this collective, albeit remote care, but increasingly it will be supplemented by direct care. Hence significant growth is to be expected within the care market.

AT&T Wireless Services is but one of many examples of product/service companies offering to sponsor sports and charities, including disaster relief. According to a background report about the company: "These donations help raise people's awareness of the AT&T Wireless Services brand name as well as benefiting the organization that receives the funding."

The care market extends to our children and grandchildren. This part of the care market is analogous to the family market, but in the present this context we shall call it care. As anyone who reads statistics is aware, the borderlines separating business segments have become ambiguous and mutable. Placing the product of a specific company precisely where the company believes that product belongs is difficult. The difficulty is compounded as the statistics become more detailed.

The U.S. toy market grew by 10 percent in 1997 and is valued today at more than $30 billion. As the biggest and most dynamic sector, video games weigh in with a market share of 31 percent. Most of these toys are bought by parents (mainly mothers) for their kids. Or they are bought by grandparents for their grandchildren. The joy of giving the gift, the joy of seeing the joy of children—these are pivotal symbols of our care and our love. As the age-old truth goes, the joy of giving can easily match the joy of receiving. Showing you care, providing care, is an important part of life, of being a human being. The symbols of care are an important part of the market. How do we best provide and strengthen the symbols of care? That is the worthwhile question that companies in this market should be asking.

Receiving Care

The examples mentioned above are largely about giving—that is, they are concerned with the segment of the market driven by the urge to give. The other part of the care market is driven by the need to receive. These are, of course, two aspects of the same thing, but it is important to distinguish among the compelling forces that create the market. We will now turn our attention to the source of the demand side.

The U.S. health market is valued in excess of $1 trillion, making up a total of 14 percent of GNP. As in other affluent countries, this share is expected to rise—in other words, we will be using an increasing portion of our income for health care. The trend is natural in a developed economy; as prosperity increases we spend less, relatively speaking, on basic requirements, and more on ensuring longevity and good health.

Up until the mid-nineteenth century, nursing, soothing, comforting, and healing were primarily a family concern—care was provided at home. If the home was not equal to the task, there was the church or the convent. Only within the last century or so have we seen a real market for caring and restoration to health. The change coincided with the scientific revolution taking place at the beginning of the twentieth century. Suddenly science could offer not only comfort and care, but cure. Curing fell within the realm of science—and science only. The alternative methods and "wise women" were a thing of the past. Or so it was thought.

Recently, however, we have witnessed a new trend. The actual caring—the emotional factor—seems to be taking over an increasing part of the health care market. The monopoly that has hitherto been the privilege of the "era of science" will wither away within the next decade or two. The health care market will also change according to the logic of the Dream Society. This is to be expected, for two reasons.

1. *Balancing Mind and Body.* In Germany, therapeutic means such as homeopathy and acupuncture are already considered "traditional" and therefore to a large degree are covered by health insurance. The news lies in Germany's 1997 adoption of legislation placing alternative medicine on the same footing as traditional practice. When applying for approval, new drugs and treatments must be evaluated by experts in each particular area.[30] Treatments involving zone therapy, say, must be sanctioned by zone therapists. Pluralism has been introduced into the health care sector. The monopoly on sanctioning new methods of treatment, hitherto held by traditional science, has thus been broken.

   New, alternative methods of treatment continue their penetration into the market, despite resistance from the medical science establishment; the reason is that new approaches are increasingly preferred by patients. The only explanation is that alternative methods of treatment usually involve a stronger element of care and sympathy; at the same time, they stress that not only the body but the soul must be actively engaged in the healing process.

   The importance of the mind in relation to state of health is not only expounded in books and periodicals about health; within the orthodox world of medicine there is a recognition of the "active placebo response."[31] It is, of course, a well-known fact that innocuous calcium tablets can be shown to have an effect. Despite a treatment, worthless from a scientific point of view, the patient does recover. In other words,

83

science is faced with a paradox. Worthless treatment does—in certain cases (often around 15 percent)—have a curative effect! But this is a paradox only to science. Any treatment, even just a placebo, gives the impression of being cared for—which may in and of itself be beneficial to the patient. Doctors themselves are increasingly accepting the placebo effect—because it works. We can expect that during the next 10 to 15 years, there will be an increased focus on the mind in curing nearly all diseases.

2. *Automated Cures.* In the United States alone, the aggregate research expenditure within the health care sector is around $15 billion. Burgeoning research will lead to previously unheard-of progress in the treatment of disease. The human genome is expected to be completely mapped within the next decade; nanotechnology and biotechnology, along with information technology and advanced scanners, will open the doors to an entirely innovative wealth of possibilities. All these developments will make actual automation within the health care sector possible. Automation is particularly relevant to hospitals, where total expenditures within the last five years have not risen as rapidly as within other sectors, such as home care. One of the reasons is that hospital procedures lend themselves more readily to automation using modern equipment. In home care, the care aspect is more labor-intensive.

A comparison to car production may be illustrative. Just as industrial robots have replaced assembly-line workers in Detroit and elsewhere, scanners and other forms of automation will gradually replace doctors. Or rather, doctors and nurses will be free to devote themselves to the business of caring.

In the long-term perspective, following this line of thought, the health care sector will have come full circle in 10 to 20 years—from its origins in the home, over the monopoly of science, and back again to placing the main emphasis on care. The difference is that technology is now available to provide an effective treatment to go along with the care. Parallel examples of how technology may liberate people to handle more emotional challenges are to be found in the financial sector, where infotechnology will free staff members to concentrate on their traditional role: instilling a feeling of security and trust in clients.

In Asia (not including Japan), $150 billion is spent annually on the health care sector. According to *Business Week,* the Economic Development Board of Singapore has estimated that this figure will grow by 70 percent, to $255 billion, by the end of the decade. Although the bulk of global health care services remains in public hands, there is ample room for a private sector offering "premium health care." Growth potential is enormous, both in rich and in developing countries. One probable scenario is that chains of hospitals, active on a global basis, will dominate the world market in 10 to 20 years—benefiting from high technology and, not insignificantly, from a thoroughly tested care concept built on detailed knowledge of the needs of sick people. These hospital chains will understand how to make automation work to their advantage, but they will also realize that the cornerstone of the service offered lies in providing comfort and care to people who are insecure and afraid of suffering and pain, afraid for life and limb. In the care market of the Dream Society, hospitals and other parts of the health care system will capture a significant share.

The church and religion form part of human consciousness. Nearly all of us need to believe that we do not rule over ourselves—that a force stronger than the individual human being exists. There has been a period during this century, particularly in northern Europe, when people expressed confidence in the ability of science to answer life's two fundamental questions:

○ Why Were We Put on Earth?
○ What Happens When We Die?

Life's existence can be exacting, meaningless, and plagued by perplexity if you do not have an answer to these questions. That is why, according to Scandinavian statistics, only 15 to 20 percent of us can exist without religion. Viewed from this perspective, it would seem that the church and religion give the most important and variegated offerings when it comes to spiritual care. All expectations that human beings with an abundance of technology and ever-increasing education levels would reject all nonscientific explanations and think in strictly logicomathematical terms have been proved erroneous. We cannot subsist merely on what can be touched and felt. Perhaps such a vision was finally buried along with the demise of the Soviet Union in the beginning of the 1990s.

The very concept of the Dream Society as the successor to the Information Society is built on the assumption that the scientific, rational way of thinking will be less revered in the future. The best indication that this, indeed, is the case is the success of the Internet, itself perhaps as much as anything a product of the Information Society. In the fall of 1996, *Time* magazine,[32] using the Internet search engine Alta Vista, found an impressive 46,000 references to Microsoft founder Bill Gates. However, a search for "God" yielded 410,000 references; "Jesus" earned 146,000 "hits." The Internet offers a hi-tech possibility for people throughout the world to discuss spiritual questions and establish virtual religious congregations—irrespective of geography. The Gutenberg bibles, mass-produced with the aid of the newborn art of printing, put Christianity in the hands of the multitudes. The Internet promises to serve a similar purpose. On the Internet, Christian sects across the world will meet one another, keyboard to keyboard—and Jews will meet Islamic Fundamentalists, modem to modem. Let us hope that the communion will lead to deeper mutual understanding among the world's great religions—to a sense of shared spiritual values, regardless of the different molds into which they have been cast in different corners of the world.

Even in northern Europe more and more people are expressing overt interest in religion—though not necessarily in the church. In the former Communist countries, the tendency is clear: Religion's "hibernation" through 70 years of scientific materialism is over, and it is once again plainly in view as a crucial part of citizens' lives. The Dream Society does not exclude the possibility that the twenty-first century will belong to religion, as the twentieth century belonged to science and technology.

4. The Who-Am-I Market

The New Orleans–based company Sazerac produces its vodka from "organically grown grain"—and the bottle is recyclable. The vodka's name is Rain and it is targeted at the ecologically aware market. By imbibing this vodka you are telling a little story about yourself, contributing to the picture: Who-Am-I.

What kind of an exciting person am I, what are my esteemed values, which stories am I able to tell? Whom do I associate with, whom am I very different from? The answers to these questions are found in the products and services I choose to buy. That is why I belong to the Who-Am-I market. This chapter will argue that the products with which we surround ourselves are increasingly becoming a way in which we stage ourselves. The market has acquired a new dimension that will gradually become the most important one—both in the eyes of the consumer and as reflected in company sales.

Louis Vuitton is a company that sells travel gear—bags and suitcases. But it does so with an added dimension. You get a story along with the suitcase, a story many customers value more highly than the practical utility of their suitcase. Louis Vuitton is a typical Dream Society company, clearly evidenced by the following, self-introductory words: "The stragegy of Louis Vuitton remains anchored in the principles which have guided our company since its origins: a constant focus on impeccable quality, direct management of a network of stores, control over production, building the value of the brand name and development of a multi-cultural organization able to react quickly to new opportunities."[33]

The story that Louis Vuitton customers tell about themselves: "I am an exciting person, gliding with perfect ease through posh hotels all over the world, and I do it in style." Champagne is associated with gaiety and merriment, and to reuse a phrase that champagne makers Moöt & Chandon attribute to Napoleon. "In victory, you deserve it; in defeat, you need it." Maybe the time has come to free champagne of its slightly old world charm and introduce it to modern-day life. That is why Moöt & Chandon has bought into the Grand Prix racing story. Winning drivers drink it on the podium during the victory ceremony. Tradition calls for some of the bubbly to be sprayed over spectators and photographers, but whatever remains of the sparkling drops constitutes a part of the victory ritual. This ritual is what the company has bought into and it shows the consumer what the champagne story is about.

"Everything I do has a personal reference, a personal sensibility. I feel it, it's who I am," says Ralph Lauren.[34] Consumers pay an annual $5 billion for his designs. Who-Am-I if I choose to buy Ralph Lauren products? "The design blends romance, innovation, and tradition with inspiration that travels across time and culture: African safaris, English aristocracy, Parisian café life, old Hollywood, the Western frontier, Russian revolutionaries, Santa Fe adobes, Eastern prep schools, and competitive sports. Mr. Lauren's vision of American style prevails with classic grace and utmost attention to detail." His collection spans everything from garments to home furnishing, and Ralph Lauren is quite possibly today's most successful designer.

Here we are dealing with an all-around story, present in all the products we surround ourselves with in everyday life. That makes sense when the story is also the bottom line. In *Fortune*,[35] Martha Stewart describes the Ralph Lauren story thus: "When people buy his products, it gives them the feeling of having class and stature." Neil Kraft, former head of advertising for Calvin Klein, adds: "Ralph's world is not unapproachable or scary. Everything is done with promise of good taste."

The fundamental story remains the same, but you can get it with variations on the main theme. Any consumer buying Ralph Lauren is in the designer's "country," and there are several versions for sale, each offering a picture of who you are.

The same is true of the Swiss watchmaker Swatch. With more than 200 million watches sold since 1983, it is the world's largest maker of timepieces, and chooses to describe "Swatch country" as follows: "It has no snob appeal, it's open to everyone, it's simply irresistible." The product line offered is a multitude of plastic watches in bold colors that vary according to the story. The exception is a collection of metal watches, called "Irony." Swatch country—as the company very aptly chooses to label it—is large, but with clear boundaries. The story stops at a certain point, going no further. Knowledgeable consumers know when they are looking at a Swatch. The point of this chapter is that more and more consumers will become aware. A story can be infused into all products, and this is what we can expect to happen.

The clothes manufacturer Esprit is marketing a story about anticonsumerism: "Our purchasing habits have enormous influence....We can buy for our vital needs, not frivolous ego-gratifying needs. We need clothes, but so many?"[36] Esprit is selling a Who-Am-I story to the environmentally aware consumer who will spend money only on what is truly necessary. It's a poignant story to be peddling in a market otherwise awash with the message that you should advertise for yourself, by staging yourself as an exciting person living on the sunny side of life. Worrying about the fate of the planet is not normally part of the story. Esprit, and the vodka mentioned earlier, are—as yet—exceptions to the rule.

On the other hand, when you are in the emotional market peddling stories, it is important to beware of anything that might ruin your story. On its home page, Gap Inc., based in California, announced that in 1996, $5 million was given to charity, primarily in areas where employees live. Gap is showing it has a heart. At the same time, the company says: "We believe that business profitability and environmental responsibility are not mutually exclusive, and we strive to keep this in mind, in principle as well as practice." Gap does not use the environment as a selling tool, but it is present as part of the background.

In the days of old, poverty was synonymous with material poverty. There was not enough money to furnish the house; there was not enough money for a separate set of summer and winter clothes. In the Dream Society, because of the widespread growth in the overall level of material comfort, there is a need for a new definition of poverty. Building a definition on material wealth will no longer suffice when perhaps 80 percent of households in the affluent countries have money to cover the essential requirements. In the Who-Am-I market you are poor if you cannot afford to buy the stories you want for staging yourself, if you are forced to wear clothes that send messages you do not identify with. The affluent in the Dream Society can afford to tell exactly the story about themselves that they want to tell.

Marketing is the key factor in the Who-Am-I market. The story must be effectively told to the market if consumers are to buy it. Storytelling has become an important part of strategy; whoever tells the best story, and whoever tells it the best, will win. Which companies, then, are best at telling stories? Some of them have been mentioned in this chapter. Furthermore, an interesting pattern revealed itself in a survey of leading publications from the United States as compared with Europe. American companies and the American market in general display a much deeper understanding of the demands of the Dream Society when it comes to telling stories. Typically, U.S. ads simply show people in certain situations, often without explanatory text. The picture is the story. An emblematic example is "Marlboro Country"—a landscape with characters. The product, whether it be cigarettes or garments, is presumed to be understood. The product becomes a by-product, as is the prevailing case in the Who-Am-I market. On average, American consumers have a 15 to 20 percent larger disposable income than Europeans; prosperity is more conspicuous in the United States than in Europe. Italian and French designers are important players in this market, but they do not have the same broad appeal as their American counterparts. This explanation also seems to indicate that the Dream Society becomes more predominant with increasing prosperity—until it becomes dominant.

Taking a longer perspective, we are looking at a future with 500 or maybe 1000 global purveyors of stories, each marketing a story "country." The strongest stories will find it easy to defend their boundaries, while the weakest will succumb to the competition. They will be "invaded" and conquered by the stronger stories. The struggle for market shares will become a struggle between stories. Some stories compete with each other; some do not. Ralph Lauren, Swatch, and Marlboro are examples of stories that are not in competition—their plots are just too different.

Since the 1950s, developments have pointed in the direction of stronger stories and less emphasis on utility value. But these have been stories fully developed by their purveyors. Perhaps the next trend will be that the customer writes the story together with the producer in a cooperative mode, letting the story develop over time with its own, inherent dynamics according to small market fluctuations. There is certainly something to be said for customer participation in the telling of the story. Pioneer, a German jeans maker, encourages customers to send e-mail with information about just who they are. "Tell about yourself—and you will be famous," so the ad goes. In one ad a selected customer—Johnny Zander of New York—is quoted as saying: "I always claim I'm a gynecologist." The Pioneer story is developed by customers along with the company—it's an interactive story.

Just as in the geographical world, the story world consists of small, medium-size, and large versions of Who-Am-I. Gucci opened its first store in Florence in 1920. Today, 180 Gucci stores exist all over the world. The Gucci motto is: "Stay small to remain great."[37] Gucci's is a story about style and luxury and would, consequently, lose its meaning if too many consumers had the opportunity to buy into the story. As mentioned previously, the same is true of a number of the other European companies.

The Versace empire designs clothes, accessories, jewelry, home furnishings, porcelain, and perfume. There are about 140 stores worldwide, with annual sales in the neighborhood of $1 billion. Giovanni Versace was a designer to the stars, to the chosen few, to the glamour set. Versace bespeaks adventure and sensuality. That—and the price tag—places a limit on how many the story should be sold to. Were a mass-marketed Versace to emerge, existing customers would flee from the story and find a new, sufficiently exclusive one.

During the last 10 to 20 years many shoe manufacturers have entered into the Who-Am-I market. This is the case whether we look at shoes for partying, for work, for leisure, for sports, or for trekking. The latest addition to Dream Society products are sandals. Under the headline "Expedition Equipment," the English periodical *Geographical,* published by the esteemed Royal

Geographical Society, evaluated 12 different brands of "All-Terrain Sandals."[38] These sandals bear names like Hitec Whitewater, Nike SCG, Air Deschutz Pro, Ecco Cosmo Mercury, and Reef Brazil Mundaka. The names convey that whoever buys these signal sandals is a connoisseur of mountains, valleys, and rivers, plus knowledgeable about the exciting challenges nature has to offer. This buyer is a lover of nature at its most rugged. An increasing number of the products that we surround ourselves with are moving from the Who-Am-I market to the market for peace of mind (see below). They are acquiring a new dimension, and producers are increasing their profits while getting more loyal customers to boot. The added story means that products are no longer judged exclusively on price and quality. The dog-eat-dog price competition is left to the companies that still sell only products and thus mainly emphasize utility value.

The Dream Society is only just emerging in the Who-Am-I market; it is not yet dominant. Most consumers still choose their purchases of clothing from an evaluation based on price and quality. Self-staging is an accompanying factor. You are aware of it, but it does not in the end determine your choice. However, as the Dream Society gains ground because of increasing prosperity, customers will gradually reach the point where they must relate to the stories the companies are selling.

"I buy clothes only to wear them. My clothes are not going to tell people who I am—I'll take care of that part myself." Such might be a typical statement from a college-educated or "sensible" consumer. This is where a paradox enters the picture. By rejecting signal value, you have chosen to become part of a story just the same. Our college grad wishes to send the signal that she or he does not wish to send any. Many companies will rush to provide this market with the proper story. The market for clothes that look worn when purchased is already emerging. These clothes must look ever so slightly threadbare, thus telling the story that the wearer does not make a great fuss about clothes; but it is important that the clothes don't look downright shabby—that might be interpreted as material poverty. We all possess the ability to register even tiny nuances in the signals we send to each other. A tie just an inch too wide may reveal that this is not a businessman, but—perhaps—a designer.

With sales in excess of $6.5 billion, Levi Strauss & Co. is Japan's largest clothing manufacturer. This company is firmly lodged in the Dream Society. Through its discrete label, the company inserts its story into every product made. The label takes up very little space but it is big enough for us to notice the inherent signal—we can decipher the code. The story is told in countless places, yet on the product itself it has been reduced to just a few inches. Customers are happy to pay extra for this story—a premium of 50, sometimes 100 percent. The story is truly global, subsuming innumerable local and national stories about garments. The Levi's sportswear story is available in several versions. An advertisement for girls' jeans in *Vogue* magazine (U.S. edition)[39] enumerates "the princess dream, the pony dream, the pretty bride dream," only to top this off with the question, "Ready for the kick the butt dream?" Little stories for an important market.

To the many people who see the Dream Society's globalization of stories as a cultural loss, the answer must be that it is occurring in an open market and that the consumer has freedom of choice; the consumer seems to prefer the global stories in favor of the local and traditional ones. In periods of momentous change it is customary for values to be cast aside and replaced with new values. And we do live in a period of momentous change. "The future always arrives when good-byes are being said."[40] Currently, we are indeed saying good-bye to many local and social traditions, and they are final good-byes. Dressing in a particular way if you belonged to a certain local region, wearing certain trousers or shirts if you happened to be a worker—all this is consigned to the history books. On the other hand, we are saying hello to the future, to new global cultural patterns. They are materializing within the marketplace, they are woven by companies, and they are changing. We are talking about collective choices made by "The Western Consumer."

Yet many Who-Am-I stories are built on national traditions. The Scottish Tartan Society has registered 2400 different patterns of tartan plaid. In 1996 alone, more than 100 new ones were added.[41]

Whether told on taxis or on Grand Prix racing cars, the story remains rooted in ancient legends of proud Scots clans, of loyalty, independence, and tradition. It also forms part of many Who-Am-I stories. The tartan pattern is a boon for modern-day designers, provided by an old and proud tradition. So is another proud tradition, still living, the Kente patterns from modern-day Ghana. Originally, Kente was part of the cultural tradition of the Asande nation. Modern designers give fresh interpretations to history, lifting it out of its cultural context and launching it on the Who-Am-I market. We will no doubt see a host of old stories being retold in a modern version to consumers unaware of the origins, cultural roots, or meaning of each story. Therefore, it is questionable whether we can call these stories "authentic" in the sense of their being true to tradition.

The Who-Am-I market does not only include clothes. It encompasses accessories—hats, shoes, sunglasses, belts, and bags—as well as cosmetics and coiffure. It embraces home furnishings—everything, in short, with which we choose to surround ourselves. Even that does not cover it all. In an advertisement for the job of TA officer, the English Territorial Army shows its brass: "Environmentalists, you say you love the earth. Eat some." The photograph portrays a soldier crawling on his belly through a puddle of mud, getting a close encounter with wet earth. Real men don't love the earth; they devour it!

"This one makes me happy; the other one is at home fixing dinner," proclaims an ad for the French compact Peugeot. The accompanying photograph shows a woman getting into the car. The story Peugeot wants to tell is obviously that here is an offer for women wishing to signal their independence; you buy a Peugeot and you flaunt it. The ad also, indirectly, implies that these days, all cars are of good quality, so we need not always talk technology. The buying incentive in this situation—where price and quality are roughly the same—lies in the story.

In an ad for the 1996 Chevrolet Monte Carlo the text, accompanied by a picture of the car's driver's seat, begins: "I want my own place. A place where I can't be reached. I want to be 'off duty.' I want to call a 'time out.' I want a mute button for reality."

The busy business executive is buying into a sanctuary, an oasis away from hectic, everyday existence where there's room to be yourself, an individual. The car is part of my story about myself: Who-Am-I.

The Western business suit has remained more or less unaltered for the last 100 years. Also, the suit has caught on in developing countries, worn by Chinese officials as well as African business-men. The reason? This is the recognized uniform for signaling confidence, stability, neutrality, and credibility. Nuances may be conveyed by choice of tie, suspenders, or perhaps color of shirt. Any company poised to tell a new story to the businesspeople of the Western world must know that it is pitted against a long and tenacious story, and not one which is easily changed. Things are different when it comes to female business attire; since it has not yet been rigidly defined, there is room here for a story.

We are entering into a future where signals will be global—almost. Certainly, many of the products named above are sold to the middle classes of Latin America, Southeast Asia, and India, but the Dream Society is currently almost exclusively happening in the rich parts of the world—in North America, Europe, Japan, Australia, and New Zealand. This is unsurprising, considering the fact that the Dream Society owes its existence directly to affluence. Even today, the metropolises of these countries offer the same merchandise. To find a culturally specific national character, you are increasingly forced to turn to museums, historical monuments, or rural areas. The stores, the items for sale, the cars, the way people dress—all these factors that used to make the atmosphere of a city unique—are becoming more or less indistinguishable.

It must be said that the game is truly afoot. It has already started, and we can begin to see the shape of the future that we are entering into. In the garment market, a number of large companies represent "countries," or "cultures" even, each endowed with an apposite story that is told and listened to everywhere in the affluent countries. In this sense, these companies might be called repositories of culture. Their stories have replaced traditional or social stories, but they function within an open market ruled by competition. The stories compete with one another. It is a future scenario that most people over 50 (including the author) find alien and a bit frightening. Many of us would prefer to preserve the old picture of great variety from country to country—from region to region even—prevailing within Europe.

We are, however, a generation doomed to experience great changes. We must learn how to live with them and avoid the feeling that "the future has let me down." In her thought-provoking book *Thinking in the Future Tense*, Jennifer James points out how we tend to see the past "wrapped in the golden glow of nostalgia." The good old days were never quite as good as we remember them.

In the 1974 Norman Jewison film *Rollerball,* the future is portrayed as owned and dominated, not by nations, but by corporations. These corporations have no need for the aggressions that lead to war, or for the expenditure required for maintaining a military defense. Therefore they create a sport—albeit an extremely violent one—through which to channel aggression. Will the movie *Rollerball*—like *Nautilus* before it—turn out to be one of those films that show us the shape of the future? Will companies turn out to be bigger and more powerful than nations in 50 years' time? If so, there is a promise of progress in at least one area. Wars, which together with disease and crop failures have been the scourge of humanity for millennia, will be a thing of the past. That would constitute a major winning at a small cost. The only problem lies in the fact that so many wise people through the ages have predicted that human beings have become so wise that they will no longer wage war. Previously, these predictions have consistently been proved wrong. A modified *Rollerball* scenario is discussed in Chapter 5.

Within the natural sciences, there is discussion about how to preserve biodiversity—the global abundance of species—as a prerequisite for continued prosperity on this planet. Among anthropologists, there is slightly less talk about preserving cultural diversity—the bounteous range of different cultures. The estimate is that out of the more than 6000 languages spoken globally, currently 2 small tongues disappear daily. For every language lost, an entire set of ideas and traditions that could enrich our lives perishes along with it.

Anthropologists also speak of people's rights to their unique cultural traditions—their roots. This view, however, is countered by a different opinion. Cultural development cannot and should not be frozen at any point in time. These are living traditions and thoughts; they must be allowed autonomous evolution. If you attempt to keep a lid on such growth, it will simply explode.

5. The Market for Peace of Mind

Alvin Toffler, author of several visionary books about society in the future, published his *Future Shock* in 1970. It immediately became a best-seller, yet its message is more timely today than ever. "Western society for the past 300 years has been caught up in a fire storm of change. This storm, far from abating, now appears to be gathering in force." This could easily be a description of day-to-day experience for many of us. One current issue of *The New York Times* probably contains more information about changes than an average farmer of the early nineteenth century would experience through a lifetime. The proportion of familiar as opposed to new information and things has been seriously altered. Too much is new and much too little is familiar. Hence the Toffler definition "Future Shock: it is the disease of change. Its symptoms are already here."

In an insecure and changeable world, there is a demand for peace of mind and permanence. In a static world, the demand will be for news and change. In other words, the things we demand are the things in short supply. When the modern-type newspaper appeared at the end of the nineteenth century, its main purpose was to deliver news—tidings of change—to readers for whom each day looked disturbingly like the next. Today, the role of the newspaper is gradually changing; it is supposed to provide a vantage point for understanding the chaos of everyday life.

As emphasized by Jennifer James in *Thinking in the Future Tense*, we have a distinct tendency to glorify and romanticize the past. The "good old days" were good, period—even though, upon reflection, we have to admit that they may not really have been quite that good. We place in demand stories about permanence, peace

97

of mind, and stable values: stories about knowing our place in life, about knowing which role to play in marriage, about working at the same endeavor throughout life, about being close with our neighbors, and about growing old with our childhood friends. At the same time, as noted earlier in this chapter, we demand change, variety, adventure. We place our demands on both markets and they supplement each other. If a survey could be done on the market shares for adventure stories and peace of mind, respectively, we would probably discover that the market for peace of mind is larger and growing more rapidly. More companies are inserting the permanence story into their products.

A prime example is Jack Daniel's Tennessee Whiskey. An ad for this product goes: "This September marks Mr. Jack Daniel's 151st birthday. Or maybe, as some say, his 147th. The exact date of our founder's birth remains a mystery to this day (folks weren't too good at keeping records in those days)." It's a product telling a story about the good old days—from before everything in this world went haywire. Incidentally, most whisky (or whiskey) labels tell minutely varied versions of this story. The focal point is the permanence aspect—the idea that the product is made from an age-old formula; that the distillery process has remained the same, just as the label has remained unchanged. A Budweiser ad describes—and displays—how the label has remained almost completely the same for more than a century. The first Bud depicted dates from the period of Custer's Last Stand. The good old days of nostalgia may even be imagined as the communist regimes of the cold war era, as illustrated by Zámek, a Czech Pilsner brew marketed in England as a product deriving from communism's "happy days" where a merry worker is seen rejoicing in the production results. This daring type of nostalgia probably would not sell in present-day, "ex-" Eastern Europe; the harsh realities of yesteryear are still too close.

How do you sell a partially mendacious picture of the past, especially when it is often evident that the product has no authentic connection to this particular part of the past? Scott Bedbury, senior director of marketing at Starbucks Coffee Co., provides the answer in an interview for *Fast Company* magazine.[42] "The common ground among companies that have built great brands is not just performance. They recognize that consumers live in an emotional world. Emotions drive most, if not all, of our decisions." We are not, then, living in a rational world; we are living in the Dream Society. Novels, after all, are not judged on the basis of whether the story is told correctly and actually took place. We read novels and we buy stories; but we also read nonfiction from which we demand objectivity. And we buy products on the basis of price and quality. The theory about the Dream Society means that the "novel" will supersede "nonfiction" on the market for products and services. This trend has not completely taken over, but it is on its way.

Starbuck's Scott Bedbury also defines brand as a concept. His is truly a wise and precise description, one that will hold the record in its field for many years to come: "A brand is a metaphorical story that's evolving all the time. This connects with something very deep—a fundamental human appreciation of mythology." Bedbury, by the way, is the man who gave the world the words "Just do it."

Is storytelling, then, just a new word for "branding"? No, but any strong brand will almost invariably contain an appeal to our emotions. A story marks the beginnings of a brand; when that story has been told to sufficient numbers of consumers for them to remember it, the company in question may claim, "We now have ourselves a brand." At the same time, the story is a much broader concept. Lots of products tell a story without being a brand—an egg, for instance. Eggs bespeak rural romanticism and animal ethics, but they are not a brand marketed by one particular company. They are a product category. One corollary of the Dream Society theory is that "brands" and "private labels" will not always constitute competing marketing methods in the marketplace of the future. During the past 20 years many theories have been proffered as to whether brands will win out over private labels. During times of prosperity it often seems that brands have the upper hand, while in periods of decline private labels seem stronger. The Dream Society theory involves a long-term trend indicating that storytelling, including brands, will prevail over private labels. Not today or tomorrow, but within 5 to 10 years. Price and quality will still be important factors, but their relative significance will be smaller.

This section is about peace of mind and permanence. Some of the best stories within these categories can be mined from the past—or, more precisely, from our way of picturing the past. The pictures of the past most commonly revisited are itemized below as a kind of Dream Society tool kit, complete with suggested narratives and myths from which to construct the stories. Myths the consumer will appreciate. Common to them are the ingredients of peace of mind and permanence. Dream along:

○ The classic England of the nineteenth century. In the wealthy English manor house, tradition and good taste are the order of the day. Existence and values are fixed and accepted by all. There is plenty of time for a spirited conversation about art or for big-game hunting in Africa. There is plenty of time to meet around the tea table in the beautiful garden in a stress-free idyllic existence.

○ The Wild West with small, comprehensible cities, where the sheriff, the undertaker, the editor, the bartender, and the local beauties meet the cowboy riding into town. Here values are fixed; justice may be summarily executed, but good prevails over evil. The task is to create a whole new life surrounded by spectacular scenery with buffalo, wild bear, and wolves.

○ Paris in the 1920s. The Moulin Rouge, the artistic milieu, red wine, and round-the-clock joie de vivre, unfettered by obligations—all bespeak resplendent beauty and amity in the bistros. It's a dream of the carefree life with romance, love, and art. Take a walk through the streets of Paris in the early hours after a long night at the Moulin Rouge.

○ The ancient world of Greece. Here Aristotle wanders the plaza among Doric columns, expounding on the meaning of life and death with intellectual rigor while his doting pupils listen. The white buildings, the blue skies, the olive trees, and a sea of jumping dolphins complete the idyllic picture.

○ The Japanese Samurai period, with its codes of honor, loyalty, and brotherhood. It is a bellicose period, but battles are fought with swords and according to rules of chivalry. Good prevails over evil. It is also about beautiful Asian architecture and tea ceremonies, about women in kimonos and green rice fields.

○ Man of the Great Outdoors, outside the reach of civilization's corrupting influences. People live in harmony with nature, the forests, and the animals. Water is drawn from clear, billowing brooks and only the most necessary animals are killed. Joy is to be found in an unspoiled existence with no change and no problems. Back to nature.

○ The Vikings of the North, who venture out to distant lands to pillage and plunder, yet preserve their purity of mind. The quiet living off the land, the love-filled home life is interrupted here and there by family feuds. The thralls know and accept their place in life with a smile. All values are fixed and permanent.

○ The Great Moguls period in India. Mighty, yet just princes live lives of refined luxury listening to music that appeases the soul and speaks to romance and unrequited love. Here power is just, beautiful, and everlasting.

The story most frequently infused into modern products is the myth of rural romanticism, whether of the classical English variety mentioned above or other versions of pastoral nostalgia (e.g., stories from the American Midwest, Mexico, Italy, or Spain). These stories of a secure, unchanging existence differ markedly from modern urban life with its attendant stress, noise, traffic, and free-floating angst. Urban life is rife with choices between different ideas, conflicts between different value systems; nothing is accepted as absolutely right by everyone. Nor is anything deemed absolutely wrong. We recoil back to an idyllic state, to a dream about the past.

The story glorifying industrial romanticism is on its way. The idea suggests itself readily: the shop floor with its workers happy and content doing hard, physical labor; the camaraderie, the joy in making progress happen—in creating civilization where once there was only nature; the gargantuan machines bending steel into towering structures that in turn become steamships

101

ploughing the waves of the seven seas. Is it that too many people are around who still remember how things really were and therefore are unwilling to accept industrial nostalgia? No. Romanticism is a myth we need, and this story will be utilized to tell many tales about products and services.

And it has begun. "The original Lee Overall. We went back and got them," announces an ad with a picture of a row of miners queuing to enter the shaft. It's a romanticized, nostalgic story about peace of mind, fixed values and camaraderie from the golden age of industrialism. The ad is hardly targeted at miners.[43]

A Finnish company has taken a tongue-in-cheek stab at industrial romanticism. The artist Alvar Gullichsen, head of Bonk Business, Inc., produces de-functional machines. They look like machines capable of making products, but they are strictly for decorative purposes, for inspiration; they are completely without practical value. Sales of these machines for offices, for canteens, for private homes, and elsewhere are doing fine; the machines make no noise and the energy consumption is low. Gullichsen, an eminent storyteller, is even planning a nostalgic look at—or a parody on—the Information Society: "Advanced Disinformation Systems (ADS)."

None of the stories mentioned above, concerning a past that gave us peace of mind, is true in any scientific sense, but all are myths we need in our search for just that—peace of mind and permanence. It is of no importance to us whether a professor would accept the reality these myths purport to describe. The Rational We gracefully takes an obsequious bow to make way for the Emotional We.

Instead of nostalgia, modern companies might find offering peace of mind and permanence as a modern-day story worth considering. Adorning products with stories culled from the past does amount to an admission of sorts. You are saying stories from the past are better than those that can be told of the present. Two examples from the world of banking demonstrate this point (and many others could be added). The Pennsylvania Capital Bank offers "private banking." On its home page we read the following: "Small by design, we deliver with dignity and discretion the direct, personalized service that has vanished from banking. Despite its mystique, private banking is in many ways simply a return to old-fashioned values and the gracious ways business was conducted years ago." First National Bank in Brookings offers almost the same story: "We strive to maintain the small-town banking atmosphere while growing and changing with the technological age."

The history of the financial sector, and of banking in particular, begins with an emphasis on security and peace of mind. Banks were offering to safekeep the customers' assets—and the peace of mind that followed—because it was safer than keeping them yourself. They were in the peace of mind market. However, following the trend as solid values increasingly disappear from business, many banks have abandoned peace of mind in favor of a story about efficiency, technology, size, and profitability. A survey of mission statements, ads, and home pages confirms the trend. The same is true within advertising, accountancy, and real estate. This change is reflected in the architectural images presented by company head offices. The older headquarters, with their marble and "Greek" columns, are still relating their story about peace of mind and security, whereas more recently built head offices, with their rectangular and utilitarian lines of concrete, impart the ideas of efficiency and technology.

We can expect that the financial sector will gradually return to the peace of mind story. The reason is not only that customers will demand these values but also that technology will become trivial—taken for granted. One possibility is that banks will rebuild branch offices to look the way they did 100 years ago: with wood paneling, green lamps, and lots of paper. Computers will be hidden behind dark wood and there will be no chains on the ballpoint pens (trust the customers!). The staged bank branch office may appear, as did the staged boutique and restaurant. The notion may seem farfetched today, but the need to tell the peace of mind story exists quite palpably. The branch bank is an obvious place to tell the story. Not that this means technology will vanish; on the contrary, it just means that technology has taken a back seat to the emotional appeal.

Andersen Consulting is an Information Society product, and considers itself as such. On its home page, the company presents itself this way: "Andersen Consulting is a global management and technology consulting organization whose mission is to help its clients change to be more successful. The organization helps its clients link strategy, people, process, and technology." This preamble reflects the "computer age" and therefore is not meant to appeal emotionally. It is about knowledge, efficiency, and technology. In the future, it may become necessary to add an emotional dimension to the story. As the examples demonstrate, however, it is difficult to transcend the Zeitgeist under which you were founded.

In the consultancy market, trust is essential; payment is agreed upon before the "goods" are delivered. These "deliverables" are a report containing concrete and nonconcrete advice. The value can be difficult to determine in advance. There is only one way to do so. The customer needs to trust the consultancy firm. The same principle applies to a future-oriented think tank like CIFS. The prerequisite for any business-customer relationship is trust and peace of mind. For this, if for no other reason, the old-fashioned business meeting complete with handshake, social conversation, coffee, and refreshments will never go out of style. This entire ritual, which is quite time-consuming, is necessary for building trust. The business-to-business market is not significantly different from the consumer market. We are all both consumers and employees.

One part of the peace of mind story emphasized by many companies is how long they have been in business. Advertising the fact that your company has operated in the financial sector for many years is part of your marketing effort—when chronologically possible.

Greenpeace, which in Dream Society terms is a global company, states its purpose thus: "To create a green and peaceful world." It and similar organizations are working to preserve nature against "progress." You could say that Greenpeace champions the idea of the past, when nature was nature and other species could live free from risk of annihilation by humankind. The idea of "sustainability"—that humans should live together with nature and not "off" nature, traces its roots back to the so-called primitive peoples, who—at least according to myth—knew how to live with respect for all living things. The story about humankind living in harmony with nature has influenced Western societies for the past 200 years; it is particularly relevant today. Now, most companies include environmental concern as part of their strategy. Caring for the environment is part of the market for peace of mind and permanence.

Today there are more than 500 million private automobiles on the planet.[44] The car-making industry is the world's largest. Together with the aviation industry, it constitutes the great industrial wonder of the twentieth century. Behind this success lie efficiency and flexibility. The car is an efficient means of transportation. There are, however, a number of emotional factors playing a significant role as well. Earlier we looked at the adventure story and self-staging. Here, we must consider peace of mind. Through observations, science has been able to ascertain that human beings have a safety zone of a little more than one yard. We do not want strangers to get any closer to us than that. Animals have a much bigger safety zone—extending up to about 100 yards. Come within this range and the animal will flee. The human safety zone is constantly being violated in the big cities, on sidewalks, and in buses and subways. Only within the closed confines of the car are we inhabiting our own space, almost like a home. And the safety zone remains inviolate. The car is an emotional thing—on many levels.

Marlboro Country, too, bespeaks the past and peace of mind. "There was a time when all this was just fields," reads the text accompanying a picture of a landscape of fields as far as the eye can see. It's a story about the era of fixed values—cigarettes with the added story of a time prior to urban life, a time before everything went haywire.[45]

As mentioned previously, the biggest peace of mind story is the one extolling rural romanticism. One of the reasons is that almost 80 percent of the people in affluent countries have grown up in the city and live their lives there. Examples include the Marlboro story and the story told by *House & Garden* and all the other magazines dedicated to interior decorating. Peace of mind and permanence is illustrated through pictures. Text is reduced to a bare minimum. Are we seeing a return to the Europe of the Middle Ages, where pictures were the lingua franca—the common denominator we could all understand?

These dream magazines are food for thought: How do we perceive our abode—the home? The home is the most emotional place we know. This is where we stage our dreams of love, family bliss, and peace of mind. These values are of course present in our day and age, but demand far exceeds supply. So we can buy the story. Companies selling home accoutrements—be they furniture, carpets, windows, bathrooms, or kitchens—almost always append a story about the past to their products. Great changes have taken place within the past 40 years. In the 1950s, the present day and the future were chic; back then, the kitchen was allowed to put new technology on display, as well as efficiency and cleanliness. Stainless steel and large, white surfaces were permissible. Today colors are permitted; the past and romance are permitted.

Maybe it happened in the 1960s. Maybe this was the decade where we lost our faith in the present and the future, turning instead to an idealized picture of the past. Alvin Toffler, whose 1970 book *Future Shock* has been mentioned, hit the nail on the head. We react to the excessive pace of changes by turning to the unchangeable past for peace of mind. We purchase a picture from the past, even if it does cost a little extra.

Happily, there is lots of past and it contains innumerable stories. The great gold mine of history will never, ever be exhausted. The possibilities are infinite: "Land's End Chinos. So easygoing it's hard to believe they descended from a starchy British officer in the Punjab"—so goes the advertisement blurb. Later on, the text makes it clear that the name of the officer is Lt. Harry Lumsden. From the rugged life of the nineteenth-century soldier at the outermost reaches of the Indian empire, to the most recent issue of *House & Garden*. As H. N. Andersen, founder of the East Asiatic Company, put it in 1919: "The Earth is not bigger than it can be girdled by thought." In the Dream Society there will be a need for many historians who can venture out into world history in order to bring back the raw material for stories about products and to create stories for companies—stories placing those companies far from our time.

The past becomes more and more plentiful as time goes by, and with the increased pace of change it is experienced as being further away from the present. The 1990s—the final decade of the twentieth century—may already have become the nostalgic past in the year 2010. Historians will speak of "twentieth-century civilization." Ads will picture us in front of what by then will be a hopelessly outdated computer, talking about this tranquil age that offered time for thoughtful reflection. Why, we even had time to create letters with our fingertips! (Computer speech-recognition capabilities having reached perfection, keyboards will have vanished.)

6. The Market for Convictions

We stand in the midst of an ongoing fusion of previously separate roles within the market for convictions. In September 1995, the English *Sunday Times* estimated that there were more than 1000 interest groups in Great Britain—ranging from Greenpeace with 4 million members worldwide to "Surfers Against Sewage"—and it is a safe bet that new figures will be higher. Interest groups have always existed but never in such numbers and never wielding such influence. These organizations are providing competition for politicians. Companies will be next to compete with politicians in the market for convictions. The number of suppliers to the market for convictions has exploded. You can buy convictions suited to practically any temperament or occasion. You can buy the politicians' fixed menu—a complete set of more or less cohesive ideas—or you may select à la carte from among interest groups.

What we are now witnessing is the start of the big convictions market of the twenty-first century. Companies are as yet a bit uneasy about having become "political companies," but this will soon become par for the course, part of their necessary strategic plan. The curtain has definitively closed on the era when a company's sole objective was profitability. That type of game—the one with rational rules—is over, but a new game is beginning, with new rules; and they are more complex. They still involve the imperative of profitability, but on top of this comes a choice of convictions.

Let us pause to consider why this change is taking place. An obvious explanation is that the consumer or voter, the one who is buying convictions, has become a well-educated, enlightened person who has lost trust in authority and who above all wishes to make independent choices. Each person is an individual. This has not always been so; previously, you shared your convictions with the social group to which you belonged, depending on whether you were a worker, a farmer, or a white-collar employee. And you placed your trust in authority, in the powers that be, in ideologies, in a certain set of values. The emancipation from the fixed menu has a clear corollary: it has become absolutely necessary to make an independent, individual choice.

Whereas previously you were issued a standard set of values, much like a new recruit is issued a military uniform, today you enter a shopping mall and are told, "Take whatever you need." Thus the demand for values and convictions is born. Politicians, organizations—and companies—react just like any other market: you match the demand with an appropriate supply.

Let us consider the conviction market of the twenty-first century as if it were a fight for people's minds. This battle will unfold as a drama, but it will not be reminiscent of the twentieth century, in which monolithic ideologies and huge social classes struggled for citizens' soul and thus for influence in shaping the laws of the land and the distribution of collective wealth. That particular conflict of the masses could be led and directed from above. This macrofront has not yet quite outlived its role, but it is about to happen.

The battle of the twenty-first century will be fought on a microfront where the bone of contention is the individual's attention. Not in the sense of gaining total acceptance of an entire system of ideas, just the conviction regarding specific questions. The range (and variety) of products on the market for merchandise has exploded to the extent that no two families today have exactly identical patterns of consumption; there is so much to choose between that chances of hitting the exact purchases are infinitesimal—like winning the lottery. The market for convictions has exploded in much the same manner. Ecology, environment, human rights, ethics, animal welfare, smoking, genetic engineering, religion, energy supply—all these burning issues have really surfaced only during the last 10 to 20 years. Or they are issues that have only recently presented themselves as concrete choices to be made and not as stable sets of values. Being a person has become more of an ordeal. You need to find your own proper place in the panoply of conviction pigeonholes, but the number of pigeonholes has increased.

Given this portrait of the present, and the future in particular, it can come as a surprise to no one that companies will gradually enter the market for convictions. The most important reason is that the consumer wants it. When you are no longer that preoccupied politicians' vast smorgasbord of ideological systems and more or less vapid visions, then you no longer just vote in the polling booth on election day; you vote every day, with your shopping cart. And a new type of political participation has seen the light of day. It has many advantages compared with the ballot, which came into being along with democracy. You may vote whenever you like, as often as you like. You may change your mind at any time, you may vote on specifics—and you vote individually. So how are people voting with their shopping carts?

At the moment a gigantic vote is being held in all the affluent countries. Should our agricultural products be made intensively, as in industry, and therefore cheaply, or should they be made ecologically and with animal welfare taken into consideration? This vote will be in progress for 5 to 10 years, but within a few years we will be able to discern trends, and see which way we are heading! Through agricultural policies, politicians will be able to delay or further these trends, but they will be unable to alter them completely. This decision-making process may not be democratic according to conventional political wisdom (the rich have more "ballots" to cast than the poor). Be that as it may, this remains the battlefield where the outcome is determined.

Needless to say, politicians will never be jobless. As Edward Mortimer put it in a commentary for the *Financial Times:* "Private choices by consumers are not the same as civic choices by citizens. Leaving everything to the market deprives citizens of the chance to make collective choices." Some decisions might perfectly well be delegated to the shopping cart while others are best left to the ballot box. There is one political sphere for politicians and another political sphere for companies. But politicians and companies alike find themselves firmly established in the convictions market. Today consumers regard the large corporations as pillars of society. There are certain expectations as to their deportment within the market for convictions.

A recent headline in the *Financial Times*[46] read "Carmaker Drops Speed and Luxury in Favour of Caring Image." The auto firm in question is Opel, Europe's number three carmaker and a General Motors subsidiary. In an ad campaign, the company emphasizes its German Standort: "We wanted to say clearly that we are a German company and that we are a good corporate citizen," explains an Opel spokesperson.

We are rapidly approaching a situation where for-profit-only companies become rarer and where suppliers and customers will be taking such companies to task, asking questions like "Does your company have no heart, no feelings? Are you nothing but a rationalistic, profiteering machine?" The future belongs to companies with firmly held convictions: the Dream Society companies.

John Naisbitt's *Trend Letter*[47] has stated: "A new trend, called cause-related marketing (CRM), ties corporate do-gooding directly to increased sales and profits—making the donations, in effect, painless." Naisbitt is referring to a consumer behavior survey that concluded, among other things, that "in households with incomes above 50,000 USD, the percentage of consumers willing to switch brands because a company was associated with a cause they supported, was 82%." The average among all those surveyed was as high as 66 percent.

But this is not only about beneficence—about charity or social politics. On its European home page, Shell calls attention to the fact that with a tax contribution of £26 billion, the company is "the tax-man's friend." BP, British Petroleum, uses its home page to report that the company's "Community Development Programme" gives support within four areas: regeneration, sustainable development, local "good neighbor" relations and arts, culture, and heritage. Similarly, Mobil's ads accentuate the importance of remaining in overseas markets despite the presence of political turmoil. Priority must be given to concern for the local population of these countries. The world's leading energy conglomerates recognize their social as well as political responsibilities. They see themselves as pillars of society.

Companies are in the market for products as well as in the market for convictions. They are in the latter because adherent convictions sell products. Some companies sell just convictions. An example of this is Greenpeace, which operates on a global scale. In one of its ads, the company proclaimed: "If you saw a crime committed, you'd call the police. When the environmental crimes are committed against the planet, people call us." The ad concludes, "Be part of the solution: support Greenpeace." The message—almost—is that we now have our global environment police. Greenpeace is nestled in the core of the market for convictions.

The new players in the market for convictions include not just companies but researchers in the field. In *Scientific American*[48] Michio Kaku reviewed a book providing a scientific explanation of the *Star Trek* saga, entitled "The Physics of *Star Trek*." The reviewer was in rave mode—a scientist taking a fantasy story seriously. There is a necessary connection. The famous futurist Arthur C. Clarke is quoted as saying, "Any sufficiently advanced technology is indistinguishable from magic." Einstein said much the same—that "imagination is more important than knowledge." Acknowledging the fact that visionary science requires imagination and magic is fine, but this is not the reviewer's only point: "Scientists must reach out to largely indifferent, and often scientifically illiterate, taxpayers and persuade them to pay our bills."

Science no longer remains the unchallenged authority. Research programs will have to venture forth, winning acceptance—and this must happen in the market for convictions. You may debate whether such a situation is desirable, but the important fact remains. Research is now "coming out" into the market—not 100 percent, maybe not even 50 percent, but the percentage is clearly rising.

Let us take a closer look at the marketplace. What will it look like in 5 to 10 years? It will be whimsical, like fashion. The international agenda is to a significant degree decreed by the media and it is like a snowball, starting with one throwaway line and ballooning into headlines. It may be questions about human rights that force companies to face the choice of staying in the market or pulling out. It may be questions regarding animal ethics or national issues, as in the case of Opel. The agenda may be supportive of or against market creations (NAFTA or the European Union). The possibilities are legion and the only certainty will be surprises.

The marketplace is global, as are the media. Affluent countries comprise one single market for convictions. The reaction patterns of consumers in affluent countries is showing a tendency to become identical—only shades and nuances will eventually distinguish them. New convictions will spread from country to country in a matter of hours; decisions will have to be made swiftly.

The marketplace is emotional. Convictions prevailing in the market may well be in flagrant opposition to "scientific truth." Companies will treat "global warming" as fact if consumers believe it to be so. Therefore, the market for convictions is not susceptible to expert opinions. But a company dealing with the market for convictions does require employees possessing high emotional intelligence (as defined by Daniel Goleman in his book of that title)—that is, employees capable of listening, feeling, inspiring, and speaking the language of the heart. In the Dream Society the emotional aspect of consumption will play an ever more important part, and convictions are part of this trend. To stretch the point a bit, a company should have a political platform roughly equivalent to that of a presidential candidate. The only difference will be that companies face election daily and not just every four years.

There are big markets for convictions, and there are small ones. The market for animal welfare is large, the environmental market is also large; therefore these are good choices for companies with many customers in many countries. You can afford to be controversial only in the eyes of a select few. On the other hand, there are small markets, such as opposition to a European Union directive to universalize escape signs in hotels. A German brewery has run ads against what is seen as bureaucracy in this matter.[49] Such concerns are suited to companies targeting a niche market.

Chapter 3

From Hard Work to Hard Fun— From Company to Tribe

Following a lecture, I met with some of the organizers for a beer. The discussion turned to working hours. They were talking about shorter hours as I began telling them about the long days I put in. They recoiled in horror: How could I be duped into such drudgery? I had to be a brainwashed victim of corporate culture. We weren't exactly on the same wavelength.

The next day, there was another lecture. This time, we rounded off the seminar with a glass of wine. Once again, the conversation turned to working hours. We began one-upping one another about our very long workday. I happened to win—I worked the longest hours and was thus the hero in that particular crowd.

How can you be chump one day, champ the next? The reason is that the concept of work is changing, and today two diametrically opposed views exist alongside one another. This chapter takes a look at the new concept and the perspectives that are in store for the future.

A revolution is in progress, taking us out of the Information Society and ushering in the Dream Society—the next and final phase in human, societal development. That was the message in Chapter 1. Chapter 2 looked at the market for products—its emotionalization, its dematerialization, and the victory of emotions over functionality.

This chapter concerns the market for labor and the shape of future corporations. What does a Dream Society company actually look like? How does work get done, and what does the work-place look like? Last but not least, what about company ownership and its duration in the future? Let us anticipate some of the conclusions reached in this chapter. They have crystalized through the reasoning found in the following pages, based on development trends in the affluent countries. If you find yourself convinced by these lines of reasoning, the conclusions will provide a recipe for success for your company as well as its employees:

○ Work will become hard fun: motivating, creative, and engrossing. No longer will the company be a satellite orbiting the family, providing it with a livelihood. In the future, our lives will have two social nuclei: the home and the company. For some, the home and family will be most important; for others, the corporation will take precedence. A lucky few will attain the coveted balance between career and family life.

○ The company will not be a legal or economic entity. It will be more like a tribe, as defined by the hunter-gatherer society. People hunt collectively and divide the prey according to preset rules. Employees are not under traditional contract; they are participants or members of the tribe. The quarry bagged may vary—tribal survival has supreme priority. Tribal life contains theater and drama.

○ Traditional methods of accounting, dating back 200 years, will be abandoned. The largest visible item in the accounts—and in status—will become the human production factor, the participant. Intellectual capital will be calculated. Physical assets will become secondary capital. After all, the computer produces nothing by itself; it has to be guided. The company or tribe is made up of the sum of its participants.

116

○ Stock owners and stock markets as we know them will wither away, since only the most engaged and active participants will be allowed to take part in the life of the corporation. The passive investor will become a twentieth-century phenomenon. Corporate capital is the property of participants only—the tribal members' reserve. These may be owners or corporate employees, but all will share in the corporate soul and partake of company rituals.

It is no wonder that the Dream Society entails revolutionary changes. This was also true of the transition to the Information Society. However, the future arrives only one day at a time, allowing us to adapt to its demands. Let us take a look at how the Dream Society may come about. First is the revolution in the concept of work; this implies the most fundamental change and is also the source of all the other changes.

From Hard Work to Hard Fun

French philosopher René Descartes, born in the village La Haye in the Loire vineyards 400 years ago, once asked a simple question (of the sort only good philosophers can pose): Are minds and bodies distinct?[50] Today we feel the answer is no—mind and body cannot be separated; but our point of focus may change. The way in which modern corporations—and this chapter— perceive human nature is a rejection of the purely materialistic and physical aspect in favor of the mental aspect, of the emotional and social environment. The reason is clear. As routine jobs are increasingly automated, there will be a corresponding increase in jobs highlighting creativity, commitment, and social skills. Technology will decree the way work is perceived in the future, and technology dictates that each and every day, routine jobs will disappear even as new ones demanding a wide range of human aptitudes are created.

The concept of work involves a paradox once nicely encapsulated by Mark Twain: "The law of work does seem utterly unfair, but there it is, and nothing can change it: the higher the pay in enjoyment the worker gets out of it, the higher shall be his pay in cash also." Meaningful jobs are better paid than those essentially routine in nature. This was the case in the days of Mark Twain, and it is true today. The only difference is that whereas meaningful jobs in those days were few and far between, today they account for the major part. As Wendy Zellner, Dallas bureau manager for Southwest Airlines, wrote in a letter to *Business Week* about this highly successful company: "Southwest's 'secret' becomes clear: Treat corporate employees right, have fun, have more fun, work hard."[51] At a seminar entitled "Leading and Managing in the Twenty-First Century," held in Wellington, New Zealand, one of the speakers emphasized that "to have a sense of fun" is crucial for visionary leadership.[52]

An important truth about the twenty-first century work concept is reflected in these sentences. Work will become hard fun—fun in the sense that it will be edifying, playful, engaging. In other words, we are moving away from work as the noble sacrifice. But make no mistake about it—the workplace of the future will not be brimming with hippies searching for their inner selves. It will be hard fun because it will demand commitment. Whenever children play, they play at their best when they are 100 percent committed to what they are playing. A Danish R&D employee at toymaker Lego defines four elements of good play:

Competition: Who is best?

Risks: It has to be possible to take risks while playing.

Emulation: People emulate each other, as in "I can do that, too!"

Giddiness: Playing should be so much fun it makes you high.

Competition, risks, emulation, and giddiness. These key notions define not only child's play but hard fun as well—the modern work concept. This is the kind of work that gets done in a Dream Society corporation. The first three notions may already be integral to many jobs, but the last, giddiness, is sorely lacking for far too many people. Not only is job satisfaction an important part of life; it also improves the bottom line—a win-win situation. But most of us will not reveal to others that we are really playing at work. Let us keep that little secret between author and reader.

To be sure, there are already a number of companies whose staff will attest to work being hard fun. Unfortunately, this vision is not the only one in the offing; it must compete with at least two apprehensions of the future of work that are widespread in academe and in unions, particularly in Europe. Both entertain the notion that jobs will disappear as a result of technological evolution—jobs will be automated out of existence. Thus the workplace will also vanish, and (if the theory is correct) this chapter will have been written and read to no avail.

As a result, many social scientists—most, I would venture to say— have duly predicted that work as such is already disappearing, that this trend can be witnessed even today—from the accountant whose auditing function is taken over by software to the corporate security guard who is replaced by electronic sensors. Sure, people are needed to write the software, but only a handful, and programming is gradually being automated. However, this theory leads to two traditional yet very different predictions about the future for the coming 20 years:

○ In the future, we will have plenty of time for our families, ample time for leisure pursuits. The leisure society will finally become reality. It will be a life of luxury, just as we picture the lifestyles of European nobility in the past. We can make money without working. Electronic and mechanical slaves—the robots—work for us day and night. That is the positive forecast.

○ The future will be plagued by mass unemployment. Therefore, we will have to reduce weekly working hours and retire earlier, starting now. In fact, work should be meted out so it is rationed equitably among those in need of it. In other words, humankind was made for work and cannot and should not do without it.[53] That is the negative forecast.

Both forecasts are erroneous. They are based on the assumption that the nature of work will remain unchanged and that we live in a static society. To gain an overview, let us look briefly at developments in the past century. When agricultural machinery—say, the binder—replaced many farm jobs, new work opportunities appeared in urban industry. After World War II, as shop floor jobs gradually became automated, the Information Society was capable of providing livelihoods for a new breed of workers—called "symbolic analysts"—those who create, manipulate, and distribute data—by Robert Reich in his 1992 book *The Work of Nations.* This group, along with those employed in the service sector carrying out more routine functions, now make up the majority of the workforce in the USA and other affluent countries. The inherent economic and technological dynamics create a new demand for jobs. Jobs vanish as others, involving different technology, appear. This is what we normally call progress. There is no reason to believe that this process will come to a standstill after the Information Society.

Today the Information Society is rendering itself obsolete. It has begun automating the very jobs it once created—especially the routine jobs, but possibly some of the more creative ones as well. Witness a Nebraska newspaper that uses a software program for writing sports stories; once the computer gets a few facts, it can fill in the rest of the words, composing a breathless report of the game.[54] Work productivity is increased by making more technology and software, as well as more raw data, available to the individual employee; the short-term cost, however, is that some jobs will disappear.

Exactly! So doesn't that bespeak unemployment? No, and no again. For one thing, most people possess an industrious drive as part of their nature—the need to be productive—to show the world that they can accomplish something. The modern corporation with its social network is a platform supremely suited for expressing this industrious drive. For another thing, the Dream Society will create work for those who are laid off by the Information Society. History, at least, teaches us that any transformation—say, from agriculture to industry—creates new jobs to replace the ones automated out of existence. Back when shop floors became more or less automated, new jobs were generated in offices, in the Information Society. Despite automation, there has not been a scarcity of jobs in the affluent countries, viewed in terms of the entire past century. This process whereby automation generates a new demand for new skills will probably continue. Every fledgling society is perched upon the achievements of those that preceded it. The agricultural society does not vanish completely—we still need to till the land. Nor does the Information Society—we still need to refine our computer systems. Notwithstanding all this, the number of jobs in these two societies is bound to fall. Only a dwindling percentage of the workforce (in affluent countries) actually works the land. Within the next 50 years (probably sooner), the blue-collar worker will be just as thin on the ground, and in the longer term, computers will have taken over most of the routine office work.

This is not a regulated process and, as with all revolutions, there will be a price to pay for families as well as for society at large. But it has begun. Like previous revolutions in the job market, it will demand adaptation, and new skills. The heroes of the Information Society will not necessarily be the heroes of the Dream Society.

Henry Ford was a supreme icon of the industrial age—creator of the efficient factory, which in turn created material prosperity and mobility to be enjoyed by all. A great boon to the people of the twentieth century. Today Bill Gates probably qualifies as an obvious icon of the Information Society. Just as the car came within the reach of everyone, so today the computer and its many applications are accessible to all. Once again, the boon means unlimited opportunities to learn and retrieve information from every corner of the planet.

The icon of the Dream Society has probably been born, but she or he is most likely still at school and is probably not the best pupil in the class. Today, the best pupil is the one who makes a first-rate symbolic analyst. In the future, it may be a student who gives the teacher a hard time—an imaginative pupil who is always staging new games that put things into new perspectives. This pupil may be attending school in the USA, in the Republic of Georgia, or in the Democratic Republic of the Congo. He or she will be the great storyteller of the twenty-first century. Dare we be audacious and name a current icon for the Dream Society? It is very early to do so, but I for one nominate Steven Spielberg, the great storyteller of the silver screen, as the closest we now have to a Dream Society icon. The reader may ponder other possible candidates—several may come to mind. Common to all will be a talent for telling stories that appeal to our emotions. This is where we find the vast, yet-to-be-satisfied demand of the future.

The transition to this new logic will place new and different requirements on corporations and employees. Many will never make the transition, or will do so only after it is too late; others will realize that their specific and unique talents are suddenly valued at a premium by the job market. Presumably, Matt Weinstein is one of the latter. He is "emperor" of Playfair, a humor consulting company in Berkeley, California. (The job title, he says, keeps people from outranking him in meetings.) A humor consulting company? Certainly, productive fun. Weinstein asks a rhetorical question: "Is there going to be any competitive advantage if your corporate employees are excited about coming to work, if they're continually surprising each other by leaving fun gifts around the office, if they're answering the phone like they're happy to be there? Of course, there's tremendous competitive advantage."[55]

Example: Hurricane Andrew's Gift to Burger King

An excellent example of tomorrow's corporate culture can be found in the company spirit that grew in the wake of Hurricane Andrew's wrecking of Burger King's Miami headquarters in 1992. Out of the ensuing chaos emerged a corporate culture based on social interaction, imagination, and having fun. But hard fun, as chief operating officer Jim Adamson commented to then CEO Barry Gibbons: "Have you noticed that you've gotten more done in the past two weeks than in the last two months?"[56]

The core of the new Burger King culture was "creative thinking, aggressive decision making, and fresh ideas."[57] Now, all days are casual days and the hierarchical structures of the past have been swept away along with the former headquarters. The former hierarchical structures had been a problem in several failed cooperative ventures with advertising agencies, and that in turn had messed up the way people saw the corporation. The Dream Society company cannot afford to have a blurry public image. The market for stories demands a full concept.

At Burger King headquarters, the new offices have no doors. All the executive offices were moved out of the choice top-floor locations. These occupants are usually away on business, so why not give people who are at their desks most of the day a chance to see daylight and an inspiring view? The layout of the new offices was conceptualized when the corporate executives noticed the enormous growth in communication after the old offices were literally blown away. People talked to one another, teams emerged, and since the company wanted this to continue, the new offices were designed to foster an easygoing, comfortable atmosphere in which employees actually managed to produce more.

Corporate survival will depend more on the ability to create an effective image, on great new ideas, than on worrying about whether the accounting system works to perfection. Future technology will see to that.

Today, the reception area of the Burger King headquarters is dominated by a giant burger stuck in the wall; the walls are decorated with giant murals in happy colors filled with happy people. In fact, the background music in the reception area is not Mozart, or anything like that, but sound effects to go along with the murals.[58] These may be jungle noises, singing whales, or the sound of wind sweeping along the rigging of a sailing vessel.

Increasingly, companies will have to deliver more than just products that satisfy material needs. The successful companies of the twenty-first century will be the ones satisfying emotional needs. The job market will have similar demands, so it stands to reason that the market for products will behave like the market for labor. Attractive pay and potted plants in the corridors will no longer suffice. That was the Information Society idea of a fine corporation. The Dream Society corporation will have to meet the social and emotional needs of its employees.

Besides meeting employees' emotional and social needs, the corporation will want to cater to consumers' emotional and social needs—something Burger King is better equipped to do now that the office reflects a distinctive corporate identity. One firm carrying this mission to the point of perfection is Nike, defining its core values in a single, handsome and aggressive sentence: "To experience the emotion of competition, winning, and crushing competitors."[59]

Employees are no longer just part of the company—alongside machines and stockholders. They *are* the company. As observed by Charles Handy,[60] Karl Marx's political vision, nearly a century old, has finally become reality. Workers have taken over the means of production, since the means of production are no longer primarily machines. The real productive factor is knowledge. Employees carry the productive factor around with them at all times; it is lodged inside each employee's head. Thus company capital becomes the sum and total of employee qualifications. Yet, in the social environment of the modern company, the crucial factor is not only concrete knowledge; it is also creativity, motivation, and—above all—cooperative skills. Production at an office is not a mechanical process that can be likened to the assembly line. It is an intellectual and primarily a social process. If this process is to work with optimum efficiency—and thus with optimum productivity—the method is hard fun.

Hard fun as the new work ethic is not the most audacious concept of this chapter. It is more of a notion aimed at bringing modern perceptions—not everybody's, but many people's—into synch with the realities of today. A survey of men's perceptions of work conducted by *GQ* magazine showed that the notion of work as merely a way of financing the family's existence is largely outdated. This notion was shared by only one fourth of the respondents—and they were predominantly among those making less than $30,000 a year. An impressive 55 percent were of the opinion that the most important thing was "getting satisfaction/enrichment from the job." A surprising number, a full 24 percent, stated that "work is the main way I express myself." About 20 percent put their weekly workload at more than 56 hours; 37 percent of the men surveyed even admitted: "I guess you could call me a workaholic."[61]

I, too, belong to this category. I express myself through my work and consider work more important than my private life—it is more exciting and more varied. At meetings with colleagues we tackle difficult questions like these (to name a few topical examples): What will the health care sector of the future look like? Will retailers disappear from our city streets and be replaced by home shopping? What is the future role of the father and mother? All these questions can boggle the mind and create giddiness; each represents a little intellectual drama (see Chapter 4). On the other hand, there is no giddiness in vacuum cleaning. Nor does this mundane activity match the excitement of knowing whether a lecture will be successful—or, when it is, the joy of relaxing afterward. Work is perfectly able to compete with family life. Not for an entire career—not while the kids are still small—but afterward.

Many indicators point in this direction. Most important, however, are the inherent dynamics. We are moving hastily beyond the old work concept generated during the industrial society at the English spinning machines, in the Welsh coal mines, and at the auto plants in Detroit. The reaction to this, in Europe, was the union movement and Marxism. Understandably, work was seen as a necessary evil that had to be made as short-lived and highly paid as possible. Pensions were the reward for a long life of toil; and the sooner you got to this reward, the better. This pattern held true for our parents and grandparents, but does it apply to us? No—or at least, it is a truth that will soon be relegated to history books.

The work concept of the twenty-first century can already be found in our sports arenas. To be sure, modern-day, professional athletes make money by excelling at their sport. At the same time, it's all hard fun. Often, interviews reveal that athletes are motivated by personal enjoyment, that sport is primarily a challenge just happening to provide a sizable income as well. In *World Soccer* magazine, the famed manager of Manchester United, Alex Ferguson, made this remark concerning his former star player, Frenchman Eric Cantona: "He would stay after training and practice for hours. Practice, practice, practice."[62]

It is little wonder that hard fun should dominate the world of professional sports. As a workplace, the sports field is relatively new. It has never looked to the traditional job market for inspiration, focusing instead on enjoyment-based leisure pursuits. But hard fun is also making its way into more traditional corporations and the criteria for success are becoming the same in sports as in business. The more you love the job, the more you get out of it. The more you can persuade colleagues to love the job, the more the company gets out of it—cashwise, too. Therefore it is only natural that successful sports coaches should moonlight as business consultants. Theirs is a message that businesses can use.

However, industrial ways of thinking are still alive and they will perhaps survive to see the millennial shift—if barely. Germany's most powerful trade union, IG Metall, is suggesting a reduction of the workweek from 35 to 32 hours. Even the Hans Böckler Foundation, Germany's influential trade union think tank, is in agreement, arguing that the last time weekly work hours were reduced—in 1985—a million jobs were generated.[63] All arguments rely on the same premise—that the total amount of work is waning and that this problem must be addressed by distributing the extant work to more people. If you take a very short-term perspective, it might be a good idea, but how long can you expect such a policy to last? Until umpteen million workers are working one-hour weeks? The answer, obviously, is that in such a situation there will not be the wherewithal to pay wages that meet living expenses. A transition is the only solution.

One element is missing, however: family relationships. When working hours can no longer be delimited within a certain time frame, but depend instead on the tasks requiring attention, a conflict between work and free time is bound to arise. *Fortune* has summarized this dilemma: Today, in the corridors of business as elsewhere, families are getting more lip service than ever. Being on the right side of work and family issues is all very PC, "but corporate America harbors a dirty secret. People in human resources know it. So do a lot of CEOs, although they don't dare discuss it. Families are no longer a big plus for a corporation; they are a problem."[64]

In a *Financial Times* interview, the author of *The Time Bind*, Arlie Russell Hochschild, explains that the contest between work and spare time has altered in the last 10 to 20 years.[65] For many people today, home has primarily become the place where a lot of routine work has to get done—duties that won't wait: doing the laundry, cooking dinner, and taking care of the kids. Home has become the treadmill. At work, there is a higher level of service; people have time to talk and have fun. The workplace has seen social product development, whereas home chores have become more of a millstone. As Hochschild writes: "In a cultural contest between work and home...the workplace is winning."

This, of course, does not constitute the only trend. Other surveys show a growing desire to cut back on working hours in order to spend more time with the family. These results, however, stem more from surveys of attitude than from surveys of actual behavior. The desire often remains just that, a pious wish. "Right now we're busy at the office, but next month things will quiet down and I'll be able to get off early"—this has long been the standard refrain offered to many a neglected spouse, and everyone knows that "next month" will be just as busy.

Pushing the matter to the extreme, American family values are actually threatened by the corporations. But can we imagine demonstrations in the streets of New York, picketing against the way large corporations are attacking family welfare? Conservative citizens who are otherwise in favor of private enterprise suddenly demand that the family be left in peace to live its own life? Picket lines carry signs emblazoned: "Hell, no—we won't work after 5 p.m.," "We demand to see more of our children," and "Hands off our family." Corporate executives are suddenly held responsible for instigating measures to secure family values, as part of the corporate vision. The demands of animal rights activists are extended to include human rights for corporate employees. No, the picket lines are not very likely to occur; corporate employees, after all, are working long hours of their own free will—almost.

This is a conflict running the length and breadth of the United States, but it is happening at a microlevel and it can only be resolved at a microlevel: by the individual company, by the families of corporate employees. This substantial conflict of values will trouble people who work in the affluent countries for many years to come, and the conflict will be intensified until universally accepted social norms in this area have emerged.

This is a fight for the individual mindset and values; it is going on right now and the trade unions ought to be playing a far more prominent role than is currently the case. The unions should come to the fore with their suggested solutions. The issue of values is far more important than the question of wages; money issues are often resolved individually without union mediation, anyway.

Let us round up three scenarios for the future of work and family:

Scenario 1.   Here, work wins the contest and the family unit becomes the place where you rest and recharge your batteries for what comes first—namely, the workplace, where most of day-to-day social intercourse takes place. This is where you find your friends—the people you meet with in your spare time as well. The kids and the traditional family values are, of course, the great losers in this scenario. But American companies do very well in the global marketplace—especially in the ongoing competition with European companies, which have to deal with powerful unions.

Scenario 2.   The family wins. There will be more time to spend with spouses and kids. Daily work hours are reduced and nearly every company has a set rule that employees must be able to have dinner with their families. Companies respecting family values can attract the most sought-after corporate employees, and thus win out over companies that are not as considerate.

Scenario 3.   A balance is achieved between work and family through intermittent negotiations between management and employees. During these talks, agreement is reached on which time slots should be devoted to giving the company full attention, and which should be devoted to the family. Corporations will lose if they make too high demands; the same is true of the family, which loses if the corporation does not succeed in the marketplace.

The compromise scenario has an enticing ring to it, and may even materialize for the fortunate few; but the fact remains that not many companies are able to predict, months in advance, which periods will be busy. Nor, we can speculate, will all employees be able to agree upon a negotiated balance between work and family. The *GQ* survey mentioned earlier showed that 37 percent of the participating males considered themselves to be workaholics—and shouldn't employees who prefer work to family be rewarded?

That leaves a choice between scenarios 1 and 2. If the developments of the past decade continue into the next millennium, the company will win at the family's expense. Daily work hours are on the rise in most affluent countries. On the other hand, a trend is only a trend until reversed, and a counterreaction remains a distinct possibility. I personally opt for scenario 1—company values—as the most likely choice in the shorter run. The company will edge out the family yet again, for a spell. We will see the company invading the family sphere with offers of paying for housekeeping—thus giving employees more spare time in their spare time. Others will become much more involved in company life—joining in business travel and in corporate social events—in order to make them more understanding when long hours at the office reduce quality time with the family.

Then, we can expect a reaction to set in, with the family gaining ground again at the company's expense. What remains important is that we recognize this as one of the major social conflicts ever, affecting nearly everybody in the affluent countries. Or is there a fourth scenario? If so, it will have to involve a melting of boundaries between work and family life. On the farms of Europe and North America such a boundary did not exist just 50 years ago. The family worked together and rested together. The same applies to the traditional mom-and-pop store. It also holds true for the major part of third world populations—work and family constitute an integrated and harmonious totality. Only in the modern societies do we find that a razor-sharp distinction is upheld.

Given the present, and particularly the future state of communications technology, the workplace can be wherever *you* happen to be at any particular moment. We will be able to communicate anything, at any time, to any place—and we will be able to do so in full color. This is the technological background for the disappearance of the workplace as we know it. We can work at home, on the plane, aboard the yacht, and on vacation in Borneo. The geographical dimension to work has been abolished.

Thus conventional wisdom about work in the future holds that increasing numbers will be working at home—or anywhere else on the planet. Witness Nicolas Kauser, executive vice president of AT&T Wireless Services Inc., who states, evidently from his pleasure boat, that "what makes the wireless office such a lucrative concept is that it operates everywhere. From headquarters to crew quarters."[66] Or take Tammy Altman, who, when offered a job 350 miles from her home, responded: "I'll just establish an online office at home."[67] Already, 7.5 million workers, or 6 percent of the U.S. labor force, work at home part time or full time.[68] But the Dream Society company is built upon the sharing of ideas, motivation, experiences, and social interaction with colleagues. This cannot be achieved by telecommuting.

In the virtual corporation employees know one another only by name—or maybe they meet once a year at the office Christmas party. The virtual corporation, pays no costly rent or cleaning expenses. Individual employees do not need a framed snapshot of the kids on their desk; their offspring may be playing at their feet. They will have more need for a picture of the boss to remind them of their duties. It all adds up to one heck of a vision, as beautiful as the notion of sitting on a Pacific islet, cocktail ready at one hand and laptop at the other—at least while it's winter in New York. The notion of the virtual corporation seems to have cropped up as recently as the 1990s, but it remains more of a mirage than a fact. Maybe this theory will share the fate of the great 1970s theory of the paperless office—a vision that ought to have become reality by now. Unfortunately, reality is aflutter with more paper than ever.

How come all these enthralling visions rarely last until the future catches up with them? The short answer is that a company is a social structure, necessitating personal interaction and contacts. This important aspect of the modern workplace is what the present chapter is about. Needless to say, modern technology will occasionally be useful for getting things done outside the office; already, workstations in the home have been established in the USA as well as in Scandinavia, but these will remain an exception to the rule.

In an interview, Robert Reich offered the following observations about the path to influence at the White House: "The decision-making 'loop' depends on physical proximity to [Clinton]: who's whispering into his ear most regularly, whose office is closest to the Oval, who's standing next to him when a key issue arises."[69] This rule about gaining power and influence also applies to companies. Staying at home, therefore, will always be a dud career move. Charles Handy, who happens to be my preferred philosopher on the companies of the future, has spoken of "the clubhouse" as the hub where corporate employees can meet, socialize, and cultivate core values—and have a drink. Such club-houses will become a necessity when a considerable amount of the work is done outside the office.

Naturally, technology does allow us to work anywhere at any time. This, however, does not mean that we will spend more time at home or at other favorite places; what will happen is that more and more work hours will spill over into what has hitherto been time off. What used to be work will become part of a daily routine that is no longer divided into work and spare time, but has become a package deal, the seamless job–life.

A case in point is the daily routine of Martha Stewart, CEO of Martha Stewart Living Omnimedia. She uses e-mail to stay in touch with all and sundry. She checks it first at 5 a.m. before venturing out on her day. Furthermore, she has computers in each of her homes and is having her basement equipped with a server to maintain PCs, phones, and videoconferencing sys-tems.[70] Does all this mean Stewart spends less time at the office? No. Does it mean she has to work less? No. It just provides her with the means to ensure that when she's at work, she really spends her time doing things that need to get done at the office. Welcome to the seamless job—never beginning, never ending— where you are never done, never off duty, but where you also enjoy true freedom and flexibility to shape your own day.

Martha Stewart is one prototype of hard fun; her idea bears close resemblance to another: that of the free agent.

Is the corporation a dinosaur? According to Daniel Pink, 25 million Americans think it is.[71] They are rejecting the life of the corporate employee and turning to the life of the free agent. Corporations that are ready to change in order to meet the needs of the new workers may be successful in keeping their workforce, but a growing number of free agents have found that their former employers were hanging on to the cubicles and the windowless office. As one free worker put it, about a project that forced her back into a cubicle for the duration: "I remember all those things I'd forgotten—pantyhose being stupid, commuting being stupid, not seeing light during the day. I want not to work there so badly I can taste it."[72]

The new workers who work to satisfy a need to create, to get more out of work than money in exchange for eight hours of toil, will not be satisfied with a cubicle. So if their company does not change, they are prepared to leave and become free agents. Free agents are responsible only to themselves, and love every moment of it. They need to finish a workday knowing they have accomplished something, created something; this is what will make people choose the freedom that they have as free agents. "I integrate my work into my life. I don't see my work as separate from my identity."[73] This statement is not unique to the free agent; it will become the general sentiment among the majority of future workers.

Himself a recent recruit to the life of the free agent, Daniel Pink sketches the emerging sphere of the free worker.[74] After being an integral part of the establishment for years, Pink opted out. He moved his office into the attic of his Washington, D.C. house and escaped from all the things he hated in the work atmosphere; he is now his own boss, but more to the point, he is free from all the bother that accompanies the office culture. This is not to say that he, or any of the other free agents he has spoken to, is working any less than was the case under the rule of corporate culture, or at the White House in Daniel Pink's case. These people simply retain the right to set their own standards and their own goals. As Liisa Joronen, of SOL Cleaning Service, puts it: "People who set their own standards shoot for the stars."[75] So it is conceivable that the free agent works even harder than the corporate employee, but the work is fun and challenging.

The interesting part is that the free agent, even after opting out of the corporate system, does not necessarily become the lonely agent. Agencies and support groups for free agents are sprouting up everywhere. Kinko's has been around for a long time, but it is currently booming in order to keep up with the growth in the free-agent crowd, which uses the Kinko shop not only as a copying facility but as a place to meet people as well—a venue where you can chat with other free agents in the network.[76] Working Solo is an agency helping free agents understand this new world order. Also, there is Working Today—a sort of antiunion—which offers free agents insurance and health care at a group discount.[77]

The Company Is a Tribe

Hard fun is the new work concept. So what will the new type of company be called? One possibility is "The Living Company." This phrase stems from Arie de Geus's excellent eponymous book.[78] As the title suggests, Geus compares the company to a living thing, illustrating a new trend in management literature. Let us once again turn retrospective in order to gain an overview of our present and our future.

In the industrial society, corporations were likened to machines. The workers, then, were the tiny cogs meshing perfectly with one another, and each little wheel was necessary to enable the big machine, the factory, to produce. Naturally, some cogs were bigger than others. Thus went the logic of industrialism. In any case, one wheel could easily be replaced by another. Like a cog, the worker was a standard piece of merchandise available for hire at a fixed price.

In the Information Society, with its networked organization, the computer provides the metaphor for the entire corporation. Great emphasis is put on channeling communication and knowledge through the correct conduits—breaking down the organizational hierarchies whenever it is expedient. Here we have the knowledge corporation, in which employees surrounded by gray computers converge in efficient cubicles to combine their collective, new knowledge—relieved by the occasional casual day.

The new, collective corporate metaphor sees the company as a living organism. For instance, a company may go through gawky adolescence, a wild youth, and a period of mature activity. Then comes the time in a corporate life cycle when the company is a bit distinguished, aristocratic; how you speak is more important than what you say. After that follows old age, when new ideas and initiatives do not come as easy as they used to—the readiness for change has gone. Finally, the company dies. The biological analogy has its strong point in that it emphasizes how machines no longer take center stage, but it overlooks the social dynamic.

The Dream Society company may be compared to a tribe with a shared set of values and rules. It is a closely knit unit whose members hunt together and divide the spoils according to certain rules. Throughout the history of our species, stretching back more than 100,000 years, organization in tribes has been the most long-lived of social structures. In this context, the family plots of the agrarian society and the factories of industrialization are but brief episodes. Now, at last, we are returning to our roots—albeit with a new technology and, to a certain degree, with new values and norms. Management consultants would be well advised to study the few remaining tribal communities. There is the distinct possibility that such studies will give rise to insights into how the family and the tribe interact. They may even contribute to a better understanding of how the family and the company interact. Other interesting study objectives for anthropological fieldwork include tribal rituals and how they strengthen cohesion. The role played by conflicts in different dynamics and willingness to change is another question that may be investigated as a modern source of corporate inspiration.

The modern corporation as a tribe. Another metaphor suggests itself: the theatrical performance unfolding with all its drama. Managing a company means staging a drama, daily. The actors/employees are given different parts to play together with colleagues and clients/customers. If the drama they are enacting is gripping, many will want to join the show. Part of the excitement lies in the fact that this drama may turn to comedy or to tragedy as the case may be. Together with clients and customers, employees determine the direction in which the show is heading. By all means let it be a big-scale production replete with heroes, villains, trolls, and scribes. In our theatrical metaphor, we are actually moving close to reality. The cold company figures, after all, do nothing to reflect the battles for contracts and clients being constantly lost and won. They do not reflect innovations and ideas being hatched at creative meetings. Above all, the emotionless balance sheet does not reflect the social interaction— the conflicts, the friendships, the collaboration, and the jealousy. The balance sheet reveals as much about corporate life as would a word count of William Shakespeare's sonnets.

Let us now turn our attention to what will happen when the social and human element moves into the center of corporate self-esteem. Hardware and software, after all, are very secondary; the office output is fairly negligible when employees have gone home and left computers to their own resources. Even as more electronic slaves are employed by companies, their human masters become increasingly important. Every single employee already has a considerable number of electronic slaves at his or her disposal, and that number keeps going up. We now have slaves copying, sending messages to colleagues and clients, keeping the books. The larger the number of slaves, the more you are free to concentrate on innovation, on creativity. The more you can concentrate on what makes work fun.

The metaphor of the company as a tribe—or the image of a drama being enacted on the corporate stage—carries an implicit revolutionary message that will transform the way business is done in affluent countries over the coming 10 to 15 years. Let us take a look at how and why.

A tribe's true productive factor does not lie in machinery, not in hardware or software; productivity comes from the participants, the members. And they, being the key to productivity, need to be measured; indeed, this is an idea whose time has come. In Europe, Swedish Scandia is the most advanced in this regard. It should be pointed out, however, that when executives at festive occasions, glass in hand, solemnly affirm that "the corporation's greatest asset remains its employees," this great asset ought also to be reflected in the annual report. As things stand today, it is not, although the adage about employees being an asset has often crept into the introduction of the same annual report. In 5 to 10 years time, we will probably see "intellectual capital" right there on the balance sheet in black and white, along with the rest of the figures.

Intellectual capital can be calculated in a number of ways: as the sum of investments in supplementary training; as a result of surveys assessing employee satisfaction with their job situation and relationships with superiors. Experience has shown that satisfied employees are more productive than dissatisfied ones. Also, paychecks may be seen as an approximate expression of employee productive value to be added to the assets, and not as a large expense. After all, salary negotiations are about trying to establish each employee's productive value, his or her value as a company asset. If salary levels are unacceptably high, red ink will appear; and if they are too low, employees will tend to disperse to better-paid jobs more reflective of their productive value.

When the value of a company's intellectual capital is reflected in the annual report, it becomes more difficult for management to fire employees. Sometimes, of course, downsizing may still be unavoidable, since a company needs profits to survive. But this way, the real cost of layoffs can be seen clearly. Just as if tossing computers out the window would destroy physical capital, layoffs involve throwing away human capital. If we are talking top-quality computers with modern software this is a bad idea. The same is true of downsizing that involves letting high-quality staffers go. Perhaps management will justly claim that the value of these employees for the company does not measure up to their salaries, and that the layoffs are thus necessary and right. But the board would have to respond to such a measure, asking how such a situation could arise. Has supplementary training been withheld? Have salaries been to high? Has the intellectual capital not been nurtured properly?

Management will change for those companies choosing to appraise their intellectual capital, and gradually most companies will do so—starting with the knowledge-intensive businesses that mainly employ symbolic analysts, such as banks, insurance companies, and accounting firms. The next candidates to value intellectual capital will be the typical service industries (McDonald's, Macy's, hospitals). Finally, the ranks will be joined by corporations with a large number of employees still manufacturing products from the shop floor (General Motors, Toyota, Boeing). Calculating intellectual capital also constitutes a departure from accounting principles that, dating back 200 years, ignore the most crucial factor in production. This oversight was less important back when the labor force consisted mainly of workers tending to a machine. Here it seemed reasonable to focus on machine output rather than worker input. Therefore, accounts emphasized the machines. Now—and particularly in the future—the individual employee will become the crucial production factor. The final "day of reckoning" for the old ways of accounting is drawing near—and it will have momentous consequences. What we are witnessing today are only skirmishes before the big battle. The outcome of this battle, however, is certain: the side blessed by the future will be victorious. Intellectual capital will reign supreme, or it will be one of *the* most important entries in the company status accounts in 5 to 10 years' time; this single entry will outshine the value of machines and computers, the value of buildings and inventory. Other entries comparable to intellectual capital will be the value of company reputation and of the brands it owns.

Perhaps we should be bold and simply call the Dream Society company of the future a social unit—a tribe with no employees, but with participants instead; a society with no subjects but with citizens, rallying around their society's goal. That, indeed, is the idea; yes, it is radical and it also defines the physical surroundings of the workplace. We stand before a revolution in office buildings and decor.

"The answer is in the furniture," says Bill Miller.[79] This is where you get a "clear" picture of what is about to happen, and this is where innovative efforts should be concentrated. The new type of work means that "they don't punch in, they live in. The all-nighter is the new rite of passage for young professionals. Whoever thought working so hard could be so much fun?"[80]

It follows logically from the above ideas about the company of the future that the traditional office will undergo a complete transformation. As described previously, Burger King headquarters in Miami has not only changed "culturally"; the physical environment has also been refurbished. The same is evident in the new media-design firm Adjancy's work facility, an enormous loft where recreational space is an integral part of the workplace. There is a pool table; people fling frisbees past others hard at work; and the large recreational room incorporates space for a game of roller hockey. The joy people experience in what they're paid to do finds expression in near round-the-clock working, interrupted by in-house recreation. There are bunks and showers and an in-line skating rink, and space is being cleared for a basketball court.[81] The interplay between the physical environment and corporate culture is pivotal, as we all know very well. You can tell a lot about a company from just a brief tour of the offices.

Some of the guiding principles for furnishing the workplace are merely a reflection of common sense: "Information is available everywhere; people are no longer tethered to their desks. As a consequence, they go to the office for new reasons: to be with one another, to collaborate, to learn, to socialize."[82] Charles Fishman offers three essential theses about how work will change: the future of work is about (1) defying gravity; (2) chaos theory; and (3) accepting the end of control. These are the basics from which Jeff Reuschel and Brian Alexander are designing the workplace of the future. They want a workstation geared to the brain, not one that requires the brain to continuously follow the orderings of a filing system. They are seeking a system that allows the creative patterns of thought to evolve, then follows those patterns. They want memos, newspaper articles, and magazines up where they are used, spread out all over the place. Reuschel and Alexander dream of creating a workplace "designed to maximize communication, interaction, and creativity; space to accommodate noisy collaborative work and private concentrated work."[83] Old-economy factories were designed to maximize standardized production. Why shouldn't new-economy offices be designed to maximize individual creativity?

Let us return to the wider perspective—to the consequences for society, and for the family in particular. Hitherto, the family has constituted the social nucleus of the affluent societies. This is where the closest solidarity is bred; this is where you stand together in solidarity—in love, in raising the coming generation, and in financial matters. Somewhere in the vicinity of this societal nucleus is where you previously found the company—as a satellite, as a job provider financing family life—a necessary supportive function lacking the high degree of common values and solidarity that exists in the family as a social unit.

Nowadays, however, the workplace has taken over a number of family functions, in that it doubles as a forum for social intercourse. Contrary to what was once supposed, new technology has far from reduced social interaction in the company. The proliferation of team-building seminars signifies a focus on employees getting to know one another, not only as colleagues but as complete human beings. Social skills—a.k.a. emotional intelligence—have never been more important in the workplace.

For these reasons, the society of the future will have not one, but two social nuclei—just like the ancient and present tribal societies. This constitutes a social transmutation with large-scale consequences for each individual and for the family. On the horizon, many see these two nuclei as equally important to a high quality of life; people will be demanding the same essential ingredients from leisure time, family, and work—namely, flexibility and substance. Others will still see the family as number 1, with the company finishing a close second. A third possibility is that people may prioritize different things in different phases of life. When the kids have left home, the company gets high priority; until then, family life is first on the agenda. In any case, the opportunity to prioritize between family and work is one of the gifts that evolution has bestowed upon this generation. If we aren't all screaming for joy the reason is that there is a downside to this new choice: the choosing. It is a difficult call and many (most?) of today's workers are beset with a perennial guilty conscience about letting down either family or work.

The company's increased status compared with that of the other social nucleus—the family—is due to the fact that corporate values will gradually become just as clearly defined as family values. Any social community is defined in terms of shared values. It follows quite logically that management literature often focuses on so-called company core values. These core values are what the corporate statements of mission, vision, and strategy are built upon. The thought-provoking and stimulating book *Built to Last: Successful Habits of Visionary Companies* reports on a number of companies with enduring success in the marketplace. The companies under survey have outperformed the stock market average by a factor of 12 since 1925.[84] The reason, according to authors Collins and Porras, is that they have held on to their core values, yet shown willingness to change—even drastically—and face new challenges. "Core ideology defines the enduring character of the organization—a consistent identity that transcends product or market life cycles, technological breakthroughs, management fads, and individual leaders."[85] These core values, assert Collins and Porras, amount to the company's genetic code.

This idea of the company of the future stands in stark contrast to the increasing importance attached to shareholder value—the notion that the first obligation of management is to generate value for stock owners. We are in for a clash of values that may turn out to be just as momentous as the clash between capitalism and socialism. Fundamental value sets are at stake—involving fundamentally different views of human nature. For instance, core values constitute those values that the company would still hold on to even if they did not lead to economic advantage. The corporation is a tribe, with values and emotions common to participants or members. In many ways, this may not wash with the interests of stockholders. The paradox, then, lies in the fact that visionary companies have generated more profits for their owners than the average U.S. business—and over a considerable period of time.

According to the same two authors, skyrocketing executive pay-checks and their widespread padding with stock options for top managers in American corporations stem from stockholders wanting to make sure that, in the event of a conflict between securing profits and securing jobs, management will choose the former. Needless to say, no business can exist without turning a profit and without yielding a return on invested capital. History has already settled this dispute—communism lost, capitalism won. But it won only one battle and the wheels of history are still in motion.

If we view the company as a forum for social intercourse, as well as an inspired drama reflecting a certain set of value norms, then we have a working definition that differs radically from other perceptions, past and present. The publicly held company is no longer merely an income- and profit-generating unit to be judged on the sole basis of whether it measures up to this requirement. Employees are participants, not just employees. Stockholders are not part of this community; they are a foreign object so long as they merely hold a financial interest in the corporation; as long as they see stocks purely as an investment whose yield can be measured in dollars and cents.

The many private shareholders and large investors operating on the stock market as we know it today are buyers and sellers of stocks, period. They are the players of the profit game; and this game is also considered beneficial to the corporations. Companies under competent management are rewarded with easy access to external capital while the inefficient ones are penalized with sagging quotes. As previously mentioned, the transformation leading to the Dream Society will involve a new conflict of interests between owners and employees. We have also seen how this conflict of interests may be resolved by companies no longer seeking intrusive (responsible) investment, but passive, external capital.

This trend is already under way. Stock options for employees is an idea whose time has come. A 1997 study by William M. Mercer Consultants found that 30 percent of the largest U.S. companies have stock option plans for more than half their employees, up from 17 percent five years earlier.[86] *Forbes* magazine concludes: "Stock options and other share-based incentive plans work wonders in keeping restless employees on the job." This group of owners/employees will be the ones who share in corporate core values. Those with an economic interest in the company's success will tend to be the same ones who participate in corporate social life: the tribal members, and nobody else. Philip Morris may be on its way to becoming a tribe of 7800 members. On March 15, 1997, tobacco workers at Philip Morris were given stock in lieu of pay hikes during the next two years. *Business Week* noted: "First executives got it. Then middle managers got in on the action. Now, it's factory workers' turn to get stocks as part of their pay."[87]

The era of the passive shareholder will end with the coming of the twenty-first century. The hectic scenes at the great stock exchanges will disappear. This does not mean the end of capitalism—the market is still the arbiter of success and failure. The state's role will be limited; but we will see a new form of capitalism. It might be called "a kinder, gentler capitalism," since economics and values are joining forces.

Of course, private individuals will still have portfolios. Stocks will still be an important part of saving for retirement; private wealth will not be dismantled. What we must imagine is that the shareholder of the future will own stock only in companies that he or she sympathizes with and holds common values with. The concern about profits is no longer the only factor. We must expect a transition in the market for stocks analogous to those in the markets for merchandise and labor.

With all this said, the trend during the 1990s has admittedly been that top management in the USA—and, to a lesser extent, in Europe and in Japan—has paid more attention to shareholder value. The wider circle of stakeholders—employees, in particular—has been somewhat neglected. Owners have demanded profits and dividends, often at employees' expense. Perhaps, "a kinder, gentler capitalism" as a trend is still below the horizon—not quite visible. But as the ship of evolution ventures into the future, new trends inevitably appear.

Then again, perhaps the "unkind, tough investor" is already becoming a thing of the past. The future will demand an ever-increasing level of investment in human beings. The two world-famous Seattle corporations, Boeing and Microsoft, represent the industrial society and the Information Society, respectively. Calculated on the basis of market value, however, Microsoft is worth more than three times as much as Boeing. The reason lies in Microsoft's ability to reinvent itself again and again—in the belief that its management is more adept at exploiting market possibilities than the competition's. Boeing's production plants are the world's most valuable aircraft construction facilities, but this is not all that counts. What matters also is faith in people and in their abilities, in the company's core values. Increasingly, investment decisions have to be made without the support of objective, measurable factors such as inventory, physical assets, and production facilities. Subjective factors, such as confidence and trust become more important—from economics to nonmaterial values.

Finally, it is worth mentioning that a number of knowledge-intensive companies, like accounting and consultancy firms, are often owned by partners—that is, participants who join actively in daily corporate life. The seed for the "kinder, gentler capitalism" of the future has been planted. Companies may still encounter a problem whenever they are short of start-up capital; but then there is always the possibility of borrowing the money from a bank. If this loan generates a higher de facto interest than what the bank has been promised, profits go to the company.

Another result of these developments relates to the company's stated purpose. The purpose of General Motors, obviously, is to build automobiles. The purpose of Shell is the extraction, transportation, and distribution of energy. If these goals can no longer be pursued and still yield a profit, then activities must be discontinued. Owners will have to invest their capital in other companies. Let's turn this around. Insofar as the company will become a social unit and come to be seen as a tribe, the natural thing for it to do, instead of closing down, will be to seek other sources of income and profit. Corporations will no longer be shackled to one line of business; they will be anchored only to

143

their values. There are clear signs that at least the very large American corporations are leaning toward this way of thinking. Values and intellectual capital being the company's greatest asset, they can be used to create new activities; there is no need to close down the company and start a new one from scratch. Built on knowledge capital, the modern corporation is more flexible than the industrial society company with its burdensome production facilities.

This way of thinking is illustrated by the Sara Lee Corporation's restructuring program. The firm has chosen to sell from its production units and focus on deverticalizing operations, using its brand name to sell outsourced merchandise in the future. As Sara Lee's chairman and chief executive officer has remarked: "The business of Sara Lee Corporation has been and will continue to be the building of branded leadership positions. The size and strength of these positions today, coupled with rapidly advancing globalization and specialization in our marketplace, lead us to deverticalize our operations. This program will significantly reduce the capital demands on our company, enhance our competitiveness, and let us focus even more sharply on our mission of building brands."[88]

This is an obvious parallel to the tribal sense of community that was given highest priority in the past; tribes would adjust by hunting new prey or finding new plants if the old ones vanished. No way would the tribe itself be dissolved. Similarly, the modern corporation will learn to adjust; despite all the differences in time and economies, it has become the tribal community of modern society.

This is creative destruction—the idea that all companies have their allotted time, a median life expectancy of perhaps 30 to 40 years, after which they will be replaced with others that are more effective and more innovative. This idea is often considered fundamental for competitiveness in the modern business environment and thus a source of increased affluence. Will this dynamic engine be stopped by the Dream Society companies? No. They will face the same need to innovate, to adjust. Only it will happen without the destruction—without tossing their collective intellectual capital overboard, without smashing social networks. Creative destruction may be allowed to take place without the prohibitive costs in money and values characterizing business today. This is the idea behind the fact that we have companies remaining more or less unchanged for hundreds of years. Every idea has its allotted time. The time has now come for companies.

How to Succeed in the Tribe—With Hard Fun as Your Work Concept

Let us follow the inherent logic in the above description of work, company, and family—and lay down some simple rules for personal success.

Success is no longer measured by the size of the paycheck. Success equals meaningful and challenging work. Charles Handy reminds us how Abraham Maslow in later years spoke about an addition to his five-level hierarchy of needs. Maybe there was a sixth need, he said, which we might call idealization, or the search for a purpose beyond oneself. Whoever finds such a purpose in work (in the sense the word is used here: hard fun) has succeeded. Of course, what was said previously still remains true. Pay is generally highest in fun jobs, and whatever you think is fun, you tend to become good at. However, the salary is really only just the trophy awarded to the really passionate, corporate participant.

"Brand yourself," writes Tom Peters in the magazine *Fast Company*.[89] The idea is quite simple. Just as the brand-name product is the winner in the marketplace, so the "branded" employee will triumph over the Brand X employee. Advertise yourself; increase awareness about your existence and your skills. Become well known for specific characteristics—say, a sense of quality, solicitude, creativity, organizational skills—and start marketing that *you* brand! Try to become well known throughout the company to increase your chances. That's the way things work in the Dream Society's corporate and social environment.

Seek to develop your social skills: your ability to connect, bond, and empathize with colleagues; your ability (as mentioned previously) to listen, to take as well as to give constructive criticism; your ability to spread happiness and cheer. In short, emphasize the fun part of the hard fun concept. Help a colleague in need. Social skills have always been valued highly, but they have never been more crucial to success in the workplace environment than is presently the case. Become proficient in the different jargons spoken in specific departments; modern experts find it difficult to communicate with and understand experts from fields other than their own—*you* be the employee who can connect!

Adapt to change. In a volatile business environment greeting every change with a smile may sometimes be difficult—do it anyway, or you risk incurring the enmity of the future. And the future makes for a dangerous enemy. Today, it is supposed that memory deteriorates and the willingness to change abates with age. If you believe this is so, it probably will be so. Often, however, it is merely because you have forgotten how poorly you remembered things when you were younger, and just how opposed to change you were then as well. A word to the wise: Do not start the countdown to old age yourself! Creativity is, among other things, the ability to combine different factors in a novel way. As the years pass, you acquire more and more factors to shift around. Thus, your potential for creativity will grow as you yourself grow older. And the will to create is something *you* control.

Last, and least: Be competent at whatever your craft is. Of course, being a good salesperson is important if you happen to be a salesperson; as is being a good leader if you are an executive. The only problem is, given today's high level of general education, superior professional competence is often taken for granted, and thus will not in and of itself distance you from the crowd. You'll need that something extra, as described above.

Titles of the Future

Let us conclude by illustrating this chapter's deliberations with a shot at a very blatant question: What will your future title be, wherever you end up being employed? Participants in the living company will have living tasks to do, along with living titles and living job descriptions. Some titles will survive from the

Information Society, but an array of new titles will begin to appear in job ads and on office doors. Here are a few examples. As yet, you cannot apply for all of them, but rest assured they will be posted on the Internet and in the papers at the beginning of the twenty-first century. Some of these titles of the future are already quite alive:[90]

Director of Mind and Mood

Director of Bringing in the Cool People

Culture Team Leader

Chief Imagination Officer

Minister of Progress

Virtual Reality Evangelist

Director of Company Future

Messaging Champion

Creatologist

VP Cool

Intangible Asset Appraiser

Others that come to mind as part of the future Dream Society company's social life include:

Director of Intellectual Capital

Minister of Core Values

Assistant Storyteller

Social Engineer

Visualizer

Chief Enacter

Court Jester

Is Hard Fun Really Work?

The description of work as pleasure-driven may come out sounding as if we are working just for fun but we are not quite ready to admit it yet. As mentioned previously, the very concept of work lies closer to playing than to anything else; but adults aren't supposed to play—they only do rational stuff. Even when such stuff is not rational, we call it that just the same. We invest it with meaning, with a purpose. The real difference is probably that play has play as its only purpose. Ask a bunch of 12-year-olds: "Why are you playing? Are you developing your motory skills? Or are you developing your social skills?" The predictable response will be a puzzled shrug—they will return to playing without answering because the only purpose of their play is play itself. We adults, on the other hand, demand that there be a purpose to the playing. This purpose lies in the demand that exists for the products or services that the company delivers.

When people reach a level of affluence that satisfies most of their very basic needs, they turn to the less basic. These are the needs that the company of the future has to fulfill. Most of us over 50 grew up acquainted with material want; thus we will perceive a large portion of the marketplace of the future as plain silly. If we want to avoid attracting the epithet "old," either we will have to learn to understand the new values or, if we can't understand them, we will have to learn them by heart.

Young people, however, will be greeted with a marketplace that holds the promise of better things for more people. The reason is that there will be a choice of a wider variety of jobs—the possibilities of ending up "where you belong" will increase; finding a job suited to your wishes and abilities will become easier.

Chapter 4

The Loving Family, Inc.—
And the New Leisure Time

We have now ventured somewhat beyond "the point of no return" on our voyage into the unknown land of the future, into the Dream Society. We have examined the theory, covering the market for products, the market for labor, and the company. Now we come to the household and the family—its home life and its leisure time. This chapter will unveil the shape of family and leisure in the Dream Society, an intriguing subject and one that lies close to our hearts, to our everyday lives. The family constitutes a basic social nucleus of society. It used to be the only social nucleus. As mentioned in Chapter 3, however, the family now has competition from the company, since the company plays a substantial and increasing role in our social existence.

At a junction where the 1900s are waning from our consciences and becoming history, this chapter will seek to describe what the phenomena we know as "the family" and "spare time" will look like when the twenty-first century has arrived. The approach will be as follows: Which products and services will the family want to buy for the household, and for its leisure purposes? Our perspective will not be for the short term—not starting next year—but will extend the horizon a bit further, using the stance adopted by companies in their strategic deliberations. Family and spare time, after all, are at the core of private consumption—the value chain usually ends in the home.

Today the average American household spends $2700 annually on furniture and household equipment alone. Consumption of foodstuffs amounts to twice this figure,[91] to which you may add clothing and housing. Household consumption is interesting—crucial, even—for most companies. How will it develop in the future?

In America, the average per capita share of GNP—an indicator of prosperity—is about $27,000.[92] In the year 2020, even if annual growth is estimated at a modest 2 percent, each American's share will be about $36,000. This growth estimate is overly cautious for the purpose of argument, yet still raises the question: How will a typical family spend this increase in disposable income, and what products and services will its members want to buy? Further, which companies will see all this reflected on a blossoming bottom line? Of course, one way of approaching the question is to look at what rich people are buying today. This is not a bad method if we keep in mind that society is changing, old values are being replaced by new ones, and technology keeps resulting in new products. The price tags on labor-intensive products will keep up with increased affluence, while machine-made products will become relatively cheaper. Thus, a private chauffeur will still be reserved for an elite few in 2020—as well as in 2070—while the prices of computers will keep plummeting.

Let us start by taking a look at the family of the future, then turn to the question of what we will do in our spare time—a spare time that, as already mentioned, will be curtailed.

The Loving Family, Inc.

Statistics can be prodded to divulge how many individuals, on average, live at a given address. In most affluent countries today, between two and three people live in each household. This statistical average has been declining up through the present century, in part because we have fewer children and in part because households no longer accommodate grandparents or other relatives. The typical household today is a nuclear family consisting of husband, wife, and kids. Large households of seven to eight people are still common in poor countries such as India; yet here, as well, they are shrinking in size. The rule of thumb is, the greater the affluence, the smaller the household. As a consequence, we must also count on the average household in 2020 being smaller, but not much smaller than it is today.

However, seeing the household as a family involves an emotional concept. Families are built on solidarity, on tender loving care, and on the task of producing the coming generation—the citizens of the future. Family values are important—a vital part of what we call "the good life." That accounts for the "Loving Family" in the chapter heading. The "Inc." is added because the family, although primarily a producer of emotions, is also a partnership founded to handle practical chores. We are zooming in on the future family from this twofold point of view: from an emotional as well as a practical angle. Both angles reveal influence on consumption patterns, but the emotional point of view will uncover the largest increase in spending; emotionally inspired spending will account for a major part of future increases in affluence. Practical spending will grow as well, but slower.

Emotional factors play a conspicuous role at work these days, and the same is true at home. Emotional elements are also predominant in the public sphere. In a summary of important 1997 events, *Time* magazine mentions a number of major occurrences (the death of Mother Teresa, the birth of the McGaughey seven, the au pair trial, and, most amazingly, Diana) and concludes: "For at least two decades, to be cool was to be 'cool.' And then, suddenly, it was not. As with all extreme cultural tendencies, something had to snap, and what began to show in the mid-1990s was an insistent desire to feel passion again and show us you care."[93] In 1998 President Clinton's private life created greater interest than tax issues—some change indeed. Emotions are now permitted—publicly as well as privately. The Dream Society theory has general validity.

Before the stage for the family of the future is properly set, we have to clarify the broader context. One necessary perspective is the historical one—the broader strokes. Most important here is the physical separation of home and workplace that occurred under the industrial society. Suddenly, the home was no longer—as was the farm—a production unit as well as a family unit. The moment people started "going to work" marked the beginning of a differentiation between work time and spare time. This differentiation is once again disappearing. Another necessary perspective has already been mentioned—the prevailing family structure of the present is no longer the large, communal family, but the nuclear family. The very concept of a family is thus undergoing constant changes, and the trend will continue in the future.

Also part of the broader context for setting the family stage of the future is the concept of growing older, since family life has hitherto followed a certain, age-determined pattern. But we are talking about new phases of life here—meaning, among other things, that old age sets in later in life nowadays; also, people remain young for a longer period than they did just 30 years ago. A few years ago, the concept was called "down-aging"—that is, it was permissible to seem young in your lifestyle and consumption pattern despite being of a ripe age. Today, a more appropriate catchphrase might be "no-aging"—in other words, you may go as you please, since the link between lifestyle and age has been dissolved. Today, only a minority fully enjoys that kind of freedom, but this minority will become a majority in the future. If you adopt a strict market segmentation according to age groups, you will increasingly fail to reach your product's entire target group. Let us take a look at the phases of life.

Children and young people might be called the independents, because they will free themselves from parents at an earlier age, acquiring their own opinions, their own patterns of spending, their own dwellings. They will become self-reliant consumers at an earlier age, and they will be approachable in separate marketing efforts.

Young adulthood might be called the free phase (version 1), because people marry later in life. In the intermediate period—

often lasting to age 30—they zap their way through life, switching jobs, educations, dwellings, lifestyles, and attitudes. They use this period to draw an overall map of life. Contrary to their parents as well as their grandparents, they are issued no such chart at home, along with a course. And those young people who do have their course charted for them at home will not be interested in following it, anyway.

The long period of parenthood with kids at home is postponed and starts later and later in life; often it lasts until well into the fifties. This is the time for homemaking, for taking care of kids, raising them while tending to your career at the same time. Therefore, this will often be the most hectic period in life, where the conflict between family and work presents itself at its most harrowing. The ideal situation is to build your career before and after you have those bundles of joy; yet this is just as logical as it is unfeasible. In short, forget it.

The period from the time the kids leave home until old age is another free phase (version 2), because the generous perks of freedom offered by life are increased. The children have moved out and often the parents are better off financially than ever before. The greatest capacity for spending will often be during this life phase. When today's young people reach middle age they will enjoy better health than did their parents—and will not yet think of themselves as old—which makes it a paradox that retirement age is being lowered. It is a paradox indeed, partially because better health allows for a longer, active career and partially because work is no longer perceived as thankless toil, but as hard fun (see Chapter 3). Therefore, we can expect the retirement age to rise in the future.

Old age is defined as the period where you are physically more or less debilitated and in need of care. Hopefully, old age will come to us later, and many people will remain in good health as they grow very old, even to the point where they will never actually experience "old age." They will be well functioning right up until death. The reasons will include better drugs, healthier food, and progress in medical science. More people will enjoy better health in old age than did their parents.

As is evident from the above, the phases of life are shifting, or even becoming irrelevant. More people—regardless of age—will be leapfrogging through life phases. Some will start the count-down to old age the minute the kids have left home, thus skipping free phase 2. Others will live their entire life in free phase 1—changing partners, homes, jobs, and outlooks every other year. Some will have more than one parenthood period. This is a gradual development, but the signs are already showing today. At this point we are ready to look at the future family setting in its proper framework: first the partnership, the "Inc." side; then the family as the place where love sprouts, blossoms, and withers.

The Family Corporation

The family may be viewed as a small enterprise with one or, more frequently, two owners or partners. The owners are employees as well. In addition, there will be one or more child workers. Often they will lack work motivation, and will therefore require a direct order before getting anything done and subse-quent supervision to ensure that the work has been adequately completed. The work atmosphere and corporate culture are generally amicable, but they are subject to greater and less pre-dictable fluctuations than is a normal work environment. At the bottom of the hierarchy there is a dog in charge of security main-tenance. Because of an unswerving loyalty, this canine worker is able to rely on a high level of service from other family mem-bers—like being the only one that gets taken for walks.

The division of labor in the traditional family corporation casts the male as hunter, venturing out into the metropolis jungle, bringing home the prey. The female cooks and prepares it. In this set-up, the household mother benefits from the hunter being skillful and spending long hours hunting. This pattern has seen a gradual decline as more and more women have entered the workforce. In more than 80 percent of American marriages both spouses work, and within a couple of decades a roughly equal proportion of men and women in the affluent countries will be employed outside the home—assuming current trends in North America, Europe, and Japan continue, as they probably will.[94] Ours is not to opine as to whether this constitutes a good or a bad trend; it simply reflects things as they are and will be. However, whether roles are distributed equally or differently, the family is still a partnership. You are partners when it comes to duties at home.

Growing affluence has brought bigger homes with more rooms; at the same time, many home chores have been either outsourced or automated. It can be argued that domestic outsourcing is far more widespread than is the case in a modern company— so widespread, in fact, that we can almost speak of the home as losing its functions. Let us take a look at what has already been outsourced by the family and what possibilities the future holds in store.

Our foodstuffs have become highly processed—not only in the form of TV dinners, but also as precooked vegetables and different types of processed meat. Work is moved from the kitchen to factories, where agricultural produce is industrially processed. Also, it will be moved from the home to restaurants and other food-related enterprises. One futurologist estimates that by the year 2000 more than half of all consumer dollars for food will be spent on eating out.[95] This will probably not quite be the case in Europe, but the trend is certain.

Entertainment has been outsourced. Hollywood has taken over. The trend will be reinforced in the future with big, flat screens displaying large-as-life actors and digital TV. Also, television will become truly interactive with games, prizes, and Internet access. As TV becomes a truly global medium producing for three continents (America, Europe, and Asia), budgets will rise. The fare available to a family wanting to gather in front of the screen will be prodigious in the future. Some researchers speak of a 50-year product cycle. That may be true if we see digital TV as a new product, but it is not true if we are talking about the product "the electronic court jester." He has come to stay. Also, there will be a European Hollywood. *Business Week* estimates that the number of European channels will rise from 100 in the early 1990s to 500 in the year 2000.[96] Hollywood, Europe will, however, probably be owned by Hollywood, California.

In the future, buying the daily groceries will be outsourced through home shopping. You will order groceries seated comfortably at home in front of the TV set or the computer. Overnight, they will be delivered to a box at your home. Visits to the mall will not be abandoned, but there will be fewer pounds to schlep to the trunk. Home shopping over the Internet will increase, but in a digital age, other possibilities will be available as well. You will not have to order your movie video, your music CD, or your book through the mail. They may be transferred electronically to a compact disk in the home. A book may be written out on your own printer, especially configured to the book format. There will be companies specializing in delivering world literature to the entire planet—all the library shelves in all the world will be accessible from your armchair. Economies of scale will mean that a few companies serve as electronic purveyors to the earth's more than one billion households; so they will probably soar among the 10 biggest service companies in the world. The year could be 2010.

Child care may also be outsourced—to a kindergarten or a professional nanny. What about the housewife? Can she, too, be outsourced? A perspicacious article in *The New Yorker*[97] answers yes; this is a trend that can already be observed. In households with two busy spouses pursuing independent careers, neither has the time for the customary chores of the true homemaker. They need to hire a housewife. Beth Berg runs a small business offering a solution. For a fee, she will invite guests over, plan the menu, fix dinner, talk to the electrician, organize moving, or decorate the house for Christmas—in short, all the tasks handled by the traditional housewife. As such companies begin to appear in several cities (and they are) and become well organized, they will be a realistic option for more than just the wealthy. Another way of outsourcing involves transferring tasks from home to company. Big corporations like Xerox, Hewlett-Packard, and Marriott are already offering to shop and handle dry cleaning for headquarters employees.

Technology, however, is by far the most substantial alleviator of the daily chores of cohabitation. Work has been automated: from the dishwasher, washing machine and toaster to the electronic home of the future, which will be able to regulate energy consumption on its own. A modern American home can be compared to an English country estate in the eighteenth century. Back then, you had numerous servants; so does the modern family, only they are electronic. The English country estate had its stables; the modern family has a garage that contains more and better horsepower. The many servants once employed in the kitchen have been replaced by gadgets and electronics; and the jester, as has been mentioned, is the TV set, while the private tutor is the computer. Most people today are actually more wealthy than the barons and earls of yesteryear.

In the future, homes will be filled with even more electronic servants. One example is your professional dietician, an electronic adviser suggesting recipes, reciting the cholesterol content of your chosen dinner, and, along with the refrigerator, able to determine which groceries should be ordered through home shopping. It will even be able to shop for you. The electronic servant will be the one to scold if there is no milk for breakfast. Does this sound impersonal? No. The digital adviser will apologize and be programmed to bring you sweet surprises or "little sins," culinary specialties that it orders by itself. You can delete this program whenever you wish, but who doesn't want to be spoiled from time to time?[98] Besides, colored indicators on the groceries in the refrigerator will tell you when the expiration date has been passed.

Also on the horizon is the vacuum cleaner programmed to navigate the house by itself, finding its own way around all the nooks and crannies and parking itself when the cleaning is done. It might be convenient if it did its stuff while we are out—that way it won't bump into us.

The digital household physician will monitor the family's state of health, offer diagnoses, and even suggest possible cures. It will ask questions about whether you are living a healthy life, whether you are getting enough exercise, whether you are smoking or consuming alcohol. And it can verify if you are telling the truth. If you aren't, it will be programmed to recriminate. It might be placed in the fitness room—fitness can be expected to find its way back into the home, along with more exciting workout programs. You will be able to race Carl Lewis— if you're fast. Otherwise, you will be conquered by a senior citizen with a cane. A video program will goad you as you run, and your results will be logged.

Each individual in the household will have a computer. Kids will have edutainment programs. They will be subjected to "stealth learning": Programs will be such a load of fun that the kids don't even realize how much smarter they are getting while it is happening, and then it is too late; knowledge cannot be deleted. Education, which moved out of the home long ago, is slowly on its way back in, thanks to digital electronics.

The home will be equipped with a master computer containing technical information about building materials and energy consumption. This master unit will control light and heat, comparing them against actual need, and will also be in charge of home security. But that is not all. It will be able to tell the story about the house and the family. The household members may each provide a short presentation of themselves. The installation of digitally electronic homes will probably be one of the major growth businesses in the coming decade. New houses will be predesigned to become "intelligent," and older houses will seem antiquated. We will be facing the most important product development within the housing market since electricity and hot and cold running water.[99]

And automated pets? Indeed, there will be electronic or virtual pets, even in the shape of dogs, cats, and fish. The robot dog will bark when it needs attention, howl when it fails to get it, and otherwise lie peacefully by the fireplace, contributing to a cozy atmosphere in the home. It isn't as thrilling as a real dog, but it saves time and provides some of the same experiences of care and fellowship as the real McCoy. Virtual pets present another possibility. They are to be found on the Internet and also require care and talk; otherwise they become aggressive.[100]

What lies behind these developments is not just the "time-saving industry"—the need to save time. New needs are also satisfied;

the simple reason is that computer electronics has opened the door to unexpected possibilities not found even in science fiction only a few years back. Computer electronics is truly a boon to the end of the twentieth century. The benefits will not diminish in the future, but our gratefulness is usually short-lived.

The following five ideas are what we at the Copenhagen Institute for Future Studies came up with on the afternoon of November 17, 1996. Some of them are already on their way to the market; others are perhaps a little close to "pop futurology." As noted by Paul Edwards, chairman of the Henley Center for Forecasting: "The value is not in the predictions, but in that it challenges straight-line thinking."[101]

1. Nature in the home. A small brook starts in the garden, runs through the house, and babbles out into the garden again. A unity between house and garden, between inside and outside, has been created. There are didactic plants; part of the living room is devoted to growing plants that will display to the family and its guests some of nature's wonders, both beautiful flowers and useful plants—rice, say, or corn and pepper.

2. An olfactory unit emitting ambience smells for the rooms. The importance of smells for our thoughts and emotions has been acknowledged for a long time, but the problem has been producing artificial smells at an affordable price—smells that sway the mind toward a mild, romantic, relaxed, or even an aggressive mood. Whoever controls the remote to the olfactory unit strikes the tuning fork for home vibrations.

3. A home audio unit. Morning birds chirp away in the bedroom; Karaoke is available in the bathroom. The sound of applauding spectators may be turned on in the fitness room or after someone in the household has told a funny joke.

4. Power sleep. While asleep, you want your sleep to be efficient—it must yield maximum rest per time unit. You will therefore want an electronic monitor keeping track of your sleep in order to determine whether your rest has been efficient—whether it has been too long, too short, or interrupted too frequently; whether you have had too much or too little REM sleep. Sleep research has established that far too

159

many people get too little true rest and resuscitation out of their sleep. We do, after all, spend from 6 to 8 hours daily snoozing. Perhaps the monitor will recommend a power nap after lunch.

5. More family rituals. We need a ritual for easing the transition to life at home, because we want to avoid bringing the conflicts and aggressions of our work life into our family life. Thus, it becomes imperative to have a mental airlock leading us from the work atmosphere into the home ambience daily. It might consist of imbibing music, coffee, tea, or a drink—or reading a story out loud. But the ritual must be marketed as a proper ritual—not on a level with Christmas, but still a sacrosanct occasion for the daily mental readjustment to family life.

Why do we buy time? Because we get less spare time, and because we still want to press in more of a social life, more of what gives us emotional experiences. All the needs that are placed at the bottom of Maslow's hierarchy of needs have to be dealt with; and a fair number of household chores are at the bottom. Actually, the level of service is somewhat higher at work than in the home. At work, you can always find coffee and food in the canteen, and spick-and-span is not something you have to think about. Even the potted plants are watered for you.

We may view the family as a company running a household, taking care of recreation, recharging batteries—and resolving these tasks with the highest efficiency possible. This section has examined how—thanks to automation and outsourcing—the functional side of the home has all but made the housewife superfluous. Statistics tell us that women are still charged with the major part of the domestic chores, but within a generation this imbalance will be corrected. Equal rights will have reached the home. Now let us return to the family as the bedrock of love.

For as Long as Love Shall Last...

Seemingly, traditional family values have been jettisoned into outer space. The family has hit upon the rocks of the future—the point where we all have doubts about which values should rule our lives, the point where we do not have a ready-made answer. Anthropologist Margaret Mead formulated a famous theory about the meetings between cultures, about what happens when two cultures collide—be they an Inuit culture of Greenland or Alaska meeting Western culture or two set images of "real life" clashing. This theory also holds true for the American family—here, the cultures colliding are the past and the future.

According to Mead, there are three phases for family and society. In the first phase, the newborn baby that parents are holding in their arms will experience the same life and the same values as his or her parents and grandparents. Children in static societies learn almost exclusively from their parents. Examples are the old, agricultural societies of North America and Europe—and the hunter societies.

In the second phase, values are no longer fixed and the opportunities for making a living change. Experience is no longer the best teacher. Something new has occurred and young people are obliged to learn from one another, rather than from their parents. That is precisely what transpired in the 1960s—in North America, in Europe, and in Japan. We saw a collective rebellion of youth, a revolt against parental values. A magnificent movie was made about this phase, starring the young Dustin Hoffman: *The Graduate.* Its theme is young people's rejection of the experiences culled by their parents' generation. Thus, the advice to get set for a career in "plastics" was nixed by the Hoffman character. Let it be shown for the record, parenthetically, that this advice—from a financial point of view—turned out to be sound; the plastics industry has grown significantly since the 1960s. But parents then were slightly puzzled by the introduction of new values, by the fact that their own experiences were no longer considered valuable. Youngsters could now learn from one another.

In the last phase, no one knows the future or what its values will turn out to be. Both adults and young people are in a quandary as to which values they should choose to guide their family lives as well as their social lives in general. That is the predicament which affluent societies are now waking up to. Traditional and modern value systems are at loggerheads, yet no generally accepted authorities are around to provide the answers. One way the prevailing situation may be gauged is through the fact that, although traditional family values are given high marks in all the polls, the number of broken homes and the divorce rates are high and still climbing. Also, marriage is quite often put off, so the "youth" period is extended. Young people need more years in order to find their values and make their choice of a social framework for living.

The affluent countries do not face invasion by a foreign culture, but the new confrontation follows the same pattern; it is a skirmish with ourselves and our own future. Technological developments, possibilities offered by telecommunications, changes in the work environment—taken together they add up to momentous change comparable to that encountered by many traditional societies when poor countries had to face Western culture. When such encounters occur, according to Margaret Mead, some will seek to isolate themselves in order to salvage their values while others become marginalized; but in a transitional phase, the opposing value norms will collide inside each individual—we stand bewildered and nervous as we face the future. Will the family exist in 50 years? Or should we prepare for a turning back to traditional family values, considering the second half of the twentieth century as an isolated period of crisis for the family? Let us look at the reasons for this cultural clash with our own future.

As already mentioned, some of the prime functions previously allotted to the household have disappeared. It is no longer a seat of production (as in the agricultural society); many of the daily tasks have either been outsourced or automated; also raising the kids and education take place largely outside the home. With women working in outside jobs, the home economy has become individualized. Solidarity regarding the financial situation is no longer necessary. We have separate bank accounts, and a phone of our own. We share the same bed and dinner table, but not necessarily checkbooks or opinions. For many families, work is a tough competitor vying for quality time. The many leisure activities being constantly offered tend to disperse family members in all directions.

Values are in crisis. The rapid speed of changes in technology means that institutions lose their power and authority. Society's traditional pillars of strength are weakened. From being infallible moral giants they have been reduced to just plain people and offices. Today we all look authority squarely in the eye, opening the field to several, competing sets of values. All of us are constantly faced with choices, with insecurity.

So changes on a multitude of levels have worked together to bring about the collision between the family and the future. Perhaps the family, if faced with just one of these changes, could merely adapt; but in such massive numbers, changes create doubts. According to traditional family values, marriage is a religious institution laying down guidelines for love as well as gender roles and financial affairs. If these values are no longer valid, marriage becomes nothing more than an alliance between two human beings. This is where doubt sets in: Which values govern the alliance? Financial partnership becomes less necessary when both spouses can make their own money outside the home. Gender roles have been debated since the 1960s; today they have, to a large degree, become individualized; each marital alliance chooses its own apportionment of the various tasks. In northern Europe there is talk of the "family of negotiation"—the family where he and she reach a bargained settlement about how roles should be divided from task to task, without any ironclad rules enforced. The daughter asks her parents: "Is it OK to be unfaithful?" Answer: "Well, I guess that depends how things are with the two of you." Or the pubescent son inquires: "Dad, is it OK to keep what you find in the street?" Answer: "What did you find?" Morals are often relative.

That leaves us with love. In the absence of any materialistic reasons for marriage to exist and in the absence of traditional family values, love remains the sole reason for marriage. Perhaps this is reflected in the sale of diamonds. The marketing story began as early as 1939 with the fixing of an image in the public imagination, the instant association of diamonds with romantic rites of passage: engagements, weddings, anniversaries. In 1996, world diamond jewelry sales totaled $52 billion, with the United States accounting for about one-third.[102] The diamond has become an important symbol of love—and for this reason, many are sold.

When love is the only reason for entering into marriage, it follows that marriages can be dissolved when love is no longer present. As evidenced by the rising divorce rates in affluent countries, this is in fact what is happening, and it appears to be the case whether or not children are involved. Where does that leave love, in our day and age? We can hardly be said to live in a romantic era, as in the early nineteenth century when the one true love—the *Romeo and Juliet* syndrome—was adored and yearned for: How can we then characterize our image of love? Has love become commercialized? No, but the high level of affluence has allowed us to purchase many expensive symbols to signal its presence. Love is alive and well.

The family's future will be determined by the outcome of a battle over our minds. How are we to perceive ourselves? How should we define ourselves in relationship to other people? Let us take a look at the changes that have occurred in the twentieth century. In northern Europe, there have primarily been two. One change is the shift from family to work as a social center. In days of old, when getting to know people at social gatherings, we would typically inquire as to familial relations: "Who are you related to?" Today, the question often centers on the job: "What's your line?" The other change is the move from collectivism to individualism. We do not perceive ourselves as part of a social context, as the daughter of so-and-so, as a member of this family or the other; we are autonomous individuals. This becomes evident whenever something criminal or immoral is done. In the old days, such an action would bring shame upon the entire family; today, only the individual is considered culpable. This is even more remarkable because the "culture of shame" still exists outside the affluent countries and it exists in Japan.

The future battle over our minds is a battle for the individual soul, the individual personality as perceived by itself. "What am I like?

Who am I?" Let us venture a guess as to which self-perceptions will fade and which will become more prevalent.

First the family, the subject of this chapter. Where it used to reign supreme, today it faces competition; in the future, this competition will be even stiffer. A 1997 survey asked American MBA students what things they considered most important in life. Heading the list was building a career (75 percent), but the family ran a very close second (71 percent).[103] Responses from these young Americans reveal the increased competition; if they stick to the ideals of their youth, these students will be facing a lifelong, daily challenge: job or family. They want both and will give up neither.

The survey also shows that other forms of social identification have gained credibility; this is true particularly of the job and the workplace. We have to envisage that the family will become more important in some life phases than in others. The reason is that relationships to the significant other and to the family are increasingly defined in emotional terms. Love is *the* precondition for entering any relationship. This means that lifelong marriage will be facing an even greater challenge than today. Most of us will probably agree that such a development cannot be a healthy one for our society at large. At the same time, it has been engendered by that society's own members, ourselves. A radical change of attitude will be required before the family can be reinstated as a fixed point throughout a lifetime. One trend spotter already sees simplicity and balance as an increasing proclivity in the late 1990s, with more people turning away from the materialism of the 1980s toward an emphasis on family life and the simple joys that life affords us in general.[104] Perhaps the trend spotters are right, perhaps not. The fight for our minds is far from over yet.

The workplace with the job as a means of social identification has gained increased importance. This development can be expected to continue and will be particularly relevant to our free phase 2: to those aged 50 plus. The connection ties in neatly with the expected rise in retirement age. Maybe future innovative employees defining corporate culture will turn out to be in the

60-to-80 age group—when it has finally become clear that there is no necessary connection between age and the ability to innovate.

Leisure time will also compete with the family. This is true of sports, the call of the wild, and cultural pursuits, as well as volunteer work where the good cause is what matters. As the array of available leisure pursuits proliferates and becomes ever more specialized, these pastimes will receive increased attention. The offers in jobs and leisure activities have been under constant product development, as they continue to be, but how do we apply product development to spouses and kids? Well-meaning efforts by families seem to produce highly varied and unpredictable results. We can provide truthful labeling for all the physical products and all services, but happily, labeling has not yet been tried on humans—though the dream still lives on.

A third possibility is that people in the twenty-first century will see themselves as true citizens, as participating members of the local community or the entire society surrounding them. So far, however, there is little indication that this will come to pass. On the contrary, after the downfall of the big ideologies on both sides of the Atlantic, grass-roots movements are becoming smaller, more ephemeral, and specialized. Also in decline is the idea that federal, state, and local authorities are organizations responsible for providing each citizen with a good life. This is true in North America and especially in Europe, where decentralization constitutes one of the strong political trends of the 1990s.

Spiritual and religious communities may well be in for a renaissance following the rampant materialism of the twentieth century—even in Europe; their role as regards the family will be positive in that they will support traditional family values.

The fight for our minds may also be called the Zeitgeist struggle; we are thus facing a family concept that cannot be taken for granted. It, too, will have to fight for position in our minds, the risk of course being that advocates extolling traditional family values do only that—simply take these values for granted. But family values no longer stand unquestioned. They are getting tough

166

competition and they can win only if these values are high-lighted and marketed as the lifestyle leading to "the good life."

The fight for individual minds is fought in the media, with celebrities filling in as mythic role models and identity beacons. They have mythic proportions because they exist both in reality and as visible bearings in the electronic screen reality. The problem here lies in the fact that precisely these role models from the worlds of art, entertainment, sports, and politics are often identified with their respective professions—they do not stand as advocates of traditional family values. With the arduous hours they work, their families are forced to take a back seat.

However, there is no law saying it has to be this way. As so often before, the future might bring us the unexpected—things that take everybody by surprise, including futurologists and others dealing professionally with the future. Let us hope that this chapter's somewhat somber view of the family's future turns out to be wrong.

With our picture of the future family we are ready to seek out what products this family will be wanting to buy. Our premise is that the family and its values live a precarious life when confronted with reality, but that the dream of a happy family life remains intact. Thus, families will want to buy products with a built-in component aglow with family happiness—products radiating the idea of love, permanent values, and peace of mind. Successful products will often be nostalgic ones, referring to the past, to the early twentieth century, or earlier still.

The paradox lies in the fact that companies selling products emanating familial happiness are the same companies acting as family life's main competitors in real life. Perhaps the connection is this: The longer we work, the more we need products signaling family happiness. Companies will sell the idea of family bliss, but will not actually support it. Mr. Rolf Jensen the employee supports his company's social life; Rolf Jensen the consumer buys the idea of family bliss. We are all employees as well as consumers; seemingly, we are able to live with this paradox. In the words of Charles Darwin: "It is not the strongest of the species that survives, nor the most intelligent; it is the one that is most adaptable to change."

As mentioned above, the products of the future are products of technology. Much new technology will arrive to ease work at home. But such technology rapidly becomes part of our everyday lives (the cellular phone, after all, only conferred status for a brief year or two), and it is placed at the bottom of the hierarchy of needs. Future home consumption will primarily be in the emotional market.

The home of the future will be electronically wired: it will be "intelligent," yet its main function will be to accommodate family bliss and the symbols of love. The more these symbols can be built into homes—inside and out—the higher the sales. The task is difficult because many modern architects and entrepreneurs think rationally, functionalistically. Perhaps this task will be better solved by the large car makers (Toyota is already producing prefab houses).[105] Designers working for the car industry are well aware that symbolic value comes first in their product—the rest is just technology and mechanics.

Cars are becoming specialized. There are cars symbolizing freedom and adventure. Then there is the minivan, symbolizing family bliss. It has room for the entire family; less important is how often it is actually used to carry the entire family.

The kitchen: a blast from the past. Shaker kitchens, kitchens evoking English social realism of the 1930s, kitchens with open stoves—the possibilities are limitless as long as you remember that efficiency is taken for granted; things simply work.

The bathroom, formerly a place reflecting hygiene only, will also tell a story, and we will see more specialized rooms: the workshop, his and her dens, the music room, the home cinema room—in short, the things only rich people have today. But they will be endowed with more stories, because flaunting riches and luxury is a bad and materialistic theme.

Modernist products pointing to a better and richer future will not sell. Consumers will take efficiency in a product for granted—

regardless of its nostalgic exterior. What they are actually buying is the emotional message. Most of the products advertised or described in magazines on interior decorating refer back to the past. These magazines are in the business of meeting consumer demands; those that do so best, sell the best. Thus we may surmise that this is the way consumers want things. The home and its products are also entering the Dream Society (see Chapter 2). The children will be affected as well. The busy working family with kids may hire a professional nanny. As a departure from the (perhaps) more cold, outside-the-family solution offered by the kindergarten, you see offers like: "Our reliable nannies are warm and loving and have excellent references."[106]

The advent of a stronger belief in family values and a deeper faith that the future will bring more happiness would totally change the market. This, however, is unlikely to occur. The tendency just described has been with us since the late 1950s—up till then, being modern was modern. From the 1960s onward, the past has become the future. This is a megatrend attributable to the value crisis and the rapid pace of technology. So, was the past really all that happy, since we seek to return there through our products? No, historians will reply; the past was plagued with disease, unemployment, social tensions, and repression, but that is of no consequence. We can still effortlessly romanticize ourselves into the past *we* need for our future.

The New Leisure Time

The *Oxford Dictionary* defines leisure time as the time remaining after we are through working; the time we have at our own disposal. As it was made clear in Chapter 3, more people these days feel that even at work, they are in control of their own time. This is because the sharp dividing line between work and spare time is becoming blurred. In the Dream Society, free time will occasionally be difficult to distinguish from work and—above all—it will be imbued with emotional content; perhaps, the Dream Society expresses itself most eloquently in the way leisure time is spent. This chapter will view the way leisure time is spent from a personal as well as from a business-oriented angle:

Which new products and services will be in demand? However, before we look at spare time and holidays, it will be useful to turn our gaze back one century—to the days before mass tourism, to a time when voyages were beset with considerable hardships.

In 1893 Samuel Barton, who was the leading investment adviser for, among others, Vanderbilt Enterprises, wrote: "I think our pleasure-seekers will discover that the lower part of Florida has as many temptations in the winter season as have any of the winter resorts of Europe. I look to see the islands in the Caribbean sea become the resort of those who seek fashionable pleasures."[107] Barton's prognosis proved uncannily accurate. Those who followed his investment advice made a lot of money not only for themselves but for their inheritors as well.

Let us, therefore, start this chapter about leisure time and tourism with a few guesses as to what Barton would have said about the leisure and tourism market during the next 20 years. Where can we be expected to spend our vacations in the future? And where would it be wise for us to invest? Where might we place a long-term investment yielding enough money for ourselves and our children, so we will never again have to study price tags before buying anything?

The first guess is shares in all sports where a monopoly is held. In the United Kingdom, there is only one Premier League in soccer and there will never be others; there is only one Olympic Games and only one Tour de France. These sports extravaganzas attract an ever-increasing share of world audiences, and in 10 to 20 years their audience will be truly global—billions of people will follow them. To be sure, they must compete with other sports and with events in other countries, but there is economy of scale in sports. The events that already exist grow bigger because they attract more investments—more than do the lesser events. In the sports market, the name of the game is being the first to be big. In this respect, the sports industry resembles the car industry. The market for spectator sports in the next 20 years will take the form of one long elimination race—with the extenuating circumstance that this is, after all, a high-growth sector with room for more and more contestants. This high growth is due mainly to television presenting these dramas to the entire planet. Digital

170

and interactive television is still not the same as being physically present, but the difference will continually decrease.

The next guess is about finding the future Florida. Our conjecture is somewhere in South Africa. It has summer when the affluent countries have winter; it has vast national parks and good possibilities for building theme parks. Just as in Florida, the prerequisites for creating a global center for tourism already exist, a plethora of offerings. It is all about creating a "magnet," with globally attractive features. This can be achieved only if the place boasts many thrills to explore—like, say, "whale watching," ballooning, and water sports. South Africa has all of this, and more. Because of expanding air transportation, several such global centers will arise—Florida is on its way to becoming the first. The only question remaining is where they will be located. Another possibility, of course, is Australia, especially the north, which enjoys the same climate and the same bountiful wildlife and nature as Florida. Queensland is an obvious choice, also because the Great Barrier Reef is located right off its shores.

As affluence continues to grow, more will join the ranks of the megarich—in the USA, in the Far East, and in Europe. This international jet set of the very, very rich is growing because more large fortunes are being inherited by fewer children, and because the possibilities of taking home huge paychecks have increased. First-class passengers on the *Titanic* had fortunes and incomes that the common folk in steerage could not even begin to imagine. The pattern seems to be returning. The megarich want to meet exclusively with one another, on small, luxurious cruise vessels, on islands and other areas shielded from the public eye. They can rest assured of exclusivity through the price—they're the only ones who can afford such places—or they may achieve it by being the only ones to pursue a specific interest or lifestyle. Where will it be expensive to meet in 10 to 20 years? There are many possibilities: luxury hotels with refined events, expensive ski resorts (like the ones today), and faraway places such as the North and the South Poles. However, luxury in the sense of conspicuously exaggerated consumption is on its way out. Big money is no longer spent on epicurean lifestyles, but on unique experiences that happen to be expensive. But where to find them?

How about in the palaces of the old, pedigreed aristocracy? As the fortunes behind these noble families evaporate in modern society, their castles and manor houses become vacant; they may be refashioned as hotels or conference centers, meeting places where history, nobility, wealth, and an extremely high level of service are combined. This has already happened in western Europe, but in Russia as well as in central and eastern Europe there are still untenanted castles. They have not yet been renovated and refurbished, but concurrently with the conversion to a market economy, they will be. The large ballrooms with their crystal chandeliers where the romantic cotillions of the czar's courtiers were held will be taken over by the megarich. India has comparable palaces from the time of the maharajas.

Other playgrounds of the megarich include Europe's old spas and resorts, and the cloisters of Tibet—places suitable for spiritual as well as physical invigoration. Finally, we will find these nouveaux riches jet-setters on the islets of the Pacific—small islands accessible only to members of the superrich club. The luxury hotel alone will not be enough; there will have to be a theme bringing people together—like a sub touring the coral reefs, or the fact that one or more are celebrities in residence. Icons from show business or the world of sports will be offered cheap palaces because they act as attractions for all of us wanting to touch their mantle.

Nobility and crowned heads have always had several abodes—the ability to relocate even as their spirits moved them. Today, the megarich also have this option. They may maintain homes on several continents. In the year 2020, the number of people owning homes in several different places across the world will have increased. They will need homes with wardrobe closets exactly the same size and a globally savvy real estate agent and adviser.

At the same time, more of the megarich will display needs that belong squarely in the Dream Society universe. To a significant extent, they will discover the joy in providing care. This is a tendency that has gained real momentum in the last few years. Individual contribution to charity has climbed 9.5 percent in the last two years, to $130.3 billion in 1996, according to the American Association of Fundraising Counsel.[108] Here we are not dealing with alms, as in the olden days; projects are usually concrete and focused. Says Bruce L. Newman, executive director of the Chicago Community Trust: "We don't talk very much about charity any more. We talk about entrepreneurialism and the ability to make change." The megarich believe they may be better suited to solve social tasks than traditional public institutions. The Soros Foundation, owned by the American philanthropist George Soros, donated $183 million in aid to Russia in 1998, nearly as much as the European Union.[109] The need to offer care exists in all of us.

Needless to say, this prudent advice is offered with no guarantee of success—the leisure business is a risky one. Here, the same rule pertains as in publishing and the movie business: first you must defray all the expenses and then see whether you can attract any customers. The possibilities of analyzing the market beforehand are meager—consumers have a hard time evaluating something they haven't seen yet.

In the future, the distinction between work and spare time will wither away—because, increasingly, the demands we put on our leisure time will be the same as the ones we put on work. We are approaching a fully integrated life. We want both our work and our leisure time to be *hard fun.* Activities must be their own reward, rich with experiences and laden with emotions; we are entering the Dream Society. On weekdays, we will see less spare time as daily work hours increase; on the other hand, we will have more days off. One pattern might be 10 years of work, followed by 2 years of free time—or 6 months of work and 1 month of holiday. Nearly all of us will go through life phases that are alternately filled with work and time on our own hands, though the time we spend on our own will increasingly reflect how enthusiastic we are about our jobs. "Working holidays" will become more common.

We are moving away from the era of mass tourism—reversing the trend begun in the 1950s, fueled by a justified need for rest and recreation and for recharging batteries worn down from the toil of the industrial society. In Europe, mass tourism was also about freedom from authority, norms and rules. In the future, people will be utilizing their spare time in a way that is more determined, yet also more emotional. Leisure time will still be generated by increased affluence. In the rich countries we have made a collective decision to have a limited amount of spare time on our hands, getting more money to spend during this time in return. Had we chosen to benefit from our advances in technology by increasing spare time instead of increasing affluence, we might have worked 20-hour weeks today. We have elected not to go for this option—we would have had too little money to spend in all this spare time and, besides, work has become more interesting, enough to rival our spare time. So our spare time is tight and we need to make the most of it, actively—and spend more money on it. The leisure time market will be a market of high growth during the coming 20 years.

Even today, international tourism is an imposing market. Total tourism revenue in the OECD countries (the affluent countries) is currently approaching $250 billion, and the number of tourists crossing a border into another affluent country is slightly in excess of 300 million.[110] Add to this the remaining part of the leisure market, which it does not make sense attempting to put total figures on. A yearly growth of 5 percent—somewhat above the overall increase in affluence—can be expected; indeed, this is what most experts predict.

We will purchase "storytelling" of all sorts in our spare time: stories about leisure time where the family may reinforce its sense of togetherness, after workdays where not enough time has been spent with one another. This might be an inspiring story told through a theme restaurant, or it might be the great story from the South Pole. It could also be the rock concert or the sports event where feelings are not only allowed, they are the whole point. This could be called "emotional jogging." Just as we exercise our muscles in order to keep physically fit, we also practice our emotions without having to be in dead earnest. This type of sentimental workout seems to be an innate need.

There is also the leisure pursuit where storytelling itself is on the agenda: storytelling where the fable creates a common bond of togetherness and absorption—of abandoning yourself, cutting loose. The National Storytelling Association, with 7000 members, boasts a list of storytellers that includes 800 individuals as well as 200 organizations and centers.[111] Here you will find headings like "The Desert Storytellers," "Bluegrass Storyweavers," "National African-American Storytellers Retreat," and "Spellbinders." We cannot live meaningful lives without stories. In *A Storytelling Guidebook,* author Jenny Nash reflects on how we learn through stories: "A child will sit enthralled through a reading of Aesop's fable "The Tortoise and the Hare" and long remember its moral that hard, steady work pays off. Simply tell a child that maxim and watch it roll off his or her psyche like water on a yellow slicker. Aesop's fables have entertained and educated listeners since the sixth century B.C., using animal characters to illustrate all-too-human foibles."[112]

Family Team Building

As mentioned above, families are busy; close and lasting togetherness in the family is often threatened. In the section on the work concept, team building was described as one of the activities strengthening core values in a company. In a similar manner, the family occasionally needs to have its core values strengthened through team building. This might happen through a common experience, or through a vacation offering time spent together without any outside, interfering demands—through the family itself. In the future, therefore, a substantial amount of leisure time will go toward family team building. The commercialized and carefully thought-through family holiday on a grand scale was first launched in 1955, when Disney's theme park opened in California. Disney theme parks are for the entire family; the shared experiences strengthen family cohesion.

In the future, there will be a desperate need of places, near and far, where family members can spend time together, sharing an experience. The nearest places are the stores, and some are already entering the future. One such enterprise is Recreational

Equipment, Inc. (REI), whose $30 million flagship store opened in Seattle in 1997. Not only a store, but also an incipient theme park, it contains a waterfall and a bike test-riding area, as well as a 65-foot-high, 110-ton, three-dimensional climbing spire surrounded by glass walls. Bob Woodward, who publishes a newsletter for outdoor retailers, states: "Somebody has to do it. It's taken the business into the modern era." REI contains 80,000 square feet of retail space and thus it is only natural to have 2 stone fireplaces, before which visitors unwind after trekking through the store.[113]

John Fry owns 16 computer stores, each with a turnover of $85 million, a figure that is considerably higher than the computer retail average. One possible explanation is that Fry hired a designer, formerly of LucasFilms (George Lucas' film production company), to concoct extravagant fantasy themes. In Woodland Hills, California, it's Alice in Wonderland.[114] Threatened by sales over the Internet, computer retail is betting on boosting the experience of mall shopping.

Nowadays, shopping is rarely considered a leisure activity, so the task facing retail chains is to create "home shopping" in the malls—meaning that stores should be designed to provide a homelike atmosphere or assume the character of an exhibition. Levi's, MGM, Disney, and Harrod's of London have taken steps in this direction. Shopping should no longer be an arduous hassle, but an experience in itself.

Other large retail chains are also redefining the idea of the store. No longer merely the place where you purchase stuff, it has become an event, an experience—offering the added opportunity to buy something as well. A prognosis for the sizable German market concludes: "Shopping will become a form of exploration and entertainment, increasingly detached from need. Consumption will rival work as a means to self-realization and identity."[115]

The excitement offered by the retail chains of the future will often be directed at the entire family—exciting experiences that can be enjoyed by all its members. Traditionally, sports has been a dividing factor for families—both live on stadium and in front of the TV. When producing the Atlanta Olympic Games, NBC Sports kept Mrs. Six Pack and the kids in mind. To keep them tuned, prime-time programming contained female-friendly sports and storytelling laced with emotion. As put, concisely, by *Fortune:* Think of it as the Oprah Olympics.[116]

NBC and retail chains concentrate on creating family fun because there is a market—a market for togetherness. This market will grow even as the family is threatened from more and more corners.

Leisure Time in the Dream Society

As world population and wealth increase, there is less and less nature to go around. In the year 2020, natural wildlife areas on dry land will be reduced to a few isolated dots on the map. During the past century, roads, buildings, and people have invaded Tarzan's domain and paved it, too. Therefore, wild nature will be a scarce amenity that we all want to visit. However, one realm remains intact in which nature can thrive without being ogled by humans— the sea. Thus, underwater tourism will be one of the twenty-first century important growth sectors. Investments in a new industry are always risky, yet there are already 45 tourist submarines in operation worldwide and their turnover is $150 million. The price for a 45-minute tour is still steep ($65 to $85), but it will drop as new technology is applied (one possibility is diaphanous, acrylic hulls), and economies of scale will facilitate mass marketing. For the megarich, it is probable that private submarines will be modern in 10 to 15 years. Following the end of the cold war, it is natural to find peaceful uses for the knowledge and capacity in this area.

Another possibility is underwater hotels with panoramic views. Today only one such establishment exists, Jules' Undersea Lodge in Key Largo, Florida, but more are on their way. The rooms are called "searooms."[117] These are the new possibilities; but diving at earth's large coral reefs and studying killer whales in Patagonia, blue whales in Antarctica, and tortoises in Malaysia are among the activities that will grow so much they will have to be regulated.

Cruises have enjoyed steady growth over the last 10 years. This relaxed kind of holiday for the wealthy with the added touch of luxury has come within the reach of the majority. If only for this reason, new developments were inevitable, and they are on their way. Mere luxury will no longer do the trick; there has to be a theme, an idea, an emotional objective to the cruise—such as a family vacation. Disney's first ship, the 2700-passenger *Disney Magic,* has been designed for kids and their parents. Cunard will let you take classes in music and art during your voyage. If you disembark on one of the restored or rebuilt great sailing ships, you can be trained as a sailor and experience the rough life that disappeared with the steamers. An ancient "Cape Horn'er" (a sailor who has rounded the nether tip of South America) will find it extremely difficult to understand how anyone today could pay for being exposed to the same trials and tribulations they were paid a salary—however miserable—for enduring.[118]

When wild nature is no longer a problem, but something needing protection—that is when "ecotourism" enters, the idea that the tourist must not encumber the natural bounty he or she visits. For the next decade or two this word will crop up in ads, only to disappear again—not because the word becomes unfashionable, but because it goes without saying that you do not damage nature. There is still an ongoing struggle concerning the preservation of natural amenities, but all agree that wild nature is a valuable asset—measured in dollars, as well—and therefore it will be preserved for our children and grandchildren.

We already see the problem: either there is too little nature left on dry land or it is too far away from the people willing to pay to see it. Therefore, another growth area will be the staging of nature: artificially constructed animal parks and national parks where wild animals are fed during winter. Thus, a word of advice to young people might be—not "plastics," as in the movie *The Graduate*—but "nature—the real thing—and whatever comes close." A lot of nature will have to be salvaged during the next 20 years; and a lot of artificial nature will have to be created— safari parks, rain forests, savannas. Some of these will lie in temperate climates, but be shielded from the cold by big bubbles made of—plastic.

The scarcity of unspoiled nature makes it interesting to ask where you can still find it. The obvious answer is Africa.

Although the poorest continent from a material point of view, it is the most magnificently endowed as regards unspoiled nature. The rain forests in the Democratic Republic of the Congo may become a greater source of revenue than its copper and diamonds. It has not quite happened yet. When it does, there will be small expeditions—"In Stanley's Footsteps" and ecotourism— then, gradually, the influx of individuals will increase.

The next attraction will be nearly uninhabited areas: the great sand deserts of the Sahara, Nabib, and Gobi and the icy wastes of the South Pole.

As far as the latter is concerned, tourism has already set in. As this is being written, 22 individuals, each paying $22,000, have set out to become the first group of civilians ever to skydive to the planet's southernmost spot. As one of the participants tells it to *Outside* magazine: "We're seen as people with a death wish, when actually we have a life wish: We want to experience as much as we can."[119] Only in the rational Information Society is there any need to make excuses for the urge to give destiny a self-assured wink. In the Pacific Ocean on January 1, 2000, there will be a "first" adventure: a race to be the first person to see the sun rise on the new millennium. For geographical reasons, this will take place on a ship. The event will probably attract several thousand people, not to mention photographers, who must have a picture of the third millennium. Being first has always fascinated humans.

Growing numbers of people will be attracted to animal wildlife. The first in-depth studies of mountain gorillas and chimpanzees in their natural habitats were initiated 30 years ago by Jane Goodall, who later wrote the book *In the Shadow of Man*.[120] These scholarly investigations have since continued, and today tourists can share the experience. We would all like to see the great simians up close; this is possible in several places in Africa, and on the islands of Borneo and Sumatra. Big hotels will spring up around these exotic locales. The same will happen around other areas where all the other animals loved by humans congregate: tigers, lions, elephants, and that great teddy bear, the giant panda.

So much for nature. But we must not forget the *story* about nature. Children are able to read about that world of wild nature lost to the affluent countries and the modern urbanite. *Time* magazine paints a dire scenario about the future scarcity of nature: a little boy reading about all the things that once were; a fairy tale about "the woodlands filled with tall trees, wild animals, and clear running streams. The scenes seemed so magical that the boy could scarcely believe in them, though his parents assured him that such wonders once existed."[121] This scenario is much too gloomy; the child of the future will still be able to see the reality described and depicted in his books, but he will have to travel far. Nature as storyteller is eminently suited to the postironic age—past the relativism concerning values—into the Dream Society, where values are alive and kicking.

Theater, ballet, concerts, musicals are all part of the future too. In the Dream Society, though, they will have to be more emotional and more interactive. Maybe they will resemble the Globe Theatre, newly rebuilt since Shakespeare's day. Back then, there was joy and merriment in the audience—none of present-day bourgeois gravity during the performances. It was OK to shout your comments to the actors and they would reply in kind. Today, it is likely that more people will choose to perform themselves, thus making the production an all-participant event, with no spectators.

In the large cities, the name of the game is economies of scale. The megacities—the metropolises that are already centers of culture—will attract the greatest throngs of visitors: New York, London, Paris, and Berlin. In the future, we must probably also include Moscow, Beijing, and Sydney as global centers. They must be conceived as great theme parks, each with its own distinctive character: Paris as the theme park for epicureans, Berlin as the theme park of history and politics, New York as the theme park 10,000 lifestyles, and London as the theme park of entertainment and shopping. After a city has been redefined as a theme park with one or more themes, city officials can lay down a strategy: What kind of leisure pursuit do we wish to attract?

The big museums are in for a revolution as well. They must create vibrant, living images of the past or present that they want to tell us about. Theme park designers will be hired—experts who are better skilled than scholars when it comes to dramatizing exhibitions. Finally, we must make note of the great, eternal attractions: the Grand Canyon, the Pyramids of Egypt, the Great Wall of China, the Mayan Temples, the Taj Mahal in Agra, India, and Ayer's Rock in Australia. Increased mobility will make it possible for more and more people to visit these.

Another buzzword to get used to in the future is political tourism. International trouble spots will become tourist venues for those wanting to form a firsthand impression of the conflict in question, those who are not satisfied with media coverage. Political tourism may range from "war tourism" (which started in the former Yugoslavia) to cultural tourism, where the objective is learning about a culture and its background.

Soon, a virtual visit to a holiday spot will be an option before actually going there. Attractions big and small will offer Baedekers on CD-ROM or guided Web sites. You will be able to click your way around New York without having to worry about traffic or lousy weather. This is not actual reality; this is marketing with addresses and phone numbers so you can book plane, hotel, and theater reservations on your own. Travel agents will be faced with a great challenge when their hitherto privileged knowledge, once their reason for existence, is now available directly to clients.

CIFS Round Table

When this section was being planned, six colleagues met at CIFS around the creative table to answer the question: name seven new leisure pursuits—ideas you do not read about every day. Below, our results. Common to the seven suggestions is that you are taking a holiday from—yourself. You become another person. You see and experience something, only that you isn't you.

1. In your leisure time, you become the product. Just as in the movie *Total Recall,* it will be possible to become another person—for a while. We are talking role games. Some of the coal mines now threatened with shutdown due to economic

failure will continue as tourist attractions. "Be a coal miner for a week"—and experience the life lived by previous generations. Get involved with the life of a coal miner.

2. Go on a social slumming discovery trip. Be a bum for a weekend. The travel agency will supply the shabby and slightly smelly equipment. You will encounter the metropolis and its people as seen from below; how the other half lives with being looked down upon; what it feels like being on the receiving end of handouts flung in a hat. Another possibility is a week in jail. The large majority—after all—have never seen the inside of a prison and need that experience. The offer might initially be given to young people wanting a first-hand impression of what crime may eventually lead to.

3. Go to the future for a holiday. First, you need to pick a year and calculate your age at that time. Next questions: What will your job be? What will your life be? Then the travel agency delivers the settings. This will be a great challenge for the travel agency, but might defray the cost of consulting companies in need of realistic advice on future strategy. A film studio is the proper physical location for this future factory.

4. Revert to childhood. You will be in a house simulating the dimensions of your surrounding world as a five-year-old. The house will be built twice as large as normal houses—the doors are nine feet high with doorknobs you can barely reach. The house canine is six feet tall. It's an eminent way for parents-to-be to spend an afternoon.

5. Relive the great battles of history. The battle between the French and allied armies at Waterloo demands about 100,000 extras to be staged on a full scale, but it may be possible to re-create just part of the atmosphere, and a film company may pay a large part of expenses. Besides, all the military historians of the world would be paying spectators. Since you were not actually there on that rainy day in June 1815, a reenactment is the next best thing.

6. Be Robinson Crusoe. Get marooned on a deserted island and test your survival skills; see if you can build a hut, collect food, find fresh water—and cope with the loneliness. This

experience will teach you how dependent you have become on modern technology, and how little you know about basic rules of survival. Often you will find that the educational experience has not done you much good.

7. Take a vacation to Mexico or Thailand, but be a Mexican or a Thai. You are a native and considered so by the natives, you live their lives along with them, experiencing everything from within. Thus it becomes possible to see the tourists from another angle—that of the natives.

Emotional Jogging

Emotional jogging refers to our need to display emotions without being really serious. We want to exercise and practice our emotional lives, just as we must keep our bodies and minds fit. A substantial amount of leisure time in the future will be spent on emotional jogging. This is an important element in sports, allowing us to express unbridled enthusiasm or disappointment. After the event is over, we are still considered to be normal individuals—the sports phenomenon means a license to thrill. The emotional drill is included in the ticket fee.

Manchester United—the leading soccer team in Great Britain (at present)—has a turnover to the tune of $140 million. Like other major sports teams in the USA, Europe, and Japan, it is enjoying rapid growth. Its regular customers, the staunch supporters, are loyal to their "brand," what they get in return is emotional jogging. In the market for products, customers will choose the best available. Not so in sports. Even the less successful clubs have a crowd of devotees showing up for games week after week, even if the team is on a losing streak. Spectator sports offer something very well suited to the future, to the Dream Society. *GQ* magazine offers the following comment on Manchester United's decision to start its own television channel: "Now it is promising to leverage the brand in the world of entertainment."[122] This is a brand selling emotions, a brand that cannot be explained through the logic of the Information Society. As a line of business, emotional jogging will figure predominantly in statistics—when statistics will have to review business demarcation lines within the next 10 years.

The U.S. music market is worth $12 billion. This is a turbulent market with stars exploding brilliantly one year and imploding into black holes the next. "The thing we need is a diva," notes Robert A. Daly of Warner Brothers.[123] Stars are needed who will shine as long as Elvis Presley and The Beatles. Young people today quickly zap from attraction to attraction. Add to this the risk in technology making bootlegging easier and easier. There is no excluding the possibility that the market for home music entertainment will evolve catastrophically within 10 years, if you can bootleg anything yourself or just snap it up from the Internet. There is, however, one segment of the music market whose future is not only secured, but will continue to grow: the grand-scale, outdoor rock and pop concerts. The Rolling Stones, U2, Spice Girls, Aqua—all these lavish corporations-on-the-go are champions of harnessing and staging emotions. Emotional jogging, that is. You might also call it neotribalism—the *neo-* prefix designates only its presence here and now; what actually makes the phenomenon different from traditional tribal rites is that it constitutes an "ad hoc tribalism." After the glitzy shebang, you change your clothes, remove your facial paint, and go back to the office; the tribal communality lasts only for the weekend. Besides, you can always switch tribes. When young people are getting acquainted with their own emotions, they need rituals to go along. We all crave to practice our feelings in the company of others—and this is something that will be increasingly encouraged by the Zeitgeist.

Transportation for kicks. As previously mentioned, cruise ships offer transportation devoid of purpose. The same is true of transportation by train. The *Orient Express* as well as trips with ordinary trains in Argentina, India, and Thailand will be supplemented by similar excursions. The great steam engines that crisscrossed the USA in the late 1800s will once again ply the prairie on romantic and sentimental journeys, not really carrying passengers to the trains' nominal destinations. Of course, the ideal remains a combination of an experience and a transportation need.

Do-It-Yourself Politics

The main portion of our time is spent in the two social circuits, the family and the company. However, many of us also spend time influencing society in a certain direction—be it in our local community or on a national scale. As the planet is increasingly perceived as a graspable and vulnerable, single platform for our life, interest in influencing global contexts has grown.

Many of us will become recreational politicians engaged in volunteer work. Involvement in local community welfare and affairs is rising, as is participation in grass-roots activities—all the things close around us are becoming more relevant. That goes for global affairs as well: the desire to save the endangered species—the tiger, the giant panda, and the whales; the ardent wish to salvage our climate from destruction by human activities. Both in North America and in Europe, local and global affairs are receiving increased attention, while national sentiment is waning. Not enough people turn up at the polls in the USA, and the number of political party members in Europe is plummeting. This may be due to the fact that the national level in particular is still encumbered by ideologies and ideas that most people consider outdated. The great era of the "-isms" seems to be over. They have more or less disappeared in the USA, but in Europe they still thrive among those who have chosen politics for a livelihood. Before returning to forecasts about leisure time spent influencing the public sphere, we need to take a look at the politics of the future in general: Who will be running the affluent countries?

Politics as we know it is on its way out. We have trouble believing in the great, impersonal ideologies with their rational logic and promises of happiness for all. They have no appeal to our brain—which will tell us that they usually do not deliver on their promises of happiness—nor do they appeal to our hearts. They belong to the time before the Dream Society.

The present calls out for politicians who address specific issues, and for politicians we may get to know not only as politicians, but as complete human beings—human beings with lives. We want to know what they are like when they step down from the pulpit; we want to know if they have a dog (yes, President Clinton has a dog) and how they pursue private pastimes. In this regard, American politicians are 10 years ahead of their counterparts in Europe and Japan. American politics is entering the Dream Society with a vengeance. In fact, the successful American political magazine *George* is built around the idea of the complete politician who can be viewed from every possible angle. "Not just politics as usual," reads the banner mission statement on the cover.[124] European politicians still try to keep their politics separate from their private lives. It's an artificial separation making it impossible to assess whether you can trust them—which, then, you increasingly don't. Trust—or specific issues—is what it all comes down to when ideologies can no longer make the blood rush.

In the Dream Society, we will need role models; for this purpose, politicians are a possibility. Others include the icons of art, entertainment, sports, and the media. All these will be in the business of courting popular adulation, and in 10 to 15 years we will probably witness how easily celebrities—the role models—move across different lines of business demarcation. This is possible precisely because they are role models whom we may trust, admire, or hate—people we can learn something from, something we can use in our own lives.

Who is going to chart the political course then—the domestic and foreign policies of a country? The short answer is that senior civil servants will take care of continuity, cohesion, and all the details that aren't actually political because there is a broad consensus about long-term goals. Politicians' dialogue with citizens is about specific issues or the emotional questions—filling in all the blanks left empty by the ideologies. Key issues include abortion, equal rights, human rights, genetic engineering/technology, and the overall debate about values—family values. Here we find the future role of the politician. Nontechnical, it requires politicians capable of speaking to our hearts, politicians who can smile as well as cry—perhaps even at the same time. The rational politician making "tough, but necessary decisions" is replaced by the politician who has principles she cares deeply about. As a result, politics may become more turbulent, less compromising, less consensus-minded, but more interactive and above all more democratic, because more engaged citizens will participate. This prediction about the politics of the future implies that developments already under way in the USA will spread to Europe. But it may also serve as a caveat to all those seeing politics as essentially a technical, matter-of-fact affair: watch out. Politics will not become more and more unprofessional; it will become more and more emotional, which is a horse of a different color.

Recreational politics evolves on a practical level with active participation. We can expect ever-increasing numbers to sign up for volunteer political work. According to a poll conducted by CNN/USA Today/Gallup, 65 percent of Americans have already done some volunteer work within the last year.[125] A small part of this work will be concerned with influencing opinions, but the major part will be practical in nature: helping to get tangible things done within the local community. People will be acting as political consumers, establishing, say, dwellings for the homeless. In short, citizens will be taking over a substantial number of tasks usually presumed under the obligation of the traditional welfare state. Likewise, the recreational politician will also be a political consumer, supporting (through purchases) companies that in turn support his or her causes of choice. You vote with your market trolley.

The theory about the "civilian society" is about citizens and companies laying down societal norms together, living according to these norms. The state is reduced to the size it had in the 1800s. We might also call this the society of responsibility—the type of society offering each citizen maximum responsibility for his or her life, as well as that of fellow citizens. Following years of massive educational effort and after the Information Society has broken the monopolies on knowledge, this might be a natural development. Knowledge and insight are now more equitably distributed, and regarding all the moral and ethical questions dominating politics in the future we are all—by definition—equal. Knowledge does not—or at least, should not—confer authority in questions involving morality.

Chapter 5

Universal Stories for Global Business

What will the global business environment look like in 10 to 20 years? The Theory of the Dream Society focuses on what is in store for the affluent countries, but these represent a minority of the world's population—slightly under 20 percent of the global population of 5.7 billion. We must turn our attention to the development of the less affluent countries—in particular, to the relations between these two economies. Once, contact between the populations of affluent and less affluent countries was limited; they literally lived worlds apart. But with the advent of modern media, notably television, this has changed. Increasingly, we will be kept apprised of how other people live; we will be aware of their values and lifestyles. What will this mean for the twenty-first century? Our forecast is globalization on the one hand—companies will increasingly be competing within an open, global market where local monopolies have vanished. On the other hand, the riches of the world are still very unevenly distributed, and so they will continue to be 20 years from now.

We will see a global encounter of cultures, and, above all, a juxtaposition of different value systems. The challenges that companies must face is to seize the global market emerging as a result, and be able to transcend cultural boundaries with their products. Those are the themes for this final chapter. What follows will provide conclusions regarding the future of the global community; then we will look at forecasts for selected driving forces. On this background, we will delineate the shape of things to come for Dream Society companies in the global economy of the twenty-first century.[126]

Overview

Global stories will conquer local stories. This means that there will be less variance in values and patterns of consumption—we will become more similar. That was one of the conclusions reached in Chapter 2. This analysis concerns the affluent countries; yet the forecast for the next 20 years is that the analysis will also become relevant for the entire world. It is estimated that today, 200 to 300 million people living in the big cities of less affluent countries nevertheless enjoy a standard of living comparable to that of the affluent countries. Global stories will reach the big cities of the world first, then they will spread to rural areas. We will see the rise of a global middle class—exposed to the same stories and adjusting its patterns of consumption accordingly. Just as jeans have replaced local traditions of apparel, so the rest of consumption will follow uniform trends, spurred by similar impulses. Cultural variations will remain; they cannot be eradicated from one year to the next, but there is no escaping the general drift: we will become more alike.

Global companies will hold center stage in the future. In the 1974 science fiction movie *Rollerball,* starring James Caan as Jonathan E., the large corporations rule politics and the economy; they have divided the planet up among themselves, and nation states have been made obsolete. This is a peaceful world with no wars— instead, sports let people blow off aggressive steam. In the film, Jonathan E. falls out with the sports managers because no one is supposed to grow more popular than the game itself. This chapter is built on a modified *Rollerball* scenario, in that it sees corporate-made stories, told through their products, as the replacement for obsolescent state ideologies. Large corporations are more in synch with the individualized, global future.

In the 1990s, the dormant megaeconomies—China, Russia, and the Ukraine—slowly arose to encounter the world economy, and in the rest of the world more and more trade barriers were lifted. We are approaching a situation where all restrictions fencing in the national economies have been done away with—where true world trade has become reality. Capital moves easier across borders than ever before. Along with ideologies, national economies presided over by governments are being consigned to the history books. Also, the role of the state has been reduced through privatizations, transferring many operational tasks from the public to the private sector. These tasks include telecommunications, postal services, rail and air transportation, research, utilities, health care, and banking. From an international point of view, we may note that many companies today boast more subsidiaries in foreign countries than their countries of origin have embassies.

The story about the state, however, still exists. This is what many young people are willing to risk their lives at war for. National symbolism strikes a powerful chord in our minds—stronger than the company. Try asking your colleagues whether they would die for their company. I tried asking around at CIFS—answers from colleagues were generally disappointing. The state as symbol, or story, will probably not disappear any time within the next century, but the state as institution and rule maker for economic activity is waning after having gained ground constantly throughout the twentieth century. Instead, we are witnessing how companies take over social tasks relinquished by the state.

The problem, however, remains global economic inequality. If we choose to say that the countries entering the Dream Society are those where an average citizen's standard of living has reached 60 percent or more of that of an American, then we are talking about 800 million out of a global population of 5.7 billion. Most are poor in comparison—more than 3 billion people make do with less than 10 percent of an average American's consumption. Never before have the riches of the world been so inequitably distributed as they are now that we stand at the threshold of the twenty-first century. However, growth statistics over the past decades indicate that this trend is reversing, and that inequality in the next century will be gradually reduced.

International trade helps reduce inequality and is currently expanding almost as rapidly as production, so today, 20 percent of the products and services we consume have crossed a national border. True, most of these represent affluent countries trading among themselves, but with China, India, Latin America, and Russia entering the fray as fellow players in the world economy, the pattern will change quickly. We are on our way toward a global economy where the greatest barriers are no longer regulatory, but cultural. Such cultural boundaries follow regional demarcation lines. A rough division might look like this:

1. The North Atlantic economies (North America and northern Europe), Australia, and New Zealand

2. The Latin, or Catholic, economies: Southern Europe and Latin America

3. Eastern Europe, Russia, and the Ukraine—the Eastern Orthodox countries

4. Countries in East Asia and South East Asia

5. The Muslim countries, from North Africa to Indonesia

6. The Hindu world—especially northern India

7. Africa—south of the Sahara Desert

These seven world regions could be said to constitute markets whose cultural borders need to be transcended by global corporations. Only problem: This way of parceling out the world's spheres of culture is not only very simplified, but misleading as well. In the first place, all the above regions contain large minorities; in the second, this carve-up does not take into account the massive cultural influence of entertainment, television, and products. This influence is strongest in the world's major cities—the cultural contrasts between big cities and rural areas in each individual region are often wider than variances between these regions. We are seeing the emergence of a global middle class, having just as much (or more) in common with people in the affluent countries as they may have with the rural population of their native region.

The global middle class is prospering along with the growth of the big cities; in fact, any general improvement in living standards always begins in big cities. On top of this, new income opportunities in less affluent countries are generally more abundant than in affluent ones. City dwellers are better educated; they are more prone to speak several languages and to partake of the metropolis' many cultural offerings. The battle for the global market of the twenty-first century will be won or lost in the world's big cities—both in affluent countries, where 75 percent typically live in the cities, as well as in the rapidly growing megacities of the less affluent countries.

Which stories will be victorious? In principle, there are many possibilities, but three stand out.

Each particular region will strengthen its unique features, its own history and values. This means that corporations with no roots in the region may find it difficult to market their products. Just as many Muslim countries have strengthened their own values and distanced themselves from other cultures, we may imagine that more regions will flourish culturally by stressing inherent values. In this scenario, world trade would stagnate and become regionalized.

The Asian countries, with their massive populations, powerful growth, and strong cultural traditions, will be able to sell the most goods and services across borders. Chinese, Japanese, and Korean design and history will experience a breakthrough in the affluent countries. Asian countries will become world trade leaders and constitute the prime trade partners for the other regions—including the North Atlantic. Just as Japan and Korea have experienced an economic miracle over the past 30 years, China will be the economic giant towering over the world market during the next 30 years—backed by a home market with more than 1 billion potential consumers.

The North Atlantic region will dominate world trade in the twenty-first century because this is the region whose companies excel in selling stories across cultural borders. In the Industrial Society, the leaders were Western Europe and later North America; in the Information Society, the USA is the present leader and this status could continue into the Dream

Society. Today's global brands are primarily American; the stories that prove most adept at crossing cultural borders are often from the USA. The fast-food establishments that have gained footholds in Moscow and Beijing are also American, as are the cigarettes, blue jeans, and movies that people demand in the big cities of less affluent countries. We may expect this self-reinforcing development to continue. The spread of English as the language of the Information Society has brought with it rising sales for products associated with the values that this language reflects.

Most credence seems to lie in the third possibility, that companies from affluent countries will win the battle, but there is no certainty. Yet these countries do have a head start compared with the others, for two major reasons:

1. English seems to have won as the leading international language, and many stories about products are sold along with that language. American corporations have been particularly successful in creating global stories.
2. The North Atlantic region is the richest today. Therefore, companies in this region have already been faced with Dream Society logic from their home markets. This gives them an advantage compared with companies in less affluent countries whose middle classes often model their lifestyles on the affluent countries' consumers.

As apparent from the discussion of communication later in this chapter, the outcome of the battle for the global market is very open-ended. The new information highways provide access to world markets for new companies and new ideas—access that was previously the prerogative of large corporations from the affluent countries. Once, export needed considerable backing in the form of capital to penetrate multiple countries: subsidiary companies had to be established, access for products had to be procured, and arrangements had to be made for shipping, distribution, and marketing. The new communication technologies will ease access to the global market. In the twenty-first century, the proverbial good idea will have better prospects than ever before—even in the absence of a large corporation with deep pockets backing it up. Progress will depend on those that can make it happen.

Setting the Stage for the Global Business Environment

Before the game can begin, we need a stage setting for the world market, complete with set pieces and a backdrop. The following seven subsections, keyed by their headings, describe the stage of the global business environment in the twenty-first century. They provide an overview of the driving forces, the factors that will redefine running a business. Together, these headings illustrate a world very different from the present, a dynamic world. This means there will be many losers and many winners. Doze off for a while, and you have fallen irreparably behind. The list of the world's Top 100 companies will look very different in 20 years' time.

Humankind Is Not an Endangered Species

We must look at population growth because, increasingly, companies of the future will offer goods and services to potential consumers worldwide—this is the kind of export market we are dealing with. For more and more corporations, the birth-rate statistics of China and Mexico are becoming highly pertinent. Keeping this perspective in mind may also keep us clear of the many prophets of gloom voicing concern in this area. For starters, we might note that we are actually moving past an explosion in world population—the greatest boom lies behind us, not ahead.

Ever since the first humans ventured out of Africa to populate the rest of our planet, and well into the nineteenth century, the world had to accommodate only a relatively modest number of people. There was ample space; cities were small and vast spaces were deserted. Humans remained more or less isolated from one another. In one community, members might live their entire lifetimes without interacting with their neighboring people. Nature with its plants and wildlife still ruled the world and the major continents were dominated by immense forest regions. In the year 1500, only 425 million people inhabited the earth, fewer than the number living in Latin America today.[127] In 1820, the first billion was reached—a doubling that took more the 300 years. Then population growth exploded, reaching its apex in the period from 1987 to 1999, where yet another billion was added in a mere 12 years. By the year 2000 we will have exceeded the 6 billion mark.[128] By 2020, 7 billion people will be treading on our dear old earth.

So to those concerned about the population explosion the answer is that, yes, we have had one, and it is becoming history—henceforth, the acceleration in population growth will diminish. We will still have growth for a couple of centuries to come—we are not an endangered species—but it is stabilizing and moving toward a rate of zero. World Bank demographic forecasts have world population at a stable figure slightly above 11 billion in the year 2150. Coming generations may subject this figure to scrutiny, but we will not be around to receive their criticism, if any.

The 1990s will always have a place in the history of humankind. This decade will be remembered as the period in which growth climaxed—an unprecedented, never-to-happen-again world population increase in a mere 10-year interval. Our era will also be remembered for indeed proving it possible to increase agricultural production so the many new mouths were actually fed. And that is not all. Since 1950, per capita agricultural production has risen as well—no mean feat, especially since arable land areas on earth have not grown significantly. Growth was made possible by increasing the yield of existing crop areas, thanks to improved fertilizing, among other things. As in previous centuries, we have not been able to escape hunger disasters in various parts of the world, but they have occurred as a result of inefficient distribution.

Conventional wisdom may debate or even quarrel over whether the earth will be able to feed 11 billion people. The one sure answer is that we cannot know for sure, but there is no red alert for the next 20 years. Not that this precludes surprises or regional problems, but a worldwide hunger disaster is just not imminent. It has already been mentioned: as far as population explosions are concerned, we have put the worst behind us.

Are these forecasts to be trusted? Yes. This is an area where we seem to be on solid ground, though it remains impossible to issue guarantees about the future. What makes the forecasts reliable is the fact that a close interrelationship pertains between the level of prosperity and population growth. The richer the country, the less the population rises. Cases in point: the Germans remain roughly the same number, while indigent Libya may expect to double its population during the next 20 years. These figures stem from the World Bank, which has hitherto prognosticated rather precisely on population growth within 10- to 20-year spans, both globally and in regard to individual countries. Only very long-term growth—within a 100-year horizon—has had to be readjusted—downward, by the way. The figures bespeak a world market growing at an annual 1.5 percent because of the rising number of consumers alone. On top of this, the market will grow as a result of the heightened standards of living, as dealt with below. The figures also predict that the densely populated countries will become even more so.

The population of China stands at 1.2 billion, meaning that one in every five human beings today lives in China, and that the world's most populous country has four and a half times as many citizens as the USA. The Chinese population continues to grow: the World Bank estimates that an additional 200 million people will live in China in 2020. The question remains whether it is possible to govern such an enormous country from a single capital, but modern means of communication and improved infrastructure increase the feasibility. India ranks second in population size. Today, there are 1 billion Indians—in the year 2020 this number will have risen to 1.2 billion. If this comparatively high demographic growth rate continues, India will surpass China as the most populous nation by the middle of the next century. India will face a similar, implicit threat: Can this vast country hold together or will it break up into a multitude of nations?

Population growth in the larger European countries is stagnating; the future will not greet many more Europeans. But there will be more Americans—50 million more, in fact, by 2020. Immigration is one of the reasons. Otherwise, growth is primarily a phenomenon occurring in very poor countries. Nigeria, which today has a population of 127 million, will have grown to almost 200 million by 2020. This places great demands on Nigerian production growth—it has to at least keep up with population growth in order to avoid a decline in the standard of living. Such a decline has in fact occurred in several African countries with a very high population growth.

World population growth happens—quite logically—because every year there is a surplus of births over deaths, 85 million to be precise. Each year, 135 million people are born, or 370,000 a day, or 256 a minute. Likewise, each year, 50 million people die; that's 137,000 a day, 5600 an hour, 95 each minute. Such figures may make for conversation in a lull, but they may also serve to illustrate how we are living on a densely populated planet and how the magnitude of joys and sorrows contained in just one single day, one minute even, is too awesome for us to comprehend. You need a poet to describe it.

The balance between affluent and less affluent countries will shift slightly, but within the present survey's time horizon of 20 years, that is of less importance. The global balance may very well look different in 20 years, but the reason will not be a surge in population. The reason will be urbanization and economic growth.

Average life expectancy in the less affluent countries is slightly above 60 years—10 years shorter than in the affluent countries. These demographics, however, hide significant variations from country to country. People living in Guinea-Bissau and Sierra Leone have the lowest median life expectancy (38 to 40 years); West Africa is one of the world's most indigent areas. Japan holds the world record in life expectancy—as high as 80 years, or 3 years longer than the USA.[129]

This leads us to another global dividing line: in the affluent countries there are many senior citizens, whereas in the less affluent countries there are many young people. While life expectancy keeps rising in the affluent countries, in the less affluent parts of the world 50 percent or more of the population will be under 25.

It is to be noted that by and large, experts do not disagree as to how much the world population will rise. However, there are very different projections as to how the growth will affect our global environment. It is unfortunate that such considerable controversy should rule among leading experts within this crucial area, if only because it creates confusion about finding the proper level of investment in environmental protection (see Chapter 3).

The Toil of Our Parents...[130]

This section is about projected economic growth and about the way the resultant bounty has historically been distributed among countries and groups of countries. The purpose is to provide a perspective for the discussion about the global economy of the future. The economy of the future is built on the knowledge and innovations of previous generations; thus we need a short overview of the economy of the past: Why, how, and how fast have we reached our present-day prosperity? This section is also necessary in order to pinpoint exactly why we can still count on economic growth and the presence of vibrant economies. The reason we speak of future growth as a likelihood of near certainty is that increasing prosperity constitutes a fundamental fact, not merely a possibility. At least, economic history teaches us that the world has enjoyed constant economic growth since 1820, even measured in per capita terms. There is no reason to anticipate long-term stagnation or recession.

The high peak, or golden age, of global economic prosperity happened from 1950 to 1973. Therefore, for those of us who are middle-aged, thanks are due to our parents; they have been industrious and competent. The second highest peak was reached in the period between the American Civil War and World War I (1870 to 1913). This was the period in which two countries in particular, the United States and Germany, created their industrial breakthroughs. The period third in position for generating growth lies close to our present, from 1973 to 1992.[131] The present-day workforce is pretty industrious as well, and there is certainly no discernible trend toward declining global growth. On the contrary, a yearly growth rate of 3 to 4 percent is the most likely prospect.

Prior to 1820, growth was more random, prone to swerves both up and down; there was no clear growth pattern. The global level of prosperity experienced by an individual in the year 1500 has been calculated at $525; it makes little difference whether this medieval person was living in Europe, in America, or in China. Global riches, or rags, were much more evenly distributed then. By 1820, the per capita GDP had only risen to $651, probably too minuscule an increase for any specific generation to have experienced life as marked by prosperity—static societies still ruled the world. After 1820, the industrial revolution set in, fueling the wave of growth and change that we are still riding. From 1820 until 1992, we had an octupling of prosperity per capita (and a quintupling of the earth's population)—meaning that this was when the really dynamic period in world economic history began.

As previously mentioned, our prosperity owes much to technology and to the increased division of labor. Increasingly, products are being made in the most cost-efficient places. This was made possible by more efficient means of transportation like trains and steamers as well as by tariff reductions. Effective tariff rates, measured as tariff revenue share of the value of the flow of goods, has fallen from a level of 15 percent in 1880 to 2 percent today.[132] The change should be viewed in relation to the growth in world trade from $7 billion in 1820 to $3786 billion in 1992—a 540-fold increase.

Global inequality also began to set in after 1820. The pattern was this: Countries having a sound economy in 1820 improved theirs even more, while countries less well-off at the time only gained insignificant ground. The affluent countries back then are also the affluent countries today, with only a few exceptions.

Together, North America, Australia, and New Zealand were the economic top scorers of the period, increasing per capita prosperity by a factor of 17. Prosperity in Western Europe saw a 13-fold increase, while Latin America improved prosperity only by a factor of 7. During the period in question, Africa had the smallest growth and—with all the provisos inherent in comparing economies from different ages and areas—by 1992, Africa had reached only the level that prevailed in Western Europe in 1820.

Looking at individual countries, Japan holds the world record in economic growth during the period from 1820 to 1992, increasing prosperity by a factor of 28. Likewise, in the period after 1950, the highest growth rates were achieved by countries in the Far East: Korea, Taiwan, Singapore, and Thailand.

All this spells ever-increasing inequality—the gap between rich and poor widens until 1950. Then, there is a change and inequalities are reduced as most regions begin to gain on Western Europe and North America. This, of course, is particularly true of the Far East, but also of Southern Europe. The answer to the crucial question about when the present trends may betoken a rough economic equality between the world's regions is that this will not occur until after the year 2100—with the exception of the Far East. Inequalities between the affluent countries and Africa are too vast, and it seems impossible for countries and regions to perform instant "quantum leaps" that drastically change their position within the global hierarchy of prosperity. This conclusion, culled from studies covering economies since 1820, may not necessarily be valid for the future, but the pattern does seem likely to continue.

Much has been said about China's economy surpassing that of the United States, thus becoming the world's largest. Using the World Bank's traditional forecasting tools, China's GDP in dollars comprises only 10 percent of the United States', and even supposing a yearly growth rate in China of 10 percent (meaning China would have to double its economy every seven years) and an American growth rate of 3 percent, it would still take China 50 years to become the world's economic leader. However, a newer method, making greater allowance for differences in purchasing power in the two countries, gives a very different result. China will surpass the USA as early as 2011. When doubling an economy every seven years, your initial parameters will determine the outcome.

Candidates for the Dream Society

When the average income of a country reaches about $11,000 per capita, measured in purchasing power, the World Bank considers it a high-income country, though there is still a long way to the American level of $27,000 or the European level of $21,000. By this reckoning, there are 25 high-income countries with a total population of 800 million—together, they constitute the countries that are on their way to the Dream Society. Not in the sense that consumption patterns of entire populations will change logic, but in the sense that Dream Society products will gain a mass market in the countries concerned. Income inequality means that all countries possess well-to-do upper or middle classes whose consumers resemble those of the affluent countries: an impending mass market. Let us take a look a the candidate countries.

The countries expected to reach the $11,000 per capita level around the year 2000 are Chile and the Czech Republic. Bearing in mind that households will often involve two incomes, these economies will offer the possibility of acquiring a car, durable consumer goods, and home insurance—as well as making trips abroad. More than previously, kids will have the opportunity of getting a higher education, possibly abroad. People will have knowledge of foreign languages and other cultures. No longer just a struggle to keep hunger at bay, life will mean the possibility of saving and purchasing for other reasons than the purely materialistic ones. For instance, ecologic foodstuffs and, not unimportantly, well-known brands will play a role in consumption—not the most prominent role, but they will be visible.

Between 2000 and 2005, the high-income candidates are Argentina, Malaysia, and Thailand—provided they sustain an annual growth of 4 to 5 percent, which is not unrealistic. Uncertainty arises from difficulty in determining comparative economic levels today. We need answers to questions such as these: What is the purchasing power of an average household in Argentina as compared, say, with Hungary? Since prices and wages are different, how much can people afford to buy? Also, there will typically be significant variations from cities to rural areas—in the latter, payments in kind will often constitute part of consumption, and in the cities we must take high housing costs into account. Answers to these questions will be sought through local analyses.

The next group consists of Hungary, Mexico, Panama, and Colombia. With four Latin American spearheads, South America will become the next high-income area—according to the definition above. Several countries in the Far East and Eastern Europe will follow suit.

Keeping in mind the rising degree of uncertainty, we can expect that, between 2010 and 2020, countries like South Africa, Russia, Poland, and Turkey will join the high-income category. These are big countries with large populations whose economies will have "matured" and whose citizens therefore often will have "money to spare." Of course, countries of this size already possess a well-to-do middle class. We will return to this question in the following section.

Still according to the above definition, China and India could become high-income countries after the year 2020. It could also happen much later; of interest in this context is the fact that it is unlikely to occur much sooner. So a mass market, say, for cars is not just around the corner in these two countries—and together they do account for one-third of the world's entire population. Of course, this is true only if we view these countries as collective markets and do not see them as separate regions. Certain regions and urban areas in the two countries will have a high-income populace long before the year 2020, but international statistics break down numbers into national states, not regions.

An overview of candidate countries will reveal that Russia joins the high-income group somewhere beyond 2013. Just as an annual growth rate of 4 to 5 percent is a reasonable assumption, we may assume that the Russian economy will begin to grow after the long transition following the fall of communism. This is important, since at this time, Russia and Europe taken together will make up the largest contiguous high-income area in the world—larger, though not richer, than North America. An educated guess regarding the period from 2010 to 2020 has globally oriented companies concentrating on two main areas—North America and Europe/Russia—followed by Latin America and China. That is the order, if we are talking about products aimed at per capita incomes of around $11,000. If Russia is not seen as the great country of opportunity today, this is because the transition to a market economy is not yet completed; but Russia is close and within a year or two will probably be an area of high growth. The figures also show that Russia will be the first country to boast a large market of relatively well-heeled consumers. China comes in second, at least 10 years later. Consequently, it is quite obvious to focus your eyes on Russia rather than China—depending, of course, on the products you are selling. India will not be a high-income economy until 2040, and will thus be a less affluent country for some time to come.

The African countries south of the Sahara, presently among the least affluent on earth, will remain poor, perhaps for the greater part of the twenty-first century. Such a long-term guess is, however, very speculative. These countries will probably prosper through the product that will be very sought after in the Dream Society: storytelling. Along with African nature and wildlife, African myths and legends, lifestyles, and rituals may become the reason that the above highly pessimistic forecast turns out to be wrong. Just as a century ago Germany increased its affluence by marketing its industrial revolution, in the next century the African nations may sell their culture and natural splendor to the rest of the world, thus creating a new economy with rapidly growing prosperity.

The Middle Classes Turn Global

We have excellent figures showing which nations are affluent and which are less affluent. The situation is different when it comes to internationally commensurable figures for the distribution of wealth within national borders. In statistics showing income distribution in different countries, the World Bank points out that international surveys in this field are uncertain. There is, however, a discernible pattern. In less affluent countries, the differences between classes are greater than in affluent countries. This is due to the presence of large rural populations living very traditional lives on the one hand, and a population of workers and white-collar city dwellers with incomes many times higher on the other. Furthermore, there is often greater inequality in a large country with many inhabitants than in a small one with fewer.

A rule of thumb has it that in the affluent countries, the wealthiest 10 percent earn between 20 and 25 percent of total income—or slightly more than twice the nation's average income. Among affluent countries, Sweden has the most balanced distribution of wealth; here, the wealthiest 10 percent earn 20.8 percent of total income. At the other end of this scale, Switzerland is the rich country with the most uneven distribution of income; the wealthiest 10 percent earn nearly 30 percent of the aggregate income.

Frequently, in the less affluent countries, the richest 10 percent earn between 30 and 40 percent of all income—or more. In Brazil, the richest 10 percent earn five times the national average, and, viewed from an international perspective, most Latin American nations have huge gaps between the classes. This imbalance makes not only the national level of income important, but domestic income distribution relevant as well if we are to describe the global middle class. As mentioned, this class is predominantly to be found in the large cities. Exactly how big is it?

Poland is a less affluent country with an average per capita income of $5400. However, if we take population size and income distribution into account, we find that 4 million Poles have an income equivalent to EU levels. This means that there is a middle class roughly the size of, say, Denmark's; as a consequence, the same types of products sold in affluent countries may in fact be marketed here. The Czech Republic has a similar middle class of over 1 million people.

The same method of calculating inequality and demographics reveals 5 million Mexicans with income levels at a par with citizens of the USA—regardless of the fact that the average Mexican makes only one-fourth of the average American. In China, where the average income is $2920, there are still about 100 million Chinese this affluent; the Indian figure lies in the neighborhood of 50 million. Globally, that gives us 200 to 300 million people in less affluent countries who actually have incomes comparable to the average in affluent countries. The result is a rich, worldwide populace of slightly more than 1 billion people. As mentioned, the global middle classes live in cities—no matter which part of the world they live in.

Needless to say, patterns of consumption, household size, and social needs are not the same for the global middle classes everywhere, and these may vary even for those living in temperate climates. Significant cultural and religious differences remain in the different regions, but in the big cities, we see a leveling out of these differences. Modern architecture dominating inner cities shows little variation the world over; the makes and designs of cars filling the streets of the affluent countries are the same as in the less affluent countries.

Airports and hotels reflect local culture only to a modest degree, and a number of global retail chains are in the process of eliminating the spirit of place. A gigantic meeting of cultures is taking place in the big cities of the world. Nowadays, everything is coalescing into a vast cultural melting pot—and local and traditional values are clashing with modern, Western ones. It looks like the latter values are winning the first round, but the fight will continue through an endless number of rounds.

From Village to Megacity

In a village you will meet only few other people, almost all of whom you know. This means that traditions are upheld and doing things the way they have always been done comes natural—children learn from their parents. The village nurtures a community spirit, but it does not incite changes. Cities, on the other hand, do just that. Here you meet thousands of people every day, people with backgrounds and lifestyles different from your own. Stores advertising their special offers, theaters, museums, universities, newspapers, magazines—everywhere, the messages conveyed to the city dweller herald the possibility of change. Because of the vast and very blatant differences in income, the city also trumpets the chance of becoming rich, the chance of improving your standard of living. The village is static, the city is dynamic.

In the affluent countries, 75 percent of the population live in cities and this number has been stable since 1980. So we will not see a massive rise in the big-city populations of Europe and North America in the coming 10 to 20 years. The opposite is the case in less affluent countries. Here, the depopulation of rural areas is far from over. Today 29 percent of the world's neediest live in the cities of the less affluent countries; by 2025 this share may well have risen to 45 percent. In absolute numbers this means that the city populations in less affluent countries alone will rise from 920 million to 2277 million—a growth of 247 percent. The explosive growth constitutes one of the major challenges facing us in the twenty-first century. It means that additional housing, schools, roads, water and electricity supplies—as well as garbage disposal and sewage—will be needed.

Around 2020—or most likely before—more than half the global population will live in cities—today that share has reached 45 percent. This means a momentous transition from a world in which the majority lives in rural, static communities, to one in which the majority lives in the more vibrant urban centers. It marks a transformation from an era where the majority has a daily experience of nature and steps on the naked earth to a new era where the majority catches only an occasional glimpse of nature and walks on concrete and asphalt. Our day-to-day experience of existence will change completely. This is one of the transformations that will be highlighted when a global history of the years around 2000 is written—even if it is in a history book written in the year 4998.

Today, 16 percent of affluent countries' populations dwell in one-million-plus cities, and this share is growing, since the giant metropolises are attracting more people than smaller cities. We relocate from smaller cities to bigger ones. This is an important point, because the spectrum of attractions becomes even wider as cities expand, and these attractions are what invite still more people. We offer lip service to small, close-knit communities, but our actions (and actions are what create facts) show that we prefer the largest communities possible. The reason is self-evident. Very large cities offer more specialized stores, more theaters, concert halls, and discotheques, more and bigger museums, and more specialized restaurants. London, for instance, has a secondhand bookstore that sells only books about voyages of discovery outside Europe.[133] This degree of specialization is viable only in a city with 10 million inhabitants and lots of tourists. The big city makes it possible for 10,000 lifestyles to develop side by side, with people gathering inspiration for change and innovation from watching one another in the streets. New ideas and trends grow and spread easily in the cities.

Only 3 of the 10 largest megacities are to be found in the affluent parts of the world (Tokyo, New York City, and Los Angeles). Tokyo is considered the largest, at 27 million inhabitants. Mexico City ranks second-largest at 17 million.[134] Rounding out the Top 10 with 12 million inhabitants is Seoul, Korea. Can we expect to see 10 to 15 cities with 30 to 40 million inhabitants each in 2020, and many with more than 10 million? Yes, if current rates of development continue, as they may well do. It is, to be sure, difficult to imagine behemoth cities with populations equal to that of Argentina, but we probably need to try. After all, the greater Tokyo area has already reached the 30 million mark.

In 2025, world population will have reached 8 billion, and if we imagine 4 billion of us living in cities, we may glimpse a blueprint of the future. A sizable portion of these 4 billion, of course, will be poor people inhabiting the slums of the less affluent countries' metropolises, but an equally large portion will constitute the new middle class—those keeping abreast of developments outside their own country, those who can afford a communicator (see the section on communication below). They will watch TV produced in other countries, and they will buy products through the Infobahn. Presumably, they will have cars and credit cards and they will, as a matter of course, be able to speak and read

English. The incipient world market may be described from many angles, but the middle class—on which everything is built—will overwhelmingly choose to live in cities. Again, the reason is that cities provide the most potent and abundant flow of outside influences and impulses.

These are the megacities in which large, globally oriented retail chains will open their stores, restaurants, hotels, showrooms, and miniature theme parks. This is where the fight for the future consumer is lost or won. Also, this is where the fight for our minds is settled—where it will be determined whether the stories from North America, Europe, the Far East, or somewhere else will win hearts and thus customers. Here the greatest part of investments in infrastructure—roads, streets, and public transportation—will be needed as well: the construction of subways, the building of airports; traffic regulation, and maybe even bicycle paths. Here we will also find the political centers. The interests of big cities will top decision makers' lists in less affluent countries, if only because the majority of the population lives there.

Tourism to the great cities will be an even larger industry than today. When the middle classes of China and India can afford to visit major cities of Japan, the USA, and Europe—when droves of people from the affluent countries start going on big-city holidays to Beijing and New Delhi—they will stop to shop. Most important, perhaps, a meeting of cultures will occur, creating a heightened awareness of inequalities and differences. All these changes mean a deeper understanding that there may be many sides to the truth in the essential life questions.

Big conferences and a number of books[135] have dealt with the specific difficulties confronting big cities in less affluent countries. Can growth in these urban behemoths be managed at all, or will we see them become mired in a pandemonium of pollution, disease, and crime? Publications seem preponderantly pessimistic. One reason is the sheer vastness of waste problems. In a city with 30 million dwellers, between 30,000 and 50,000 tons of household refuse needs disposing every day, while a similar amount of foodstuffs must be delivered to the megalopolis by truck or train. We have no way of knowing for sure whether these teeming cities will function better or worse than today. Presumably, we will witness a situation more or less like the present—many big cities will in fact adapt to high growth, while other cities will suffer the occasional breakdown of utilities and supplies. It is certainly no law of nature that cities of the future will be almost uninhabitable. It does, however, seem close to a law of nature that humans will rise to almost any challenge—and seek to solve problems as they arise.

Seize the Global Market!

There are seven reasons that the twentieth century can be described as the century of communication: radio, television, newspapers, phones, computers, cars, and planes. These seven contraptions have spread all over the globe and are the main reason we can speak of the planet as having shrunk. As for the one means of communication coming closest to utter global penetration—the one medium that most strongly knits the people of the world together—we would have to name television, despite the fact that it did not become widespread until the second half of the twentieth century. In the affluent countries, practically everybody has one or several TV sets, but the less affluent countries have their share of sets as well. In China, there are 252 TV sets for every 1000 people, or about one set for each household. In Brazil, this figure is 289; in Argentina, 347; and in Russia, 386.[136] The people of the world unite in front of the TV set.

On the global scale, phones are not as ubiquitous. In the two great countries of China and India, only 34 and 13, respectively, out of every 1000 individuals own a phone. Cell phones will provide the solution for many less affluent countries, changing these figures dramatically within the next 10 years. In terms of international telecommunications, however, the affluent countries will continue to dominate. In 1995, Europe and North America as a whole consumed 70 percent of the world's international telecommunication minutes.[137]

World newspaper circulation is a similar matter; newspapers are not widely distributed in the less affluent countries. Information carrying wider significance than what stems from the immediate community arrives through television. Spoken media, and particularly the visual medium, have the added advantage of transcending illiteracy. This is important, considering the fact that today 25 percent of the adult population in the less affluent countries cannot read or write.[138]

In the affluent countries, statistics covering computer sales are tallied almost monthly because the rapid development rate means that last year's figures are of practically no value. Worldwide statistics, however, can be completed only with a relatively large delay factor. Yet even with figures that are not quite up to date, one unequivocable conclusion can be reached: Everyone in the affluent countries will soon own a computer, but the less affluent countries still have a long way to go. In China and India, only 10 of every 1000 people have a computer.

Figures for now indicate a stable and continuous development toward a truly global state of communication with access to information and dialogue for everybody. The notion of stable development will be advantageous in most areas—for example, cars where technological advances move ahead at the pace of a few percent a year. The affluent countries' collective fleet of cars will be approaching 500 million or more as prosperity keeps growing; but then, that's it. The same does not apply in computer technology and electronics, where productivity for the past many years has doubled every 18 months. Sales projections from the 1970s regarding computers in the 1990s completely missed the mark, because the developments in productivity were underestimated. Besides, these projections did not even include the personal computer, which as yet was uninvented. Similarly, communications projections will have to include ideas for hitherto unthought-of products and surprising technological advances in order to get a precise grip on the future.

Digitized communication will girdle the globe completely within a decade or two. The world Infobahn will extend to every household's doorstep, and inside too. The much-touted comparison to highway systems is appropriate, and quite illustrative. Today, each household has (perhaps) only a single, dingy garden path leading into its home. The path will allow you to speak on the phone, view a certain number of channels on TV, and maybe wander the Internet. Still it remains but a garden path compared with future prospects. The reason lies in the digitizing of the "info-cars" cruising the highways. In the future, billions of cars will be able to pass through your living room—not just the few constituting today's traffic.

This road system, built from cables and satellites, will permit each household to receive thousands of interactive TV channels, creating a global marketplace for products and ideas. At the same time, the TV set, the computer, and the phone will merge into a single communicator offering users contact with the whole world. The Internet is intensely "private"; nobody owns it and everyone may emit and receive information. In a similar sense, we will witness a "privatization" of the world's telecommunications and television corporations. Monopolies will be broken and replaced by a wide-open, global market. The result will be an entirely new ball game. The consequences of privatization are difficult to assess, but let us try.

Global home shopping seems one incontrovertible result. Featured will be those products and services most eminently suited to being sold on the digital highways: information and education. Next come all those products that are overpriced in relation to their weight. Costs of sending these goods halfway around the world will be within reason. The appearance of giant virtual bookstores has been mentioned in Chapter 4, but the new perspectives really arise when you start asking yourself: "Can we transform our physical product so it may be sold without transportation costs?" (And the time for asking this question happens to be right now.) The digital Lego block, the digital Barbie doll, like books and entertainment, are possibilities that readily suggest themselves and are becoming reality. Travels are another option. The virtual voyage to Siberia may in fact be preferable to the real thing, at least the first time around. In many companies, R&D departments will be donning their "thinking caps"—a good and timely idea may be worth millions.

Television's one-way, monopolizing type of mass communication is being replaced by digital highways where there is ample room for everyone. All may go exactly where they want—at the exact moment they want—and with nobody interfering with their pursuits. Besides, they can be in constant dialogue with a great number of interlocutors. Unlike the gridlocked physical highways, the digital superhighways have plenty of room. There is one rule of the road, though, one that nobody will presumably be opposed to, and that is the language: English. For all those not conversant in this language there will be software to take care of translating into their own native languages. So we may be looking at an Egyptian maintaining contact with the entire world from her village. She may purchase goods, education, news, and entertainment. Most Egyptians are poor, and will continue to be so for many years to come. Therefore, we have to ask the price of the communicator. No one knows, but given mass-production advantages and the aforementioned technological advances, it may well become a realistic option even for people with only 10 percent of the affluent countries' standard of living.

Today physical distance is what determines who we know and who our friends and acquaintances are. Gradually, the confines of our geographical prison will break down; planes, high-speed trains, and cars will increase our cruise range. If we happen to be interested in tropical butterflies, however, these means of transportation will not help us find like-minded lepidopterists elsewhere on our planet. On the spacious digital superhighways, this will be easier. In the coming 10 years we will see "cybernations" evolving—people sharing an interest, exchanging information, and possibly arranging to meet with one another. It will happen on a global basis and provide the distant village dweller with the opportunity to make contact with any person, anywhere in the world, whose passionate interest is also tropical butterflies. Companies selling products to people with an interest in tropical butterflies will be able to assess their global market.

Flat-earthers will be able to form a cybernation of their own, and those who are worried about how their own culture can possibly survive in this frontierless world—well, they too will be able to meet and debate their shared anxieties. We may also see the birth of a Scots cybernation populated by most of those living in Scotland, but with the addition of many more having roots there. Ireland will have a similar chance of creating a cybernation larger than the Hibernian isle itself. The threat thus posed to the traditional formation of states, with their physical borders, is obvious.

The many religious minorities of the world will be given an opportunity to feel less isolated. At the same time, competition will be stiffer—we will see a global supermarket of religions, a full-fare smorgasbord of ideas and values operating outside the old religious organizations. Along with the universities of Europe, the different religions are among the oldest organizations boasting continuous traditions—some of them have been around for millennia. The twenty-first century may constitute the biggest threat yet to their existence, greater than the wars.

War Without Soldiers?

We must consider what could cause potential conflicts and how wars may be fought in the twenty-first century, for the simple reason that wars have always occurred. Lamentably, nothing indicates that human nature will suddenly change, replacing wars with conferences and dialogue. But in the Dream Society, wars may progress differently, and the values fought over may be different ones.

In the agricultural societies, wars were about particular values—land, forests, fields, and crops—and about maintaining control over the peasants who produced things of value. Peasants were useful for harvesting crops as well as soldiering. For centuries, wars were fought as a result, and the king or feudal lord who had the most land was also the most powerful. From a modern point of view, Napoleon's world seems simple; his war objectives were easy to determine.

Twentieth-century wars were defined by industrial society. The outcome of World War I, and of World War II in particular, was determined by combatants' industrial output, and their objectives were chiefly to take out the opponents' industrial centers. Nazi Germany had lost the war the minute the Ruhr and Essen could no longer deliver and there was no longer gasoline for transportation or factories to build planes and tanks.

The Information Society has fought only one major war—the Gulf War in the beginning of the 1990s. This war was won by computer technology and communication; the opponent possessing the most information and capable of manipulating it in the most skillful manner was the victor. In all probability, the wars of the coming decades will develop according to a similar logic. So we are now far removed from the Napoleonic world view, facing a situation where nations with access to advanced electronic equipment are the ones that should be feared the most by potential adversaries. The Gulf War was primarily about material values—namely, control over the vast oil reserves in Kuwait and northeastern Saudi Arabia. World production and transportation are based on fossil fuels; thus access to the carbonic pool is crucial. This situation will continue, probably until the mid-twenty-first century.

So much for an historical background on which to view wars in the Dream Society. Following our theory's logic, wars will be about access to nonmaterial values—to attitudes, to feelings. Maybe these conflicts have already begun to rise, given the rich countries' increased insistence on human rights and democracy. These are notions centering on systems of government and freedom of expression. As far as the conflict in former Yugoslavia is concerned, power over television channels is important and it is conceivable that the key to the solution of this conflict may lie precisely in making sure that the "proper" attitudes are relayed to the populace. That is why the North Atlantic Council authorized NATO peacekeepers in Bosnia to take all actions necessary to "suspend or curtail programming that is hostile to the spirit of the Dayton accords."[139] Subsequently, radio and television stations have in fact been subjected to such suspension and curtailment. In the bloody Rwandan war there was a widespread understanding that jamming the radio programs exhorting people to take up arms would have checked or stopped the carnage and bloodshed.[140]

As noted above, the future of communication means an end to state-held information monopolies. The fusion of computers and TV sets into interactive communicators not subject to state censorship means the definitive end to any such national information monopolies. This will not happen from one year to the next, though; and a number of nations will believe that the state can survive only as long as it is able to control or influence the opinions disseminated among its citizenry. Here we may have the seeds of several conflicts and potential wars: civil wars where national opposition factions demand leverage regarding the news flow; international wars where one country demands the right to relay its own information to citizens of another country. In the long run, digitizing the information flow will lead to freedom of information and freedom of speech, but in the coming 10 to 15 years, latent conflicts will be mounting.

Today only a few of the world's countries can lay claim to having freedom of speech, and many countries will be facing a considerable challenge as technology confers freedom of speech irrespective of state authorities. After all, this is a question not only of access to different sides of an issue, but of allowing the dissemination of various ideologies—including those extolling the use of violence to groups large and small—and inciting revolt against the state itself. The conflicts in Bosnia and Rwanda were about stopping the forces calling for violence. Another goal will be to ensure that many views are represented, that the information flow is not one-sided.

If conflicts arose only between nations and local factions, the problem might be manageable, but the fact that, in principle, everybody—be they citizens, companies, or global organizations—has access to info-expressways makes wars and conflict seem almost inevitable. Grass-roots organizations direct-mailing every Chinese citizen with their views on how the world and the Chinese government in particular should behave are playing an entirely different game from the USA expounding on its human rights positions in negotiations with Chinese government officials. We cannot rule out the possibility that 10 to 15 years from now, many will find it regrettable that every single citizen has access to making his or her views known to the entire planet. The result will not only be peace messages; there will be calls for violence and upheaval as well. This could quite possibly be the section turning out to have most relevance for international

216

affairs in 2020—not necessarily because the book's forecasts turn out to be right, but because the issues raised here will be the ones preoccupying leaders of the world community.

Experience teaches us how difficult it is to predict the sequence of events in the next war. Technology will have changed and with it ways and means of victory versus defeat. So this is where we stand as to forecasting the wars of the twenty-first century. We may conjecture and marshal the various parameters, yet we still face considerable uncertainty. The great wars of the twentieth century have been exceedingly bloody and have victimized innocent civilians to a far greater extent than those fought in the 1800s. Dream Society wars, on the other hand, cannot be expected to focus on front lines and battlefields—military technology as such will not be the decisive factor. What is at stake is who gets to use the information highways leading to individual citizens. By its nature, this battle need not be a blood-and-guts conflict, or one involving lots of people. It may well be violent, but the violence will be of the sort that police have the monopoly on exercising.

A wish may develop to outlaw organizations urging the use of violence or violating various perceptions of the human rights concept. You cannot prevent these messages from being sent, but you may track down the people sending the missives. Such may be a typical twenty-first century police task, far removed from the traditional definition of war. Companies will be major consumers of information highways; they require attention for their products and therefore will want these conduits to be as wide and as wide open as possible. But they also want a peaceful world where messages that may threaten this peace are not allowed.

Do We Want to Postpone the Dream Society?

If they are tenable, some of the more gloomy prognostications for the state of our planet even within a short time span would seem to warrant that the Dream Society should be postponed or even canceled. While experts round the world may debate scientific details, they are—by and large—of one mind as to the future of our planet. Not so when environmental problems are on the agenda; here, disagreement reaches near-religious proportions, and this detail just happens to concern the future of all humankind. On the one hand, we have the "prophets of doom" (the quotation marks indicate that this is the moniker used by adversaries, not by this author) such as the director of Worldwatch Institute, Lester R. Brown. The blurb on the back of the 1997 edition of *State of the World* reads as follows: "...if these trends continue unabated, the pressure on the earth's natural limits will undermine food security....Indeed, food scarcity may be the first economic manifestation of our environmentally unsustainable global economy."[141]

On the other hand, we have the "irresponsible optimists" (same use of quotation marks as above). Among these are Gregg Easterbrook, who writes in the conclusion to his 1995 book *A Moment on the Earth*: "Not all that far into the future—perhaps within the lifetimes of the children of those who read this book—the biosphere of Earth will have become once again pure and pacific and yet stronger than it was before intellect, befitting from the thinking ape's rise from brute force to cautious wisdom."[142]

The same basic data may lead to diametrically opposed conclusions. Let us once again resort to the past for clarification. In Great Britain during the 1880s there were widespread fears that British coal reserves would be gone within a few decades.[143] People were well aware that there was lots of coal left in Australia and China, but the idea of being dependent on your colonies was unpleasant. This problem, however, took care of itself when the world switched to oil for its transportation and heating needs. Similar forecasts, dating from the 1970s, as to when the world will run out of oil could also be used as an argument that the "prophets of doom" are barking up the wrong tree. Oil reserves today are no less plentiful than previously—thanks to new finds— and more have become economically viable as a result of improved technology. When the Club of Rome published its famous report *The Limits to Growth*[144] the year before the grave oil crisis of 1973, the first serious doubts about the future started. The report had grave tidings about the imminent depletion of the earth's resources—we were to run out of gold in 2001 (today the date has been put off until the middle of the next century). The report was alarmist and added extra momentum to the ongoing environment discussion.

History has taught us the lesson that things never go as bad as we think they will; new technology tends to solve problems, and people are capable of dealing with threatening situations in a rational manner. The only problem is that we don't live in history; we live in the present. In earlier times, environmental disasters were local phenomena. A famous example is the Easter Islands off the coast of Chile. Here, the indigenous people—without knowing it before it was too late—made their soil barren through a ruthless deforestation. Some historians believe all these trees were cut down because islanders needed the trunks for moving their large, incredibly heavy statues from the quarries to the shore.[145]In our present day and age—and particularly in the future—environmental disasters may well be global. Caution, therefore, is more important than ever. We do not know the laws governing nature as well as we do our human-made laws—despite the fact that violation of certain natural laws gets you the death penalty, without the right of appeal. Yet this is exactly what the world community humbly acknowledges today. A large majority of responsible politicians in the world take the environment seriously and are ready to invest in cleaning it up. Environmentalists may turn out to be wrong after all, precisely because they pointed out the problems and because they were listened to while there was still time.

Correspondingly, nearly all companies in the affluent countries have turned their attention to their own production processes; most of them even prefer to keep a couple of steps ahead of the minimal requirements set by legislation—and they do so because they are courting an environment-conscious consumer.

We do not know for sure whether we will be facing an environmental disaster—or several. Scientific research cannot provide us with a clear and unambiguous answer to, say, the question of global warming. There is no excluding the possibility that after a century of technology and optimism, we are now moving into a century where nature will rule, full of threats and pessimism. The jury is still out and it could be some time before it returns with a verdict on our future: Are we guilty of having destroyed our planet or will we be acquitted? We don't know. So it would be a chipper author who simply ruled out the possibility that the Dream Society will be postponed or canceled. Like the reader, I would prefer the vision of the future presented by this book to turn out to be wholesome truth.

The Global Business

We still need to cultivate the land and produce goods. Even in 2020, agriculture will account for the major part of jobs here on earth. Some 35 to 40 percent of the workforce will have to provide food for everyone else; this figure is 10 to 15 percent lower than it is today. These farmers will predominantly work in the less affluent countries: in India, China, and Africa. In the affluent countries, agricultural production will be almost fully automated.

The production of goods will probably still move from affluent countries with high wages and high basic costs to countries where costs are lower. Sometimes it may prove expedient to place the modern, automated factories in proximity of the markets where the products are sold, but the overall picture is that the industrial areas of the world will have moved to countries like China and India by 2020. This is where the world's steel will be produced, as will ships, and a major portion of the world's consumer electronics and clothing. World trade—measured in tons—will have moved to Asia. This will mean layoffs for the affluent countries, but Dream Society theory stipulates that new jobs will be created to replace those lost—so we will not see mass unemployment in the affluent countries because of the new economic structure regarding physical production.

More accurately phrased, the affluent countries will hold on to jobs as well as growth, if they understand the Dream Society and the need for storytelling that develops when more basic needs have been satisfied. This is not a given thing. As already mentioned, however, companies in affluent countries have the best possible head start, since their domestic markets have already begun to seek out stories. Branded products today originate in affluent countries, and are then spread to the global middle classes in affluent as well as in less affluent countries.

The market for love and friendship, as well as secure family life, is in excess of 1 billion people. The market is not just about single products; we are talking about stories that—in principle—may be sold in connection with any product whatsoever. This is not to say that Disney should be selling cars in 2010, but an obvious idea is for Disney's family-friendly products to be shaped like cars along with the Disney logo and the appropriate values. Disney is already moving into cruise ships and cities. From here, there is but a short step to planes, cars, kitchens, and all the what-nots we surround ourselves with in everyday living—provided, of course, that we feel like buying the story about the happy family.

Here we spy the beginnings of a global story that can be expanded to encompass every physical product and every service. In itself this is a fantastic perspective, pointing to the modified *"Rollerball* scenario" mentioned earlier: the global market subdivided into a few big stories that are sold worldwide. The physical products representing the stories may be produced anywhere in the world, but this is not where the biggest profits lie. The money is made through selling the stories themselves. Consider the story about care, marketed globally through hospitals and health centers, clinics and pharmacies. The manufacturer that is best at telling this story may become owner of the market for care—not in the sense of owning the hospitals that the global middle class will want to use, but in the sense that hospitals will need to buy the story for their facility, in order to attract enough patients.

As mentioned, there is economy of scale inherent in story marketing, but along with the new communication thoroughfares comes fiercer competition—reaching the households of the global middle class will become cheaper. In the digitized world of the future a small enterprise, be it German, Japanese, or Indian, may gain access to a billion households through the communicator. The prerequisite is that they tell good stories. That in itself is a great challenge, because stories need development over several years through a dialogue with customers. Even so, digitizing makes establishing a dialogue with the customer easier.

As an added requirement, stories must be able to transcend cultural borders; they can't afford to be impeded by the big religions or the perceived quality of life. Many stories will turn out to be culturally specific. Thus the story of the Lone Ranger surpassing the most incredible obstacles and riding victoriously into the sunset may not prove to be popular in the cultures of the Far East and Africa, where group results count for more than individual accomplishments. But again, we cannot know for sure—no one holds the answer to how quickly the multitudes of cultural encounters will equalize differences. We only know it will happen first in the world's big cities and last in rural areas.

The market for convictions—the market for goodness—may be roughly the same in affluent countries. Animal welfare, the condemnation of child labor, priorities given to the environment—all are values that companies may confidently tell stories about in North America and in Europe. Telling them through products and services is still somewhat novel, but here is a growing storytelling market. However, we must ask if this is a global market—or if it will become one. Obviously, as things stand today it will confront many cultural barriers on the world market, and even within the global middle class. Again, we do not possess the full answer; perhaps we can venture the conclusion that tendencies point toward shared convictions among steadily increasing numbers of the world's population, but we dare not affix a precise year to when this sun will shine through.

Notes

1. The History Factory, at www.historyfact.com.

2. Michael D. Eisner: The Walt Disney Company 1996 Annual Report.

3. Arie de Geus: "The Living Company," *Harvard Business Review,* March–April 1997.

4. Alvin Toffler: *Future Shock,* Random House, New York, 1970.

5. Daniel Goleman: *Emotional Intelligence. Why It Matters More Than IQ.* Bantam Books, New York, 1995.

6. Craig Wilson: "Disney Gets Real: It Takes a Leave from Fantasy to Create Actual Florida Town," *The Detroit News,* October 22, 1995.

7. William Rademaekers: "Going Gaga Over the Aga," *Time,* December 23, 1996.

8. The NASA home page, at www.nasa.gov/.

9. Samuel P. Huntington: "The West and the World," *Foreign Affairs,* November–December 1996.

10. Estimates based on data from "The World Competitiveness Report 1995" (The World Economic Forum, Geneva, Switzerland, 1995), *The Economist,* January 18, 1997.

11. "Lightweights," *The Economist,* January 18, 1997.

12. Richard Conniff: "Racing with the Wind," *National Geographic,* No. 3 (1997).

13. Gary Hamel: "Killer Strategies," *Fortune,* June 23, 1997.

14. Marc Gunther: "Get Ready for the Oprah Olympics," *Fortune,* July 22, 1997.

15. "Sport and Television: Swifter, Higher, Stronger, Dearer," *The Economist,* July 20, 1996.

16. "Leading Men: Humphrey Bogart," *The Economist,* May 17, 1997.

17. *The Economist,* November 9, 1996. Further research results.

18. Bob Ridell: "Hard Drive," *Wired,* February 1997.

19. William Rademaekers: "Sky Unlimited," *Time,* June 16, 1997.

20. "Neighbours of Hercules," *The Economist,* May 17, 1997.

21. "Mr. Knowledge," *The Economist,* May 31, 1997.

22. Erick Schonfeld: "Virtual Vice and Victuals," *Fortune,* June 24, 1996.

23. "The Convention Business," *The Economist,* June 14, 1997.

24. "The Business of Bereavement," *The Economist,* January 4, 1997.

25. "Making Strategy," *The Economist,* March 1, 1997.

26. J. M. Keynes: "The Economic Prospects of Our Grandchildren," an essay recently presented as a speech. In 1930 held as a lecture in Madrid. Later on published in two sections in "The Nation and Athenaeum," October 11 and 18, 1930, during the crisis.

27. "Sikke et hundeliv," *Berlingske Tidende,* April 14, 1997.

28. *Wired,* April 1997.

29. Quoted from the Salvation Army Act of 1980.

30. D. Charles: "German Law Embraces Alternative Medicine," *New Scientist,* June 28, 1997.

31. "Collected Works," *New Scientist,* April 19, 1997.

32. "God and Cyberspace," *Time,* December 16, 1996.

33. Quoted from the Louis Vuitton home page: www.vuitton.com/lvpage.htm.

34. Quoted from the Ralph Lauren home page: www.ralphlaurenfragrance.com/corporate/ralphbio.html.

35. Susan Caminiti: "Ralph Lauren," *Fortune,* November 11, 1996.

36. Quoted from the Esprit home page: www.esprit.com/history/history1990.01.html.

37. Quoted from the Gucci home page: www.made-in-italy.com/fashion/fashion/gucc/gucc.htm.

38. "Expedition Equipment," *Geographical,* July 1997.

39. *Vogue,* November 1996.

40. Quote by Elazar Benyoëts.

41. "Stretching the National Fabric," *The Economist,* February 8, 1997.

42. *Fast Company,* August–September 1997.

43. *Details,* August 1997.

44. "Living with the Car," *The Economist,* June 22, 1996.

45. *GQ* (U.K.), April 1997.

46. *Financial Times,* September 1, 1997.

47. *Trend Letter,* July 18, 1996.

48. *Scientific American,* March 1996.

49. *Punch,* October 12–18, 1996.

50. "Science Does It with Feeling," *The Economist,* July 20, 1996.

51. "Southwest's Love Fest at Love Field," edited by Sandra Dallas. *Business Week,* April 28, 1997.

52. "Leading and Managing in the 21st Century," Wellington Seminar by Malcolm Menzies, *Future Times Journal,* Vol. 2 (1997).

53. Richard J. Barnett: "The End of Jobs," *Harper's,* September 1993.

54. Edward Cornish: *The Cyber Future: 92 Ways Our Lives Will Change by the Year 2025.* World Future Society, 1996.

55. Matt Weinstein: "Are We Having Fun Yet?" Weinstein home page at www.speaking.com.articles.w/weinsteinarticle1.html, November 28, 1997.

56. "A Hurricane Blew Away Burger King's Headquarters—And Its Old Culture," "Burger King's Culture Change," at www.prcentral.com/rmma95bk.htm, November 27, 1997.

57. "A Hurricane Blew Away Burger King's Headquarters—And Its Old Culture," "Burger King's Culture Change," at www.prcentral.com/rmma95bk.htm, November 27, 1997.

58. "A Hurricane Blew Away Burger King's Headquarters—And Its Old Culture," "Burger King's Culture Change," at www.prcentral.com/rmma95bk.htm, November 27, 1997.

59. James C. Collins and Jerry I. Porras: "Building Your Company's Vision," *Harvard Business Review,* September–October 1996.

60. Charles Handy: "The Sixth Need of Business," *Focus,* Zurich Insurance, 1997.

61. Alan Deutshman: "Men at Work," *GQ.*

62. Kevin Palmer: "Great Minds Think Alike...and the Subject Is Progress," *World Soccer,* December 1997.

63. "Chopping and Changing," *The Economist,* May 17, 1997.

64. Betsy Morris: "Is Your Family Wrecking Your Career?" *Fortune,* March 17, 1997.

65. Victoria Griffith: "Work, Dear Work," *Financial Times,*

66. Advertisement for Ericsson Radio Systems AB, *Business Week.*

67. Julie Rilsner and Larry Armstrong: "The Office Is a Terrible Place to Work," *Business Week,* December 27, 1997.

68. Julie Rilsner and Larry Armstrong: "The Office Is a Terrible Place to Work," *Business Week,* December 27, 1997.

69. Justin Martin: "Robert Reich's Labor Pains," *Fortune,* May 12, 1997.

70. Ira Sager and Amy Cortese: "The New Cool Tools," *Business Week,* November 24, 1997.

71. Daniel H. Pink: "Free Agent Nation," *Fast Company,* December–January 1998.

72. Daniel H. Pink: "Free Agent Nation," *Fast Company,* December–January 1998.

73. Daniel H. Pink: "Free Agent Nation," *Fast Company,* December–January 1998.

74. Daniel H. Pink: "Free Agent Nation," *Fast Company,* December–January 1998.

75. Gina Imperato: "Dirty Business, Bright Ideas," *Fast Company,* February–March 1997.

76. Daniel H. Pink: "Free Agent Nation," *Fast Company,* December–January 1998.

77. Daniel H. Pink: "Free Agent Nation," *Fast Company,* December–January 1998.

78. Arie de Geus: "The Living Company," *Harvard Business Review,* March–April 1997.

79. Charles Fishman: "We've Seen the Future of Work," *Fast Company,* August–September 1996.

80. Ana Marie Cox: "Wide Awake on the New Night Shift," *Fast Company,* August–September 1996.

81. Ana Marie Cox: "Wide Awake on the New Night Shift," *Fast Company,* August–September 1996.

82. Charles Fishman: "We've Seen the Future of Work," *Fast Company,* August–September 1996.

83. Ana Marie Cox: "Wide Awake on the New Night Shift," *Fast Company*, August–September 1996.

84. James Collins and Jerry I. Porras: "Built to Last: Successful Habits of Visionary Companies," *Harvard Business Review*, September–October 1996, pp. 65–77.

85. James Collins and Jerry I. Porras: "Built to Last: Successful Habits of Visionary Companies," *Harvard Business Review*, September–October 1996, pp. 65–77.

86. Carolyn T. Greer: "Sharing the Wealth, Capitalist Style," *Forbes*, December 1, 1997.

87. Aaron Bernstein: "At Phillip Morris, Blue Chips for Blue Collars," *Business Week*, March 27, 1997.

88. Sara Lee Corporation press release, at www.saralee.com.

89. Tom Peters: "The Brand Called You," *Fast Company*, August–September 1997.

90. *Fast Company* online archives, at www.fastcompany.com (December 1997).

91. Economic Indicators, September 1997. Joint Economic Committee *105th Congress Paper*. U.S. Department of Commerce, Bureau of Economic Analysis, Washington, D.C., 1997.

92. *World Development Report*, World Bank, Washington, D.C., 1997.

93. Roger Rosenblatt: "The Year Emotions Ruled," *Time*, December 22, 1997.

94. Betsy Morris: "Is Your Family Wrecking Your Career?" *Fortune*, March 17, 1997.

95. Marvin J. Cetron, Fred J. DeMico, and John A. Williams: "Restaurant," *The Futurist*, January–February 1996.

96. William Echikson et al.: "Move Over, Hollywood!" *Business Week*, December 15, 1997.

97. Margaret Talbot: "Dial-a-Wife," *The New Yorker*, October 20–27, 1997.

98. "The Kitchen Assistant," *Wired*, February 1997.

99. Brigitte De Wolf-Cambier: "Chronicles of a Domestic Revolution to Come," *I&T Magazine,* July 1995, published by the European Commission.

100. VirtualDog, at www.virtualdog.com; ComputerWorld, at www.hp.com/go/fish.

101. Ian Pearson: "An Epidemic of Futures," *Financial Times,* December 22, 1997.

102. "The Diamond Business: Glass with Attitude," *The Economist,* December 20, 1997–January 2, 1998.

103. *Fortune,* April 1997.

104. The Trend Research Institute of Rhinebeck, N.Y. Floral News Bureau, at www.safnow.org/afmc/releases/feb2396.htm (1997).

105. Brian Bremmer: "Toyota's Crusade," *Business Week,* April 7, 1997.

106. Jackie Williams: "Hiring a Professional Nanny," at www.ilovemynanny.com/hire.html.

107. Dave Walther (ed.): *Today Then.* American & World Geographic Publishing, 1992.

108. Richard A. Melcher et al.: "New Breed of Philanthropist," *Business Week,* October 6, 1997 (European ed.).

109. "Western Man's Burden," *The Economist,* December 12, 1998.

110. "OECD in Figures—Statistics on the Member Countries," *OECD Observer,* No. 200 (June–July 1996).

111. National Storytelling Association, P.O. Box 309, Jonesborough, TN 37659.

112. *The Economist World in Figures,* Penguin Books Ltd., London, 1995 pocket ed.

113. Eric Ransdell: "Adventures in Retail," *Fast Company,* December–January 1997–1998. Scott MacCredie: "For Those Who Want to Play Outdoors," *Smithsonian,* Vol. 28, No. 7 (October 1997).

114. Ann Marsh and Scott Wooley: "The Customer Is Always Right? Not at Fry's," *Forbes,* November 3, 1997.

115. Günther Rosenberger: *Consumption 2000: Changes in Consumer Life.* Campus, Hamburg.

116. Marc Gunther: "Get Ready for the Oprah Olympics," *Fortune,* July 22, 1996.

117. Beatrice Newbery: "In League with Captain Nemo," *Geographical,* Vol. 69, No. 12 (December 1997).

118. Cathy Carroll: "Where to Go Next," *Travel and Leisure,* Vol. 27, No. 11 (November 1997).

119. Susan Enfield: "Dispatches: News from the Field," *Outside,* Vol. 22, No. 1 (December 1997).

120. Jane Van Lawick-Goodall: *In the Shadow of Man,* 1971.

121. "Child of the Future, Prologue," *Time,* November 1997 Special Issue (Vol. 150, No. 17a).

122. "Village People," *GQ,* December 1997.

123. Elizabeth Veomett: "Unfortunately, Elvis Is Still Dead," *Business Week,* September 1, 1997 (European ed.).

124. Mike Wallace et al.: "Party Time," *George,* August 1996.

125. Lexington: "The Worker and the Volunteer," *The Economist,* April 26–May 2, 1997.

126. Unless otherwise indicated, data in this chapter are taken from *The States of the Developing World: World Development Report 1997,* and *World Population Projections.* World Bank, Washington, D.C., 1997 and 1994.

127. Angus Maddison: *Monitoring the World Economy, 1820–1992.* OECD, Paris, 1995.

128. *World Population Projections.* World Bank, Washington, D.C., 1994.

129. *World Development Report.* World Bank, Washington, D.C., 1997.

130. Angus Maddison: *Monitoring the World Economy, 1820–1992.* OECD, Paris, 1995.

131. Angus Maddison: *Monitoring the World Economy, 1820–1992.* OECD, Paris, 1995.

132. *World Economic Outlook.* International Monetary Fund, Washington, D.C., May 1997.

133. Antiquarian and Second-Hand Booksellers, Voyages, Travels. Reg and Phillip Remington, 18 Cecil Court, London WC2N 4HE.

134. U.N. Population Division 1995 figures. Quoted in *Time,* November 1997 Special Issue (Vol. 150, No. 17a).

135. *The Gaia Atlas of Cities: New Directions for Sustainable Urban Living.* Gaia Books Ltd., London,

136. *World Development Report 1998/99.* The World Bank, Washington, D.C., 1998.

137. "Telecommunications Survey, Down with Distance," *The Economist,* September 19, 1997.

138. *The States of the Developing World: World Development Report.* World Bank, Washington, D.C., 1997.

139. Jamie F. Mentzl: "Information Intervention," *Foreign Affairs,* November–December 1997.

140. Jamie F. Mentzl: "Information Intervention," *Foreign Affairs,* November–December 1997.

141. Lester R. Brown: *The State of the World,* W.W. Norton & Co., New York, 1997.

142. Gregg Easterbrook: *A Moment on the Earth.* Viking, New York, 1995.

143. Robert Routledge: *Discoveries and Inventions of the Nineteenth Century.* Bracken Books.

144. Donella Meadows, Dennis Meadows, Jørgen Randers, and William W. Behrens III: *The Limits to Growth.* Potomac Books, Washington, D.C., 1972.

145. Clive Ponting: *A Green History of the World.* St. Martin's Press, New York, 1992.

Index

Active placebo response, 83–84
Adamson, Jim, 122
Added value, 11
Adjancy, 138
Adventure, market for (*see* Market for adventure)
Advertising, 53–54, 65, 99, 104, 193–194, 220
Aesop's fables, 175
Affluence, 7, 13–16, 32–33, 71–72
Africa, 41, 95, 100, 178–179, 192, 195, 198, 201, 204, 220
AGA, 39
Age:
  phases of life and, 152–154, 161–162, 165–166, 198–199
  retirement, 153, 165–166
Agricultural society, 11–13, 45–46, 49
  automation in, 7, 14–15, 119–121
  family and work in, 12, 129
  origins of, 2
  wars in, 214
Air Deschutz Pro, 92
Alaska, 161
Alexander, Brian, 138–139
Alps, 55
Alta Vista, 86
Alternative medicine, 83
Altman, Tammy, 130
American Association of Fundraising Counsel, 173
Andersen, Hans Christian, 42
Andersen Consulting, 104
Andes, 55
Animals:
  adventure market and, 59–60, 177–180
  animal husbandry, 12, 13
  animal rights, 3, 78, 109–110, 113
  electronic pets, 76–77, 158
  endangered species, 42–43, 185
  pet market, 77–78
  wildlife areas, 177–180
  (*See also* Nature)
Aqua, 184
Argentina, 184, 202–203, 210
Aristocracy, 172
Aristotle, 32, 33, 100
Aston Martin, 58

AT&T Wireless Services, Inc., 81, 130
Australia, 10, 39, 42, 95, 171, 181, 192, 201, 218
Automation:
  in agricultural society, 7, 14–15, 119–121
  of communication, 35–36, 67–68, 129–132
  in Dream Society, 2–3
  fear of, 119–121
  of feelings, 35–36, 48–49
  in health care, 84
  in the home, 156–159, 168–169
  in industrial society, 6–7, 13–15, 119–120, 137, 220
  in Information Society, 2, 4, 7, 17–18, 120–121
  (*See also* Computers; Machines; Technology)
Automobiles, 94–95, 168, 211

Ballet, 180
Ballooning, 54
Banking, 30–32, 102–103
Barbie, 78
Bars, 65–66
Barton, Samuel, 170
Bathrooms, 168
Beatles, 184
Becky, 78, 79
Bedbury, Scott, 98–99
Bentley, 38
Berg, Beth, 156
Biotechnology, 21, 84
Blixen, Karen, 42
BMW, 58
Boeing, 137, 143
Bogart, Humphrey, 57–58
Bonk Business Inc., 102
Books, 156
Borneo, 179
Bosnia, 215
Brand identity, 65, 99, 194, 220–221
"Branded" employees, 145–146
Branson, Richard, 54
Brazil, 205, 210
Breitling Orbiter (hot-air balloon), 54, 55
British Petroleum, 111

233

242